The DIY Investor

The DIY Investor

How to take control of your investments and plan for a financially secure future

Andy Bell

Harlow, England • London • New York • Boston • San Francisco • Toronto • Sydney • Auckland • Singapore • Hong Kong
Tokyo • Seoul • Taipei • New Delhi • Cape Town • São Paulo • Mexico City • Madrid • Amsterdam • Munich • Paris • Milan

PEARSON EDUCATION LIMITED

Edinburgh Gate
Harlow CM20 2JE
United Kingdom
Tel: +44 (0)1279 623623
Web: www.pearson.com/uk

First published 2013 (print and electronic)

© Andy Bell 2013 (print and electronic)

Pearson Education is not responsible for the content of third-party internet sites.

ISBN: 978–1–292–00066–4 (print)
978–1–292–00067–1 (PDF)
978–1–292–00068–8 (ePub)
978–1–292–00737–3 (eText)

British Library Cataloguing-in-Publication Data
A catalogue record for the print edition is available from the British Library

Library of Congress Cataloging-in-Publication Data
Bell, Andy, 1966–
    The DIY investor: how to take control of your investments and plan for a financially secure future / Andy Bell.
        pages cm
    Includes index.
    ISBN 978-1-292-00066-4 (pbk.) – ISBN (invalid) 978-1-292-00067-1 (PDF) – ISBN (invalid) 978-1-292-00068-8 (ePub) – ISBN (invalid) 978-1-292-00737-3 (eText)
    1. Portfolio management. 2. Investments. I. Title.
    HG4529.5.B453 2013
    332.6–dc23
                    2013027158

10 9 8 7 6 5 4 3 2 1
17 16 15 14 13

Cover design by Dan Mogford
Print edition typeset in 9pt Stone Serif by 3
Printed and bound in Great Britain by Ashford Colour Press Ltd., Gosport

NOTE THAT ANY PAGE CROSS REFERENCES REFER TO THE PRINT EDITION

Contents

Publisher's acknowledgements

We are grateful to the following for permission to reproduce copyright material:

Figures

Figure 9.1 from IMA website, www.investmentfunds.org.uk, Investment Management Association (IMA); Figure 9.2 from AJ Bell Research Centre, www.ajbell.co.uk, AJ Bell; Figure 18.1 from Vanguard Asset Management website, www.vanguard.co.uk

Screenshots

Screenshots 9.3 and 9.4 from Invesco Perpetual website, www.invescoperpetual.co.uk. Screenshot 9.5 from Trustnet website, www.trustnet.com; Screenshot 13.1 from UK Debt Management Office website, www.dmo.gov.uk

In some instances we have been unable to trace the owners of copyright material, and we would appreciate any information that would enable us to do so.

About the author

Born in Liverpool in 1966, Andy Bell was educated at Rainford High School and then went on to study at Nottingham University. He graduated with a first-class degree in Mathematics in 1987 and subsequently joined a large insurance company as a trainee actuary.

Somewhat disillusioned with the financial services industry, Andy took a sabbatical in 1990, which lasted for three years on and off, to coach football and tennis (of a fashion) in America, followed by an extended period of travel and growing up.

When Andy returned to the UK, he resurrected his actuarial career and qualified as a Fellow of the Institute of Actuaries in 1993, while working at a small actuarial consultancy.

AJ Bell was established in 1995 by Andy Bell and Nicholas Littlefair in a 149-square-foot office, funded by £10,000 of personal loans. It has since grown into one of the largest investment platforms in the UK, with over £20bn of assets under administration. AJ Bell has offices in Manchester, Tunbridge Wells and London, employing approximately 500 staff. It looks after a wide variety of retail clients, many of them DIY investors.

AJ Bell (www.ajbell.co.uk) offers investment solutions to DIY investors as well as clients of financial advisers and other financial services companies. Its award-winning DIY investment platform is called AJ Bell Youinvest (www.youinvest.co.uk), formerly known as Sippdeal.

AJ Bell also owns the popular *Shares* magazine (www.sharesmagazine.co.uk) and specialist investment information websites MoneyAM (www.moneyam. co.uk), StockMarketWire (www.stockmarketwire.co.uk), Broker Forecasts (www. brokerforecasts.co.uk), Directors Holdings (www.directorsholdings.co.uk) and DIYinvestor (www.diyinvestor.co.uk).

Andy was ninth in *Management Today*'s 2010 Britain's top 100 entrepreneurs and AJ Bell is one of only a handful of companies ever to appear in the *Sunday Times* Profit Track and Fast Track (top 100 UK private companies with the fastest-growing profits and revenues respectively) in the same year – 2010. Both Andy and the company have won numerous other business and industry awards.

Andy lives in Lancashire with his wife Tracey, their four children, a dog and an ever-growing menagerie of farmyard animals. His interests are skiing, playing 5-a-side football, flying helicopters, boxing (training, not fighting) and watching Everton and St Helens RLFC.

Andy set up his own charitable trust in 2011 and has a number of other charitable and business interests.

List of acronyms

AER	annual equivalent rate
AIM	Alternative Investment Market
AMC	annual management charge
ASP	alternatively secured pension
AVC	additional voluntary contribution
BP	British Petroleum
CFD	contract for difference
CPI	Consumer Price Index
DIY	do it yourself
DYOR	do your own research
EBIT	earnings before interest and taxes
EIS	enterprise investment scheme
EMS	exchange market size
ESMA	European Securities and Markets Association
ETC	exchange-traded commodity
ETF	exchange-traded fund
ETN	exchange-traded note
ETP	exchange-traded product
EU	European Union
FCA	Financial Conduct Authority
FSA	Financial Services Authority

FSAVC	free-standing additional voluntary contribution
FSCS	Financial Services Compensation Scheme
GAD	Government Actuary's Department
GIA	general investment account
HMRC	Her Majesty's Revenue and Customs
ICVC	investment company with variable capital
IFA	independent financial adviser
IMA	Investment Management Association
ISA	individual savings account
ISIN	international securities identification number
IT	information technology
KIID	key investor information document
KPI	key performance indicator
LSE	London Stock Exchange
MIR	minimum income requirement
NAV	net asset value
NS&I	National Savings and Investments
OEIC	open-ended investment company
ORB	Order Book for Retail Bonds
PAYE	pay-as-you-earn
P/E	price-to-earnings
PEP	personal equity plan
PIBS	permanent interest-bearing share
PIIGS	Portugal, Ireland, Italy, Greece and Spain
PSB	perpetual sub bond
QROPS	qualifying recognised overseas pension scheme
RDR	Retail Distribution Review

REIT	real estate investment trust
RIE	recognised investment exchange
RNS	Regulatory News Service
RPI	Retail Prices Index
SEDOL	Stock Exchange Daily Official List
SIPP	self-invested personal pension
S&P	Standard & Poor's
SPDR	S&P 500 Depository Receipt
TER	total expense ratio
TESSA	tax-exempt special savings account
TIB	trustee in bankruptcy
UCIS	unregulated collective investment scheme
UCITS	undertakings for collective investments in transferable securities
VCT	venture capital trust

Preface

I can't abide intellectual arrogance. I have no time for people who think they are cleverer than they are or, even worse, people who deliberately try and sound intelligent at the expense of others. Most subject matter, when explained well by someone who understands it, makes sense. So I have a simple rule in life, and that is if I don't understand something then it must be the fault of the person who has just explained it to me. Hopefully that doesn't sound like intellectual arrogance.

So what does this have to do with DIY investing? Well, what puts most people off looking after their own finances is fear. A fear of the unknown. A fear of not being able to understand the subject matter. A fear that they might feel stupid.

The world of investments can appear impenetrable – full of statistics, jargon and acronyms – but being a DIY investor can be as simple or complicated as you want it to be and you *can* become a DIY investor, if you want to. And remember, if you don't understand this book, it is not your fault, it is mine.

So, who should read *The DIY Investor*, and why?

The 'who should read it' question is easy. The answer is anybody who is thinking of, or is currently, managing their own investments. Today's and tomorrow's DIY investors – a group that industry experts expect to increase from 2 million to up to 7 million in number over the next few years.

The answer to the 'why' question is to gain the knowledge, understanding and confidence you need to take control of your finances and meet your investment objectives.

The best way to grow your assets is through the stock market, which is statistically proven to have beaten returns from banks and building societies over long periods for more than a century. This book gives you the tools to invest, cutting out unnecessary costs and putting your money directly into the wealth-generating sectors of the economy. You will learn how to invest your money efficiently and avoid expensive mistakes. It is designed both for beginners and existing DIY investors who want to hone their skills and trim their costs of investing.

This is not a 'get rich quick' book, nor is it anti-establishment. Financial advisers, wealth managers and fund managers all have a vital role to play in managing investments and many do a fantastic job. But the abolition of commission from the start of 2013 means financial advisers now have to charge explicit fees, meaning financial advice is fast becoming a luxury that only the wealthy can afford.

I have tried to structure this book in a logical format and, where possible, explain new concepts as I introduce them to you, but at times I have chosen to leave the detail until the relevant chapter. If you come across a term or concept that you don't understand then there are two great websites that will help you out: www.monevator.com and www.investopedia. com – just type in what is confusing you and there is every chance that a simple explanation will pop up.

Where I refer to a tax rate or allowance, unless otherwise stated, these will be the rates applicable to the 2013/14 tax year. There is a dedicated section on www.diyinvestor.co.uk that will keep you up to date with important changes to allowances or legislation referred to in this book – until the next edition is published anyway.

There are lots of people involved in writing a book and the blame is rightly mine if it doesn't hit the spot. If it does, the credit should go to the many people who have helped me on this journey. Thanks go to my friends and family who have been brutally honest proofreaders and to my colleagues, too numerous to mention, for helping me to rearrange a random collection of words into something resembling a book.

One thing about being a DIY investor is that you have no one to reproach but yourself. Most people find this quite liberating and, when things go wrong, you don't find blame and anger eating you from the inside out. DYOR is something you will come across quite regularly on financial websites – Do Your Own Research – often accompanied by some very helpful tips. What this politely means is I am happy to help, but I accept no liability and you can't sue me.

Being a DIY investor is not hard but it does require a measure of effort and engagement on your part. All you need is a computer, an internet connection, your bankcard and the time it takes to read the parts of this book relevant to what you want to achieve.

So welcome to the world of the DIY investor. It can be exciting and nerve-racking in equal measure. But it can also deliver real financial rewards. I hope you enjoy what I am sure will be the only book I will ever write, and don't forget: I am here to help, but DYOR.

Andy Bell

one

What being a DIY investor is all about

Introducing DIY investing

Why be a DIY investor?

'Because nobody cares as much about my money as I do.' This quote came out of a survey that AJ Bell commissioned to find out why people had chosen to become a DIY investor. It accurately reflects the primary reason why anyone would want to take control of their financial future.

The lack of engagement many people have with their investments never ceases to amaze me. Many of us spend hours scouring the internet to save a few quid on a new phone, eat at restaurants we otherwise wouldn't be seen dead in to take advantage of a coupon discount scheme, or buy three items for the price of two when we only need one.

That is human nature – everyone likes a bargain. But translate that to far bigger financial decisions and most people simply haven't got a clue. Ask many people how much they have in their ISA (individual savings account) or pension, what charges they pay, how much they need to retire or what their investment goals are and a look of quizzical bemusement takes over.

The fact that you are reading this book means you probably don't fit into this category or, if you do, you are desperate to break free. Learning how to become a DIY investor enables you to set basic goals and implement a simple strategy to achieve them. You will strip out a whole layer of charges that will free up your investments to grow quicker and hit your desired targets sooner than would otherwise be the case.

Follow the strategies, ideas and tips set out in this book and you will learn how to create the sort of portfolio that you would get from a professional adviser, without incurring the charges.

I am often asked, 'What is the minimum fund size you need to have a SIPP (self-invested personal pension) or to become a DIY investor?'. My reply is always the same, after checking for eavesdroppers to avoid embarrassment. 'It is not about size, it is about your state of mind.' There is a DIY solution for everyone, irrespective of how much you want to invest. But you do need an appetite for taking control of your investments.

Why everyone should invest – DIY or otherwise

However you choose to invest for your future, the necessity of doing so is an imperative for us all. The government has made no secret of the fact that it expects us to provide for ourselves, both before and during retirement.

If providing for your children is one of your investment objectives, this could be for a number of reasons: to pay for school fees, university fees or to help with their first house. Providing for private school fees is expensive enough, but we have also seen university fees triple in recent years.

Or your primary goal may be more focused around your own retirement.

Retirement ages are increasing and anyone in their early thirties today will not get their state pension until the age of 68 at the earliest. State pension age is being linked to longevity, so as life spans increase, so the day you get your pension recedes further into the future.

I attended an actuarial conference a few years ago and the heading of one session was, 'Immortality is no longer a pipe dream'. While the speaker may have been stretching the point, the heading succinctly highlights the direction of travel. Increasing longevity means longer in retirement, which may sound great but it is also making saving for your retirement a real uphill battle.

Just how much longer everyone is living can be hard to digest – the statistics are phenomenal. Back in 1952, only 300 people in the UK made it to the age of 100. Just over half a century later, 8,000 people a year are receiving their telegram from the Queen. Experts predict the first Briton to reach 120 is already receiving her pension, meaning she will be in retirement for half of her life.

And every new generation seems to be living longer than the last. A baby boy born in 2012 is expected to live until 91, and a baby girl to 94. And these are average figures, meaning roughly half of people will live longer. What's more, they include those who will become overweight, smokers, heavy drinkers and those with long-term health conditions. You may not believe it, and you may not even want to believe it, but these days if you are of above-average health you are in with a decent shot of making it to 100.

This means if you want to retire aged 60 then unless you have got a final salary pension, you will have to put away a small fortune to pay the bills for a retirement that could run into three, four or even five decades.

Put all these financial challenges against a backdrop of financial uncertainty and it is clear doing nothing is not an option.

Why new laws for financial advisers are turning more people into DIY investors

Since January 2013 financial advisers, whether in banks and building societies or in firms of IFAs (independent financial advisers), have been prohibited from receiving commission from fund managers and insurance companies for distributing their products.

Nowadays, a financial adviser can only work for you if you agree to pay them a fee, instead of them receiving a commission from the product providers that they recommend. The change is part of the Retail Distribution Review (RDR), an initiative to raise the professionalism of financial advisers and to remove commission bias from their recommendations.

Many self-help books are anti-establishment, and this is particularly so in the world of DIY investments. I take a different view. Having worked with many excellent financial advisers and wealth managers over the years, I have always been impressed by their knowledge, commitment and the personal responsibility they take for their clients' money.

For those individuals wealthy enough to be comfortable paying fees for a financial adviser or wealth manager, the RDR will make investing a much more transparent experience.

But experts predict millions of people who had been happy to deal with commission-based advisers in the past will not be prepared to go to them if they have to pay a fee.

Banks are already putting up the 'closed' signs on their high-street financial advice businesses, so they can target top-end clients. Lloyds Banking Group and HSBC only offer face-to-face advice to wealthy customers, while Barclays has closed its financial advice arm, Barclays Financial Planning, altogether.

Independent financial advisers and wealth managers are moving upmarket, targeting only wealthier individuals.

What does being a DIY investor entail?

Being a DIY investor can involve as much or as little effort on your part as you want it to. You could set up a well-researched, low-maintenance investment portfolio from scratch in less than an hour, which only needs an hour or two every six months or so to review it. Or you can create a more complex portfolio that may require daily or weekly monitoring.

The choice is yours, but please don't dive in at the deep end. Read this book and then ask yourself the question, 'Am I a DIY investor?'. If the answer is yes, you will no doubt have identified with one or more investment styles and strategies highlighted here and you are ready to go. If the answer is no, then you need to seriously consider appointing a financial adviser.

You may have accumulated one or more old pensions or savings policies. The policy documents may be getting mouldy in your filing cabinet and at some stage, as part of this process, you will have to dust these down and consider consolidating them all onto your investment platform. These will give your portfolio a decent kick-start, but more on this later.

Being a DIY investor does require some commitment on your part. Because you are not paying for advice, you are buying on a *caveat emptor*, or 'buyer beware', basis. This means that you will be the person responsible if things go wrong; for example, if you make a mistake and buy a share or fund that you thought was something entirely different, or if you misunderstand a tax planning strategy, then you will have no one to blame but yourself.

The extent to which you should engage as a DIY investor should reflect the person you are. If you are someone who finds numbers particularly difficult to grasp then don't worry, just keep it simple. Buy a few index tracker or actively managed funds and you will get the hang of it. Don't do what many people do and think by going direct to one of the household-name fund managers in response to a press advert you will be cutting out the middleman. That is, contradictory as it might sound, about the most expensive route to buying investments there is. You will end up paying the same, if not more, than if you bought through a financial adviser.

You also need to have the discipline to review your investments at least once a year and preferably twice a year, to make sure they are performing as they should. A few carefully considered Google alerts can keep you abreast of any key changes to your investments in the interim.

The skills and commitment you will need will also depend on the type of investor that you intend to be. If you are going to adopt a long-term buy-and-hold strategy, you may need no more than a couple of hours a year to review your portfolio. That said, once everything is set up, checking your investments online is so straightforward that most people find themselves regularly looking to see how their investments are faring anyway. Several investment platforms now have mobile phone applications, which you may find compulsive. But don't forget, a watched pot never boils. On average, most DIY investors look at their portfolio once a week, though people do tend to look more when the market is rising than when it is falling.

Investment platforms

An investment platform is a web-based service that offers the DIY investor at least three types of account (SIPP, ISA and a Dealing Account) through an overarching account, accessed by a single log-in. It is the service that facilitates the execution of your DIY investment strategy, so choosing the investment platform with the right charging structure, choice of investments and investor tools is very important.

The functionality that today's investment platforms offer means it has never been easier to be a DIY investor. It is no exaggeration to say that the internet has genuinely revolutionised the process of investing, in particular DIY investing. Investment platforms today give you online access to real-time dealing, along with data and information that only a decade or so ago were exclusive to professional advisers and fund managers. What to look for when choosing an investment platform is covered in detail in Chapter 20.

Different types of investment accounts

Efficient DIY investing involves using the right type of account, sometimes referred to as a product, tax wrapper or savings vehicle, at the right time. The two main tax-efficient products you will see are a SIPP, which stands for self-invested personal pension, and an ISA, which stands for individual savings account. As well as a SIPP and an ISA, you will most likely need a Dealing Account for any investments that fall outside these two accounts.

The SIPP is a very tax-efficient, long-term savings vehicle and allows you to save relatively large amounts of money, benefiting from tax relief on your contributions, although access to the funds held in your SIPP is restricted and cannot normally be accessed until the age of 55. Contributions into an ISA do not attract tax relief but money saved within an ISA grows largely free of tax, and you can access it at any time. These different types of accounts are all covered in subsequent chapters.

Different types of investments

As a DIY investor you should only invest in assets you fully understand. This book devotes a chapter to each of the main different types of asset you will come across. The key assets you are likely to use are quoted equities, which are shares in limited companies listed on a recognised stock exchange, investment funds such as unit trusts and OEICs (open-ended investment companies), exchange-traded (or tracker) funds, investment trusts, corporate and government bonds, and a number of less mainstream assets for the more adventurous DIY investor.

In Part 4 you will find an explanation of how to blend these different assets into a portfolio that reflects your personal attitude to risk.

How to save money on charges

There are a number of ways of saving on charges and I will look at them in more detail in later chapters. First, by not having an adviser you have an immediate saving, but you don't have the benefit of their time and expertise.

Buying funds through a DIY investment platform means that you will often be able to eliminate any initial charge on the fund and possibly also get a rebate on the annual charge. The RDR has seen a whole new range of fund classes introduced that slightly confuses the situation, but the principle remains.

By funds, what I mean is a unit trust or OEIC. For this purpose they are interchangeable, and I will refer to them as funds. They do not include investment trusts and if I am referring to a tracker fund or exchange-traded fund then I will make the reference explicit. All will become clear later.

As well as shopping around for the best-value investment platform, you can save money by thinking about how you invest and what you invest in. There are various types of DIY investors, ranging from those who adopt a long-term buy-and-hold strategy, to day traders – the people who sit in front of a screen all day, every day.

Buying and selling investments frequently can be expensive, as you will incur dealing commission, stamp duty on purchases and also suffer the spread cost, which is the difference between the buying and the selling price of an investment. So, the less you deal the less you pay in charges.

If you buy funds you will incur a management fee, a charge imposed by the fund manager for managing your money. You will need to understand the main types of charges so that you can compare funds.

You can minimise these management charges by buying low-cost funds. Tracker funds are the best example of this.

You can avoid management fees altogether if you buy shares directly yourself. Even if you are a novice investor you can put together a portfolio of big defensive shares that pay healthy dividends and just sit on them. It may not be a very sophisticated strategy, but it is one that can be quite cost-effective and plenty of experienced investors do it.

These shares may underperform a rising market and outperform a falling market, but whatever the weather they are still generating dividends. An alternative strategy, along similar lines, is to find out what the popular fund managers are holding in their funds and replicate their key holdings.

One advantage of being a DIY investor can be highlighted by imagining both you and a professional fund manager get advance notice of an impending stock market crash. You are in a position to convert your holdings to cash in an instant. The fund manager can't because their holdings would be too large to offload quickly without causing its own market crash. The DIY investor can be nimble and fleet of foot.

You may think fund management charges look pretty tiny, so why should you be bothered about them? The simple answer is that, over a long period, small differences in charges can make a massive difference to the size of your investment pot. Over a 30-year timeline, 0.5 per cent per annum difference in charges will mean the difference between a pension fund of £505,365 and £459,946, on a £5,000-a-year contribution, assuming 7 per cent a year net growth. That is a difference of more than £45,419 lost by investing in a product with a charge 0.5 per cent higher.

table 1.1	Fund management charges	
	7 per cent per annum return after charges	If additional 0.5 per cent per annum charges are incurred
Return after 30 years on £5,000-a-year contribution	£505,365	£459,946

Save money on tax

Tax planning is as important to effective saving as slashing the costs of investing and choosing the right investments.

Tax relief on pensions can be as high as 45 per cent, meaning it costs just £5,500 to credit £10,000 into your SIPP. You can withdraw a quarter of your fund as tax-free cash, and money held within your SIPP grows mostly tax-free and in many situations is outside your estate for inheritance tax purposes.

ISA tax privileges are also valuable, and come with the added advantage that you can access your money when you want.

And when it comes to withdrawing your money as income at retirement, carefully planned use of both growth and income investments across a SIPP, ISA and Dealing Account, possibly split between a husband and wife or civil partners, can dramatically minimise your tax bill. Details on the tax treatment of different asset classes and the tax privileges of different products are covered in their respective chapters. Chapter 16 looks at tax planning in a broader context.

The above is just a flavour of some of the issues I will cover in later chapters. If none of what I have said floats your boat then it is eBay for the book and to the *Yellow Pages* for a financial adviser. But if I have whetted your appetite for more information, then it's on to Chapter 2 to understand how to set your investment objectives.

2

Setting your investment objectives

t is impossible to invest effectively without a clear understanding of your investment objectives or goals. Once you have clarity on your investment objectives, making investment decisions becomes a lot easier.

For many people, putting away as much as they can afford is their investment objective. Saying 'I will save as much as I can' is certainly better than doing nothing, but it is like going for a drive without having decided on your final destination. You will have a far greater chance of getting where you want to if you know where you are going from the start.

Creating a realistic set of investment objectives can be difficult, so at first allow yourself to be as specific or as vague as you like.

As with all good objectives, your investment objectives should be achievable and measurable. Owning your favourite football club, for example, is unlikely to be a realistic, or a sensible, investment objective for most people. Clearing your mortgage by the age of 50, on the other hand, may well be.

You need to be able to measure progress towards these objectives and have a half-decent chance of achieving them. Most objectives will be set in a time frame, though you should not get too distressed if you find you do not meet your milestones on time.

When quantifying amounts you want to achieve in the future, don't forget the impact of inflation.

Visualising your investment objectives

You may think this sounds like psychobabble, but visualising what you are trying to achieve is the first step to achieving it. Visualising an objective makes it more vivid in your mind, making you more attached to the idea of turning it into reality. As a DIY investor there is nobody to encourage you along the way, so you need to remain motivated if you are to achieve your objectives.

The examples of objectives set out in the box below will hopefully get your mental juices flowing. There are no rights or wrongs when setting investment objectives – they are unique to you and your family. Also, they will inevitably change over time as your circumstances change and should be reviewed at least once a year.

Ideas for your investment objectives

- Repay my mortgage by 2025.
- Retire at the age of 65 with a fund to provide a £20,000-a-year income, in today's money.
- Provide an immediate income of £10,000 a year, with the additional prospect of future capital and income growth.
- Accumulate enough to fund a house deposit for my only child in 10 years' time.
- Achieve an investment return of 5 per cent a year greater than the rate available on cash deposits, after charges, while retaining reasonable access to my capital.
- Save enough money to pay for a round-the-world cruise at retirement.

What I find useful is to start with a blank sheet of paper and draw a time line. Break it into five- or ten-yearly intervals looking forward, and focus on when you think you will reach key milestones. These key milestones could be leaving university, getting married, buying your first home, having children, seeing them through college and retiring.

Think how you would like to be able to structure your finances to be able to respond to these events.

You may feel self-conscious at first, but seeing your words written on a piece of paper will help you untangle in your mind what your investment objectives really are. I mentioned earlier the importance of keeping these objectives under regular review. You may be promoted or find a new job paying a far higher salary, take on a big mortgage, inherit some money, get divorced or find your family increasing in size when you weren't expecting it.

At the highest level, investment objectives normally focus on providing income or capital over a period of time or at a specific date. You may have other objectives, such as minimising tax, but this should never be an objective in isolation. You may have an overriding objective that your money should be accessible at all times or at reasonably short notice.

If you do find yourself struggling to identify your investment objectives and it really is just a case of investing as much as you can afford, then just try and clarify two things – the time frame of your investment and whether you are looking for income and/or capital growth.

Most people hate budgeting. But if you don't know what your family income and expenditure is you won't know how much spare cash you will have. This book is about DIY investing and not about the wider issue of family finances. A back-of-the-envelope calculation will suffice to determine how much 'free money' you have to invest.

The trick is, don't be too ambitious – invest or save only what you can realistically afford. If not, you may find yourself having to rethink your investments six months down the line so you can meet your everyday living costs.

If the time horizon within which you need access to your capital is less than three or maybe even five years, then I would suggest that DIY investing is not the right solution for you. You probably need to be investing in cash-type products, such as bank or building society accounts or national savings (see page 204, Chapter 14).

Short-, medium- and long-term objectives

DIY investing is suitable for meeting medium- to long-term objectives. Most people have a blend of short-, medium- and long-term objectives. It is important to prioritise these, although it is never easy. A new car in three years or repay the mortgage in fifteen? Most will choose the former.

Psychologists have described this human trait as 'hyperbolic discounting'. It's the hard-wired tendency to place a far greater value on something that will be received in the near future, such as a holiday, than something in the distance, such as a pension, even if the thing further away in time is far more valuable.

Overcoming this desire for immediate gratification is incredibly hard, with the unfortunate consequence that most people only realise they need to start saving for their retirement when it is going to cost them far more to do so, as Table 2.1 below demonstrates.

The newspapers are full of shocking statistics about just how poorly prepared Britons are for retirement. One of the most chilling was a 2012 report ('Retirement income and assets: the implications for retirement income of Government policies to extend working lives') by the Pension Policy Institute, an independent research organisation, which found that 45 per cent of those over the age of 50 will have to work an additional 11 years past state pension age (currently between 61 and 68) if they want to achieve a retirement income of just £11,000 a year.

Fixing objectives in the context of retirement can be particularly difficult because of the shock many people experience when they realise just how much of their salary they will need to save to achieve the retirement income they expect. And the longer you leave it, the more you have to pay to get there.

table 2.1 Proportion of salary someone earning £50,000 needs to pay into a pension to build an income of 50 per cent of salary from age 65

Age	Pension contribution
25	14 per cent
35	23 per cent
45	40 per cent
55	95.5 per cent

Retirement objectives

As this table shows, the later you leave it to start saving for retirement, the more expensive it gets. This is not surprising given the 55-year-old in this example is hoping to save for a retirement in just 10 years that could last 30 or 40 years.

Increased life expectancy is of course a fantastic development for society, but it is making retirement planning incredibly expensive. The princely sum of £100,000 will give a male 65-year-old an inflation-linked annuity of £3,275 a year, or an income paid out of a SIPP – under income drawdown rules, which I will explain further in later chapters – of a little more than £5,000 a year. To be able to draw an income of £25,000 a year in retirement you would need to build up a pot of between £400,000 and £500,000.

But don't get put off by the magnitude of the challenge of saving for retirement. Burying your head in the sand is not an option, and the sooner you start, the longer your pension fund will benefit from compounding growth. And remember, most people find their earnings increase as they get older, so if you are only paying a fraction of what you need to, at least you are making a start.

There are a number of pension calculators on the internet that will work out how much you need to save to deliver a set income in retirement. These calculators may give your results in real terms, meaning they take into account inflation between now and your retirement. They may also factor in the tax relief you get on your savings. Try www.aviva-pensioncalculator.co.uk to see whether your retirement planning is on course.

How long-term factors can impact your objectives

I mentioned the impact of inflation earlier. As a rule of thumb, if inflation is running at 3 per cent per annum, then £100 today is worth £75 in 10 years and £55 in 20 years. If inflation is at 5 per cent per annum, these figures reduce to £61 and £38 respectively.

Planning for income in retirement is even more difficult, as you not only have to factor in the impact of inflation, but also increasing longevity. Increased life spans mean the cost of buying an annuity is likely to increase in our lifetime to a level that will make it unattractive for most people. So, unless you are one of the lucky ones in a final salary scheme, the chances are you will enter retirement with a pot of money, and the challenge of investing this to provide a long-term income in retirement. The good news is DIY investing is the perfect way to meet this challenge.

Avoiding emotional investing

Before we turn to understanding the detail of the tax wrappers and investments you will encounter, I would just like to comment on the psychology of investing. It is important to recognise that you will need to adopt a dispassionate and emotionless attitude if you are to become a successful DIY investor.

If you are an incessant worrier or your life is an emotional roller-coaster ride, or even if you find yourself watching poker on TV when you should be asleep, you will need to take a moment to sanity-check any decision to become a DIY investor.

Understanding the way your brain is programmed to react to investment situations can stop you having expensive knee-jerk reactions. This is particularly important for DIY investors who do not have an adviser to guide them when investment markets are volatile.

Human beings are psychologically programmed to be bad at investing. Buying at the top of the market or selling at the bottom are two classic mistakes inexperienced investors make. Holding onto a good share too long and missing the chance to take a profit is also a classic mistake.

Psychologists have carried out research that shows we tend to overreact when markets move significantly. When our investments rise in value we can be overcome with a feeling of euphoria and a sense of invincibility – when they fall we become stressed, fearful and wracked with regret.

The truth is, you should only ever decide whether to buy or sell an asset on your assessment of the basic fundamentals. As the well-known regulatory disclaimer goes, past performance is not a guide to future performance. One could argue that this is nonsense. It is like saying that the fact that Manchester United have been at or near the top of the premier league table for the past decade is no guide to their future performance, when it clearly is.

Past performance is one of the most commonly used benchmarks by professional advisers when deciding where to invest. But the principle behind the regulatory warning is both clear and sensible: don't follow performance graphs blindly.

Strategies for taking the emotion out of investing

- **Pound-cost averaging.** This is one of the simplest ways of spreading risk and smoothing the volatility of investment markets. The key point about pound-cost averaging is that you invest small amounts on a regular basis. So, when prices are high your monthly investment will buy fewer shares or units, but when prices are low your investment buys more shares or units.

- **Diversification.** Different types of asset tend to rise and fall in value at different times in the market cycle. So, by diversifying your portfolio across different geographies, asset classes and even across different sectors within an asset class, you can dampen much of the market's volatility out of your portfolio.

- **Use fund managers.** While you still need to choose a fund manager, this is a lot easier and less risky than choosing individual investments. You are leaving the big decisions to them and paying them for taking the pressure off you.

- **Use tracker funds.** You need to choose the index to track and the fund with which to track it, but thereafter you can put your feet up and leave the fund to grow, hopefully, without too much interference.

- **Use model portfolios.** Many DIY investment platforms now offer a guided investment or model portfolio option. This is a basket of investments that constitutes a ready-made portfolio of assets – typically actively managed funds but it may extend to tracker funds chosen by the investment platform or a firm they appoint. Model portfolios look and feel like recommendations from professional financial advisers, but they are not. They are generic recommendations offered without assessing whether they are suitable for your circumstances.

- **Control your emotions.** As a DIY investor you will need discipline and cannot afford to let emotion get in the way. If you want to become a real DIY investor, you have to be prepared to take some losses. Selling all your holdings as soon as you suffer a loss can often be the worst thing to do.

Investment objectives, appetite for risk and investment strategy

Your investment objectives are only one part of the investment equation. You try and achieve these objectives by implementing an investment strategy. Any investment strategy needs to be set in the context of an appetite for risk – how much risk are you willing to take to achieve your objectives?

People often confuse these three concepts, but it is important to keep them separate. Think of your investment objectives as the destination, your investment strategy as the route you have chosen to get there and your risk appetite as how fast you are willing to drive to get there!

We will cover risk appetite in Chapter 18 and as for investment strategy, well that is pretty much the rest of the book. It is all about what you invest in to achieve your investment objectives.

The DIY investor's toolkit – the products

The ISA – individual savings account

Individual savings accounts (ISAs) offer you the ability to invest in the stock market or to keep your money in cash, in a tax-efficient way. All investment income is tax-free and there is no tax to pay on capital gains.

The tax efficiency and easy access to your money offered by ISAs means they can be used for both short- and medium-term saving and can also sensibly form part of a DIY investor's retirement strategy.

If, like me, you dread filling in your tax return, then one of the advantages of an ISA is that the taxman isn't interested in it and details do not need to be supplied as part of your self-assessment.

The history of ISAs

Launched by Gordon Brown in 1999, ISAs have become one of the most useful tools available to savers and investors. They followed in the footsteps of other tax-exempt savings accounts, such as personal equity plans (PEPs), tax-exempt special savings accounts (TESSAs), mini ISAs and maxi ISAs.

All PEPs have now been converted to stocks and shares ISAs and all TESSAs have been converted to cash ISAs. ISAs have matured with time, with the complex and confusing mini and maxi ISAs being replaced by the more clearly labelled cash ISA and stocks and shares ISA in 2008.

As PEPs and TESSAs have faded into distant memory, the core attractions of a shelter from income tax and capital gains tax, combined with immediate access to your money, have seen ISAs earn a place in the hearts of the nation's savers. Their popularity has grown to such an extent that in 2011/2012 a whopping £53bn was saved into ISAs, with approximately 70 per cent of this being into cash ISAs.

How ISAs work

You have an annual ISA allowance, which is the amount you can pay into your ISA every year. In the 2013/14 tax year it is £11,520.

This ISA allowance comes in two parts – you can either invest the whole lot in a stocks and shares ISA or put up to half, i.e. £5,760, into a cash ISA and the balance into a stocks-and-shares ISA.

Allowances traditionally go up each April in line with inflation. You can pay into a different ISA each year, but you are only allowed to pay into one stocks and shares ISA and one cash ISA in any one tax year.

ISA allowances operate on a 'use it or lose it' basis. If you haven't used your full allowance by 5 April in any tax year, it is lost forever.

Just to be clear, investment returns such as interest, dividends or capital gains from existing ISA investments do not count towards your ISA allowance. You can withdraw money from your ISA at any time, but paying it back in again uses up more of your ISA allowance and is only permitted if you have not exceeded your annual allowance.

Your ISA investments can grow free of capital gains tax, and there is no tax to pay on any investment income that your ISA receives.

- **Cash ISA** – interest is paid to your ISA gross, i.e. without any deduction of tax.
- **Stocks and shares ISA** – interest is paid to your ISA after tax at 20 per cent has been deducted at source. Dividends are paid to your ISA with a 10-per-cent tax credit, but this cannot be reclaimed. More later on this.

Paying money in

You can pay money into an ISA either on a monthly basis or in single lump sums. Payments into an ISA are known as 'subscriptions'. Most investment platforms accept subscriptions into stocks and shares ISAs of as little as £50 a month, with some having no minimum payment for subscriptions at all when they are made by direct debit. If you are opening a stocks and shares ISA with a one-off lump sum, there is typically a modest minimum subscription required.

There is normally no charge for making a subscription into a stocks and shares ISA. But once your money is inside the ISA wrapper there are a variety of charges you may encounter. (These are covered in Chapter 20.)

By investing on a monthly basis and spreading your purchases over the year you not only spread the pain of money coming out of your current account but you also considerably reduce the risk of buying all your shares on a day when the price is high. This risk-mitigation strategy is known as 'pound-cost averaging'.

ISA or SIPP?

It depends on your personal circumstances. If you are young and don't want to tie up your investments until you are 55, then you should focus your savings on an ISA rather than a SIPP.

Your ISA contributions are, however, being funded out of taxed income, whereas SIPP contributions attract tax relief at your marginal rate.

This means paying into a SIPP becomes particularly attractive if you are a higher or additional-rate tax payer now but expect to be a basic-rate tax payer in retirement – because your pension is taxed as earned income. Other factors to consider when deciding whether to pay money into a SIPP or an ISA are covered in later chapters.

Who can pay into an ISA?

To make a payment into a stocks and shares ISA you have to be aged 18 or over (for children see the section on Junior ISAs, below), resident in the UK and have not subscribed to another stocks and shares ISA in the current tax year. Crown employees, such as diplomats and members of the armed forces, and their spouses and civil partners, are also entitled to hold an ISA.

UK residents over the age of 16 can invest in a cash ISA.

Bed and ISA

'Bed and ISA' is the name given to a strategy for people with unused ISA allowances, but no spare cash to invest, to use up their ISA allowance by placing other investments such as shares into their ISA in lieu of a cash subscription. Your investment platform will explain the mechanics to transfer investments from your Dealing Account to your stocks and shares ISA and may offer reduced dealing commissions, to ease the costs of selling and then re-purchasing your investments. As well as dealing commission, other likely costs are the spread, being the difference between the selling and buying price of the shares and stamp duty of 0.5 per cent on the re-purchase.

Don't forget, the sale of personally held investments in this way will be a sale for capital gains tax purposes. This may be useful if, for example, you have capital gains elsewhere in your portfolio and are trying to use up your annual capital gains tax allowance.

What you can invest in

Stocks and shares ISA

When it comes to investing in a stocks and shares ISA the range of possible investments is bewildering. Many providers will give you access to a wide range of funds, investment trusts, government and corporate bonds and quoted shares.

Stocks and shares ISA – permitted investments

- Shares, corporate bonds, investment trusts and exchange-traded funds listed on a recognised stock exchange including the Alternative Investment Market (AIM).
- Unit trusts and OEICs, either Financial Conduct Authority (FCA) authorised or European equivalent.
- Gilts and corporate bonds with five or more years to maturity, including those gilts that are undated or irredeemable.
- Cash awaiting investment.

These different types of asset are explained in greater detail in later chapters. ISAs have been able to hold AIM shares since August 2013 when the government removed the restriction preventing shares on the junior investment market being held in ISAs.

Cash ISA

The cash ISA component of your allowance can be invested in cash deposits, typically with high-street banks and building societies.

Watch out for cash ISA providers that lure you in with a table-topping rate, only to slash it to almost zero 12 months after you give them your money. Many of the biggest providers pay derisory rates of interest to existing customers after the introductory rate has expired, so it usually pays to shop around for the best deals and keep transferring your cash ISA holdings every year.

You will come across two terms in relation to a cash ISA that are worth a brief explanation. The first is the AER, which stands for annual equivalent rate. The second is the gross rate.

The AER is the rate you want to be most concerned with as this is the true annual return you will get from your cash ISA. It takes account of the rate paid throughout the year, the frequency of interest payments and compound interest, meaning that if you get interest paid monthly, this interest will earn interest. A cash ISA with an AER of 2.25 per cent will return interest of £22.50 after a year on a £1,000 investment into a cash ISA.

The gross rate is the interest rate payable at the outset, including any initial bonuses. It will make no allowance for the frequency of interest payments or compound interest.

A cash ISA advertised with a gross rate of 2.25 per cent will return a lesser amount if, for example, the actual rate paid drops to, say, 2 per cent after a 3 month introductory bonus. Only ever use the AER when comparing cash ISA rates.

Junior ISA

Junior ISAs replaced Child Trust Funds, which ceased being offered to those born on or after 3 January 2011. A Junior ISA can be opened for anyone under the age of 18 who was born before September 2002 or after 3 January 2011. Children born between these dates must save in Child Trust Funds instead. These products will be merged in due course, with Junior ISAs prevailing as the investment product of choice for children.

You can establish a Junior ISA for a child as long as you have parental responsibility for them. The child must be resident in the UK.

The maximum you can pay into a Junior ISA is £3,720 for the 2013/2014 tax year.

Junior ISAs and inheritance tax

If a parent, grandparent or indeed anyone else pays a subscription into a Junior ISA on behalf of a child then it is treated as a gift. If the person paying the subscription, the donor, subsequently dies then the gift may be subject to inheritance tax. There are, however, a number of exemptions that would render this unlikely and the rules below apply to gifts generally and not just subscriptions into Junior ISAs.

- **Annual exemption** – gifts of up to £3,000 per annum in 2013/14 are normally exempt. You can also carry forward unused allowances up to one tax year.

- **Gifts out of income** – Gifts paid out of surplus income, where the donor's standard of living has not been reduced as a result of the donation, are normally exempt.

- **Potentially exempt transfers** – if a gift is subject to inheritance tax, the tax payable reduces to zero once seven years have elapsed between the date of the gift and the death of the donor.

The money can be invested in either a cash Junior ISA or stocks and shares Junior ISA, up to the £3,720 annual limit. A child may not hold more than one cash Junior ISA and one stocks and shares Junior ISA at any given time.

Funds held in Junior ISAs cannot be accessed until the child reaches 18, at which point it becomes their money. Funds held in a Junior ISA are rolled into a standard ISA at the age of 18, which means tax advantages are retained.

In the tax year the child turns 18, the full Junior ISA allowance can be paid before the 18th birthday and the full adult ISA allowance can be paid afterwards, meaning both allowances can be used in the same tax year.

Why have an ISA?

The ability of ISAs to shelter investments from income tax and capital gains tax makes them an immensely valuable weapon in the DIY investor's armoury. Successful DIY investors will be making a combination of capital gains and investment income, hopefully above and beyond their normal tax allowances. By maximising the use of ISAs, unnecessary tax liabilities can be avoided.

Tax advantages

Capital gains tax

Capital gains tax can be costly for anyone cashing in assets that have risen in value considerably. For investments held personally, for example in a Dealing Account, capital gains tax of 18 or 28 per cent is chargeable on all capital gains above an annual allowance (£10,900 in 2013/2014).

The 28-per-cent rate is payable if the gains above the threshold, when added to your income, would take you into the 40-per-cent income tax band. Certain assets, such as private company shares, may be subject to a lower capital gains tax. Assets held within ISAs, on the other hand, do not create any capital gains tax liabilities at all.

However, it should be noted that losses on assets held within ISAs cannot be set against capital gains elsewhere in your portfolio.

Income tax

It sounds obvious, but there is no income tax liability on any money you draw out of an ISA.

Transferring your existing ISA

You may find you are not happy with your existing ISA provider and want to switch to a different one. You may want to bring all your assets into a single place, or want access to lower charges, better service or a wider range of investable assets.

The process of transferring your ISA

A cash ISA can be transferred into a new cash ISA and/or into a stocks and shares ISA. A stocks and shares ISA can, however, only be transferred into another stocks and shares ISA.

For subscriptions placed with providers in previous tax years, you can transfer some or all of your holdings to a different provider. But you are only allowed to transfer your current year's ISA subscriptions if you transfer them in their entirety.

If you are transferring from an insurance company or bank-run stocks and shares ISA then re-registration may not be possible and your existing ISA provider may have to sell your investments and send cash to your new ISA provider, for you to then invest.

You could, of course, choose to sell all of your ISA investments prior to transferring, which may speed up the transfer process as only cash is being transferred. But, it will mean that you are out of the market for a period of time and you will be incurring unnecessary costs to sell and then re-purchase your ISA investment holdings.

Some investment platforms may impose a transfer out or re-registration charge, often based on the number of lines of stock, meaning the number of separate investments, you hold. As DIY investment platforms all desperately want your business, it is quite common for the receiving ISA provider to offer to pay some or all of your exit charges. Even if there are no advertised offers, it is worth asking your proposed new ISA provider if they will pick up these exit charges.

Re-registration of your ISA investments from one platform to another can take between four and six weeks. This may sound a long time in today's digital age, but the reason for this delay is that industry-wide systems are not yet fully developed to automate the transfer of investments between different providers.

The re-registration process may appear relatively slow, but it is seamless, meaning you will not be out of the market at any time. Crucially, transferring your ISA holdings in this way does not crystallise gains or losses for tax purposes, and assets remain within the ISA wrapper throughout the process.

Where do I find an ISA provider?

Cash ISAs

Many DIY investment platforms do not offer cash ISAs, though one or two do. You will typically find that the best rates for cash ISAs are available direct from banks and building societies, so you may have to accept that your cash ISA will sit outside your main investment holdings held by your investment platform.

If you take out a cash ISA, remember to create a diary note for 11 months in the future to check the market again for the best rates and switch your money to a better account if necessary. Go to one of the comparison websites to compare cash ISAs: www.moneysavingexpert.com; www.moneysupermarket.com; www.money.com; www.gocompare.com. All have comparisons of the top cash ISAs.

Stocks and shares ISA

The websites listed above also all have details of which companies offer a stocks and shares ISA. Two websites that provide a comparison tool to allow you to compare charges of the main DIY investment platforms are www.diyinvestor.co.uk and www.candidmoney.com. If you just want to invest in funds and are not interested in investment trusts, exchange-traded funds or shares then you will find a useful comparison tool at www.rplan.co.uk that looks at the charges of a number of 'funds-only' ISAs.

The Dealing Account

The Dealing Account, sometimes known as a general investment account (GIA) or funds and shares account, is where the DIY investor holds assets that aren't held within a SIPP or ISA. This can be because you have put all you want or are able into your SIPP and ISA, or because you are investing in asset classes not allowed in these tax wrappers.

History

Without Dealing Accounts there would be virtually no DIY investors. Developed from the online brokers that emerged with the growth of the internet in the late 1990s, the history of the DIY investor is bound up in the history of the Dealing Account.

In the days before the internet and electronic trading, anyone wanting to buy shares had to phone up a stockbroker and place an order over the phone. If you wanted to buy funds then this was typically done through a financial adviser or direct from the fund manager. Broking commissions were eye-watering when compared to today's levels.

Those laborious processes were revolutionised by two key technological developments – the advent of electronic share dealing in the 1980s and the emergence of the internet a decade later.

Online share dealing first started in the United States in 1994, with the services arriving in the UK shortly afterwards.

The fast, simple and convenient process offered by these early-day investment platforms made DIY investing attractive to an increasing proportion of the population. By the late 1990s anyone with an internet connection and a computer could access real-time dealing, live valuations of shares and funds, as well as an increasing amount of market data to help them with their investment decision making.

The proliferation of the internet fuelled a rapid growth in the number of online share dealing services. It was a growth that tracked the technology bubble of the late 1990s, of which it formed a part. The number of web-based brokerages is believed to have grown from around 12 in 1994 to well in excess of 100 by the turn of the century.

With share prices on a seemingly one-way upwards trajectory, there was also a significant increase in the number of online investors. Interest in investments among the UK public was also fuelled by the demutualisations that made shareholders of millions of building society savers. The bursting of the dot-com bubble in March 2000 brought a sense of reality to people who were giving up well-paid jobs to trade shares, spending all day in front of their computer screens.

The story of Joseph Kennedy pulling out of the stock market in 1929, just before the Wall Street Crash, after he was given share tips by a shoe shine boy is now etched into folklore. Back in March 2000, I had my own shoe shine moment while out for dinner with a friend who runs a building company. He mentioned that his security guards were spending most of the day buying and selling shares, a far more profitable venture than working for him. The following morning at market opening I sold all of my technology shares, only hours before the market went into freefall.

Genius? Well it might have been had I not bought all the shares back a week later thinking I had ridden the storm. The shake out of the dot-com bubble took a while – the Techmark 100, the index of the UK's largest technology stocks, fell steadily, in the way that a brick falls steadily, between March 2000 and early 2003, losing about 90 per cent of its value.

Every decade or so sees a stock market crash or major correction and you should always bear this in mind when you are investing. Some of the professional investors were caught out as badly as private investors, so the fear of a crash is no justification for not being a DIY investor. It is back to the emotional investing point I made in the first chapter. If it looks too good to be true, it probably is. Intelligent and normally rational people were buying into the dream of dot-com companies that never had and, under the bounds of common reason, never would make any money. It sounds daft now, but of course hindsight is a wonderful thing.

Online brokers recovered from this temporary setback and continued, albeit with more sober and realistic business models and projections. With so many players in the market, and with DIY investors becoming increasingly well informed and demanding, the cost of dealing and investing fell, and continues to fall to this day.

The last two decades have seen a massive growth in the range of funds, shares and other investments that can be bought and sold through Dealing Accounts and in the research tools available to assist DIY investors make their decisions.

Some of today's DIY investment platforms have their origins as a stockbroker, either a traditional firm that has embraced the internet or an internet-based start-up. Some investment platforms have grown up as financial advisers who have embraced the idea of offering funds with no advice and no initial commission. Some have developed their proposition into that of a fully-fledged investment platform, extending their investment range to include shares, gilts, corporate bonds, investment trusts and exchange-traded funds.

Others, often referred to as discount brokers or fund supermarkets, have kept their funds-only model and are being challenged by the advent of the RDR (Retail Distribution Review). From the end of 2013, these discount brokers have to charge an explicit fee and won't be able to receive commission from fund managers. It is hard to see much of a future for those discount brokers that don't extend their investment range to a full service-offering. Therefore, this book focuses on those investment platforms that can offer the full range of investments.

What you can invest in

The world is your oyster when it comes to the range of assets available through Dealing Accounts and is only restricted by the investment platform itself. ISAs and SIPPs offer access to literally thousands of funds, investment trusts, government and corporate bonds and quoted shares. Dealing Accounts offer all of these and more – including those asset classes that can't be held within the tax-advantaged ISA and SIPP wrappers, such as shares trading on niche exchanges and derivatives.

Dealing Accounts – what you can invest in

- Shares issued by companies listed on recognised exchanges around the world.
- Unit trusts and open-ended investment companies (OEICs).
- Investment trusts.
- Gilts.
- Government bonds from countries overseas.
- Corporate bonds.
- Exchange-traded funds (ETFs).
- Structured products.
- Permanent interest-bearing shares (PIBS).
- Real estate investment trusts (REITs).
- Venture capital trusts (VCTs).
- Contracts for difference (CFDs) and other derivatives.
- Foreign exchange.

How Dealing Accounts work

Setting up your account

Before setting up an account, you need to decide which investment platform is the best one for your needs. Not all platforms are cheapest for every part of the process, and can be more or less expensive depending on whether you are using them for a SIPP, an ISA or a Dealing Account, and depending on the frequency, size and type of investments you are buying or selling.

For most people it makes sense to hold your ISA, SIPP and Dealing Account with the same investment platform, although DIY investors who are frequent dealers may decide that different providers work out as more cost effective for different parts of their overall investment. Before selecting a Dealing Account, check the detailed section on comparing investment platforms in Chapter 20 to decide which one is best value for you.

Once you have decided which provider to go with, registering and applying for an account online should take just a few minutes. You must be over 18 to open a Dealing Account, and you can open one in joint names with your spouse or partner if you wish, giving some tax advantages that I will cover in later chapters.

Also, some investment platforms allow you to link accounts so that one person can manage all the family's accounts.

Paying money in – cash

Before you can start investing, you need to pay money into your account. You can pay money in, whether online or over the phone, with a debit card, or you can normally send a cheque in the post.

Drip-feeding money into the market on a monthly basis allows you to spread the risk that you buy on a day when the investment you are buying is particularly expensive. You can drip-feed money into the market whether you pay by monthly direct debit or in a lump sum. Where a lump-sum payment is to be drip-fed into the market, the cash sits in the cash account and a monthly instruction to invest is set up.

Paying in shares

You can pay shares into your account by sending the certificates to your investment platform with a stock transfer form, which is available from any investment platform.

This process of moving your shares and funds from one investment platform to another investment is called re-registration and is the same as the process described in Chapter 3 for ISA transfers. You can transfer investments held in your Dealing Account without raising a potential capital gains tax liability and without incurring stamp duty costs, although the investment platform you are leaving may have one-off charges for processing the transfer away from them.

Capital gains tax

This book is not intended to be a tax guide, but I will cover the high-level tax issues you will face as a DIY investor. When you sell an investment for more than you bought it for, you create a capital gain. There are, however, a number of exemptions available that mean, in reality, many people escape capital gains tax altogether.

The first and probably most important exemption is your annual capital gains exemption. In the 2013/14 tax year this is £10,900 and will increase by £100 in each of the subsequent tax years. Everyone gets this allowance, and without stating the obvious (though there is little obvious in tax), a husband and wife or two civil partners each get their own allowance in full.

Your taxable gain is the total of your capital gains less your annual exempt amount.

The second exemption to be aware of, if you are married or in a civil partnership, is the fact that gifts to a spouse or a civil partner do not create a capital gains liability. The original cost of the investment transfers to the recipient, for calculation of their capital gains tax liability when they ultimately sell it.

You may have already worked out how these two exemptions can be used together to mitigate tax. More on this later.

The rate of capital gains tax payable is 18 per cent if your combined income and taxable gains are less than the upper limit for basic-rate income tax. Any taxable gains above this amount are taxed at 28 per cent.

If you own investments jointly with your spouse, any capital gains or losses are shared equally between you.

You can offset capital gains in the current tax year against capital losses in previous years. You must first net off any gains and losses in the current tax year, and only once you have done that can you take advantage of prior-year losses. You can go back up to four tax years, so in the 2013/14 tax year you can offset losses as far back as 2009/10. There are certain restrictions, but the guidance available on HMRC's website is reasonably user-friendly in this area.

Exempt assets

Certain assets are normally exempt from capital gains tax:

- Your main home.
- ISA.
- SIPP.
- National Savings Certificates.

- Certain approved share option schemes.

- Betting and lottery wins.

- Private cars, boats, caravans, etc. whose expected life is less than 50 years (I have never come remotely near to making a gain on any one of these!).

- Tangible moveable property, such as furniture and jewellery, worth less than £6,000.

Typically, where an asset is exempt then any losses in respect of that asset will not be allowed to be offset against a gain.

Note that on your death, no capital gains tax is paid, but inheritance tax is paid on the full value of your assets after using up any inheritance tax-free allowance.

'Bed and breakfast'

'Bed and breakfast' is, in the context of investing, the name given to a scheme to crystallise gains or losses on investments to offset crystallised losses or gains elsewhere in your portfolio and reduce your overall liability to capital gains tax.

This term originates from a practice, common years ago, when investors would sell investments to crystallise a gain equivalent to the capital gains tax allowance, go to bed, wake up, have their breakfast and then buy exactly the same investments back again. The going to bed, waking up and having breakfast bits were, of course, all superfluous. The idea was to take advantage of the annual capital gains tax allowance without being 'out of the market' for any period of time.

HMRC moved to stop this loophole in 1998 by introducing a rule that says if you buy back the same investment within 30 days, then the sale is disregarded for capital gains tax purposes.

'Bed and ISA'

'Bed and ISA' and 'bed and SIPP' strategies offer the same ability to wipe out capital gains tax liabilities but with the additional attraction of being able to place investments within a tax-advantaged environment.

'Bed and spouse'

'Bed and spouse' is not quite as saucy as it sounds, but is still good solid tax planning. Married couples and civil partners can minimise their capital gains tax bill by making the most of any unused tax allowances the other party may have. This can involve giving investments to the spouse or civil partner with unused tax allowances, made easy by the fact that transfers between spouses and civil partners do not crystallise a capital gains tax liability. There are no time restrictions involved, and you can transfer investments to a spouse or partner who can then sell them immediately to take advantage of this.

There is no liability to stamp duty on the transfer, nor do they create a potential inheritance tax liability. The original base cost of the shares will carry over to the recipient, so the ultimate gain or loss is not affected. All you are doing is making best use of two capital gains tax allowances instead of one. Using any or all of the unused allowances of a spouse or civil partner to reduce your own tax bill is known as a 'bed and spouse' strategy.

Gifts between spouses and civil partners can also cut the couple's overall income tax bill. Putting income-generating investments into the name of the spouse or civil partner with the lowest total income will mean tax on that investment income will be paid at a lower rate.

example

Bed and spouse – sharing allowances

Katie and Peter are married. Katie has a large portfolio of shares and wants to sell shares in a pharmaceutical company that have increased from £20,000 to £40,000.

If she simply sells the shares herself she will crystallise a capital gain of £20,000, £9,100 of which is liable to capital gains tax after her £10,900 capital gains allowance is taken into account. As she is a higher-rate taxpayer she will pay capital gains tax at 28 per cent, totalling £2,548.

By transferring half of the shares into Peter's name she pays no capital gains tax at all, as her capital gain is now just £10,000. Peter also has a £10,000 capital gain that is within his annual allowance.

Peter is earning less than Katie, and only pays basic-rate tax. So, if the capital gain on the sale of the shares had been greater and exceeded both their annual allowances it would have been more tax efficient for the majority of the shares to be held in Peter's name, as he would have been liable to capital gains tax at only 18 per cent and not the 28 per cent payable by Katie.

5

SIPPs

S IPPs have become the retirement savings product of choice for investors wanting pensions that offer transparency, control, choice and competitive pricing.

A SIPP, which stands for self-invested personal pension, is a type of personal pension plan. SIPPs differ from personal pensions offered by insurance companies by virtue of the fact that they put you, the DIY investor, in complete control of where you invest your retirement savings.

SIPP overview

SIPPs offer exactly the same tax advantages as traditional personal pensions, meaning basic-rate, higher-rate and additional-rate taxpayers can get 20, 40 and 45 per cent tax relief on contributions respectively.

Investments held within a SIPP grow free of income and capital gains tax. Tax deducted at source on dividends cannot be reclaimed, although there is no additional tax to pay. Where investment income is paid into the SIPP gross, for example in the case of gilts, most corporate bonds, property and cash deposits held within a SIPP, no tax is due.

While mainstream pension plans typically only offer access to a predetermined selection of funds, SIPPs allow you to invest in a far wider range of assets, including unit trusts, OEICs, shares, bonds, exchange-traded funds and commodities. Online SIPPs allow you to view and adjust your holdings 24 hours a day, giving real-time pricing of the assets held in your SIPP portfolio.

A quarter of the value of a SIPP can be taken as a tax-free lump sum from the age of 55, making SIPPs an extremely efficient way of saving for the long term. SIPPs also give you the flexibility to remain invested in stocks, shares and other investments while you draw a pension income, as an alternative to ever buying an annuity.

You can have a SIPP even if you are a member of a company pension scheme – for example, if you want to save more than the amount offered by your employer's pension scheme. However, if you are a member of a company pension scheme it normally makes sense to take advantage of that offer before setting up any alternative top-up arrangements.

You can use a SIPP to buy commercial property, whether it be your business premises or purely as a stand-alone investment, although you will need what is often called a 'full' or 'full-fat' SIPP. You will find that most DIY investment platforms offer a low-cost online SIPP, but few if any of these will allow investment directly in commercial property. Costs for full SIPPs are normally considerably higher than their online counterparts due to the more complex administration involved.

More esoteric investments, such as unlisted company shares and some unregulated collective investments, can also be held within a SIPP. Again, a full SIPP may be required if these assets are to form part of your SIPP portfolio.

History

SIPPs evolved from personal pension plans, which were first introduced in 1988 by the Conservative government in a bid to encourage people to save for their own retirement rather than rely on the state.

In his Budget speech of 1989, Chancellor Nigel Lawson promised to 'make it easier for people in personal pension schemes to manage their own investments'. Shortly after, SIPPs were launched, enabling savers to invest in a far wider range of asset types than the personal pensions traditionally offered by insurance companies.

The growth of the internet around the turn of the millennium gave online SIPPs a massive boost and their popularity has increased year on year ever since.

A radical liberalisation and harmonisation of the rules surrounding pensions introduced in 2006 saw the Treasury float the idea of allowing residential property to be held within SIPPs. It eventually pulled back from taking this controversial step, but the press coverage that SIPPs got during this period was instrumental in bringing them to the fore as a mainstream savings product. SIPPs are as popular with DIY investors as they are with savers who use financial advisers.

If you want to minimise charges, I would challenge anyone to find a lower-cost pension than a low-cost online SIPP invested in a handful of mainstream tracker funds. Your all-in annual charge could be as little as 10 or 15 basis points – that is, between 0.1 and 0.15 per cent.

Compare this to the much-lauded 'low-cost' stakeholder pension with its 100 basis points, or 1 per cent annual management charge. Other pension products charge even more than stakeholder pensions, and if you are unfortunate enough to have an old-style pension that is invested in what are called 'initial' or 'capital' units then you could be paying as much as 3 or 4 per cent per annum in charges.

Yet more liberalisation of the rules surrounding SIPPs was seen in 2011 with the removal of the obligation to buy an annuity at the age of 75. Some may argue that this obligation was removed in 2006 with the introduction of the since-rescinded ASP (alternatively secured pension) rules but these earlier well-intentioned rules were fundamentally flawed and ineffective.

In 2011 the income drawdown rules, which hitherto had only applied up until the age of 75, were extended with no age limit. This removed the much-feared black hole scenario, where pension savers over the age of 75 could lose virtually their entire pension savings after their and their spouse's death.

The other concept that was introduced at the same time was flexible drawdown. This allows SIPP holders to draw income amounts from their SIPP as large and as frequent as they want. To the surprise of many, this could include extinguishing the full value of the SIPP as a lump sum, subject to income tax. But before you get too excited there is a big proviso here. The SIPP holder has to be in receipt of a guaranteed income of at least £20,000 per annum before they are allowed to take 'advantage' of flexible drawdown.

This condition can be fulfilled by having a pension annuity, company pension or a state pension in aggregate at least equal to the £20,000-per-annum threshold. Sadly, other forms of income such as investment income or salary do not count.

Why do the government impose this condition? Well, they seem to have an irrational fear that someone who has been prudent enough to accumulate pension savings throughout their working life will suddenly turn into a spendthrift and fall back onto state benefits.

SIPPs have only been regulated since April 2007, the same date from which operating, or administering, a SIPP also became a regulated activity.

In a little over 20 years, SIPPs have evolved into flexible, transparent, tax-advantaged savings vehicles offering investors choice and value for money. With over 800,000 individual plans now in existence, holding assets in excess of £90bn, SIPPs have been one of the genuine success stories in the financial services landscape.

Key reasons to have a SIPP:

- Tax relief on contributions at your marginal rate of tax.
- Investments grow free of income and capital gains tax.
- A quarter of the value of your SIPP fund can be taken tax-free from the age of 55.
- Pension income can be drawn directly from your SIPP instead of buying an annuity.
- Lump-sum benefits payable on death are free from inheritance tax (though there is tax to pay on lump sums paid on death if you have commenced benefits).
- Investment flexibility, before and after retirement.
- Transparency of charges.
- Low cost.
- You are in control.
- All your pensions are accumulated in one place.

Key reasons not to have a SIPP:

- You are in a company pension scheme that meets your pension needs.
- You don't like the restrictions that go hand in hand with pensions:
  - You can only access your benefits from the age of 55.
  - You can only access your SIPP in the form of a lump sum and taxable income.
  - SIPPs can't invest in certain assets, such as residential property.

Tax relief and contributions into SIPPs

One of the key incentives offered by the government for pension saving is the tax relief provided on the amounts paid into pensions by savers and their employers.

When you or your employer make a payment to a pension this is known as making or paying a 'contribution'.

You don't have to pay contributions to be a member of a SIPP, you can instead just transfer funds from pensions held elsewhere. However, if you want to increase the value of your pension, as well as aiming to maximise the growth you achieve from your investments, topping up your pension with contributions will help.

Contributions can be paid to a SIPP either as a one-off payment called a single contribution, or an instruction can be set up so that an agreed amount is paid each month, referred to as a regular contribution. Most SIPPs have modest minimum amounts for both single and regular contributions.

To make a contribution to a pension and claim tax relief, basic eligibility requirements must be met, but most UK residents will be eligible. There are limits on the amounts that can be paid into a pension and receive tax relief each tax year.

The concept of an annual allowance was introduced in 2006, this being the main control mechanism used by HMRC to ensure that you don't pay too much into your pension. If your total personal and employer contributions exceed the annual allowance then you may face a tax charge on the excess, although you may be able to carry forward any unused annual allowance from earlier tax years.

The annual allowance is £50,000, but will reduce to £40,000 from the start of the 2014/15 tax year.

As well as the annual allowance, there is a further restriction on how much you can pay into a SIPP, or indeed any other type of pension.

Personal contributions, though not employer contributions, are further restricted to a maximum of 100 per cent of your annual earnings or £3,600 – whichever is higher. 'Annual earnings' excludes investment or pension income.

Contributions – eligibility

Anyone can make a contribution to a UK-registered pension scheme, but there are limits on eligibility for tax relief on personal contributions.

In order to be eligible for tax relief on personal contributions, you must be a 'relevant UK individual' for the tax year in which a contribution is paid.

To qualify as a relevant UK individual you must:

■ have relevant UK earnings that are chargeable to income tax in that tax year, or

■ be resident in the United Kingdom at some time in the tax year, or

■ have been resident in the UK at some point in the previous five years and have been resident in the UK when you joined the pension scheme to which the contribution is to be paid, or

■ be a Crown employee or the spouse of a Crown employee in the tax year.

Tax relief on personal contributions, but not employer contributions, is only available to those under the age of 75.

Provided any of the 'relevant UK individual' criteria are met, tax relief will normally be allowed on personal contributions paid to a pension scheme, subject to your having sufficient unused annual allowance.

Additionally, personal contributions in a tax year must be no greater than either £3,600 or your UK earnings in that tax year, whichever is the greater.

Contributions – personal contributions

Personal contributions made to a SIPP are paid net of basic-rate income tax (20 per cent for the 2013/14 tax year).

For example, if you pay a personal contribution of £800, then your SIPP administrator will reclaim £200 from HMRC and credit this amount to your SIPP cash account once it has been received.

This reclaim of basic-rate tax will typically be credited to your SIPP between 6 and 11 weeks from the date of paying the contribution. This delay reflects the timing of the monthly tax reclaim process carried out by your SIPP administrator.

In the example above, you will be treated as having made a contribution of £1,000 to your SIPP for tax purposes. This is the total of the net personal contribution and the basic-rate tax reclaim associated with it.

Any higher-rate relief that you are entitled to is usually reclaimed via your self-assessment tax return.

In the above example, if you are a higher-rate taxpayer you will claim back an extra £200 via your tax return, making the cost of a £1,000 contribution equal to £600, as you would expect if you are paying a 40-per-cent rate of tax. If you are an additional-rate tax payer you will reclaim £250 via your tax return, making the cost £550 for a 45-per-cent tax payer.

You should be aware that there is no relief for either employer's or employee's National Insurance if a personal contribution is paid.

Most SIPP operators will not accept any personal contributions to a SIPP once someone has reached their 75th birthday, since they are not eligible for tax relief from that age.

Contributions – employer contributions

Your employer may also pay contributions into your SIPP.

All employer contributions are payable gross. By gross, I mean that if your employer agrees to pay you a £1,000 SIPP contribution, then that is how much they actually pay. As we have seen above, if you want to pay £1,000 as a personal contribution you only pay £800 and the tax system then kicks in to ensure you get the correct level of tax relief.

The employer will normally receive tax relief on any contributions they pay to your SIPP as a normal business expense and you, the employee, will not normally be taxed on these contributions.

Employer contributions are not restricted by the 100 per cent of UK earnings limit (or the £3,600 maximum) but they do count towards the annual allowance usage.

If an employer contribution is made on your behalf, no PAYE tax or employer's or employee's National Insurance is paid. So you may hear people say that an employer contribution is more 'National-Insurance efficient' than a personal contribution, which it is.

Contributions – third-party contributions

It is possible for another person to pay contributions to a SIPP on the SIPP holder's behalf. This would typically be a payment by the SIPP holder's spouse, parent or grandparent.

Any such contributions paid will be treated as the SIPP holder's own personal contributions for tax and allowance purposes. Third-party contributions are paid net of basic-rate tax.

Up to £3,600 can be paid irrespective of the recipient's earnings. To pay a £3,600 contribution, £2,880 is paid as a net contribution and after tax relief has been reclaimed by the SIPP operator, this increases to £3,600.

Contributions – annual allowance

The annual allowance is used by HMRC as a means of restricting tax relief on pension contributions. The annual allowance is £50,000 for the 2013/14 tax year and reduces to £40,000 on 6 April 2014.

When the annual allowance was first introduced, it was set at £215,000 for the tax year 2006/07, with predetermined staged increases to £255,000 in 2010/11. This was then reduced to £50,000 for the 2011/12 and 2012/13 tax years and further reduces to £40,000 for the 2014/15 tax year and beyond. The direction of travel is now quite clear – downwards.

To complicate the calculation, annual allowance usage is not always based simply on what you (and your employer and any third parties on your behalf) have paid to your SIPP (and other pension arrangements) during the relevant tax year.

Each scheme under which benefits are accrued has what is known as a 'pension input period'. Most SIPPs use the tax year as their pension input period but company schemes will often use their accounting year, which serves to make life very complicated. If you are only accruing benefits in a SIPP then you are probably safe to assume that your pension input period is the same as a tax year and you can ignore this concept.

You will then just need to ensure that your total pension contributions are within the annual allowance in the relevant tax year, with the additional test that your personal contributions do not exceed 100 per cent of your earnings, or £3,600, in that tax year.

If you are accruing benefits in several schemes, particularly where one or more is a company scheme, then you will need to aggregate the value of all types of contributions paid in all pension input periods ending in a particular tax year. A bit of further research on HMRC's website is advisable if this is relevant to you.

Contributions – carry forward of unused annual allowance

In some circumstances it is possible to reduce the impact of the annual allowance by the use of carry forward of any previously unused annual allowance.

Carry forward allows unused annual allowance of up to £50,000 from each of the three previous tax years to be swept up.

As long as you were a member of a registered pension scheme (whether or not you were contributing to it) in the tax year from which you wish to carry forward unused annual allowance, and you have sufficient UK earnings in the tax year in which you make the contribution, then you can use carry forward if your contributions exceed the annual allowance in that tax year.

Carry forward cannot be used unless you have exceeded the annual allowance in the current tax year. An example should help to explain the rules.

If we look at someone who has exceeded the annual allowance in 2013/14, their position could be as follows in Table 5.1.

table 5.1 Carry forward of unused annual allowance

Tax year	Contributions paid	Carry forward available for 2013/14
	£	£
2009/10	20,000	N/A – too long ago
2010/11	20,000	30,000
2011/12	50,000	NIL
2012/13	20,000	30,000
Total carry forward available for 2013/14		60,000

So, in the above example, the individual can pay up to £110,000 in 2013/14, being the £50,000 annual allowance in 2013/14 plus the £60,000 unused annual allowance carried forward.

If this is paid as a personal contribution, then this is subject to earnings being at least as high as the contribution. In reality, you would want your earnings to be a good bit higher than your contribution to maximise the tax relief. As tax relief is given at your marginal rate tax, if your earnings are the same as your personal contribution then you are getting a blend of nil-, basic-, higher- and possibly additional-rate tax relief.

If the annual allowance in any tax year is exceeded (after any available carry forward has been used up) then an annual allowance tax charge will apply. The mechanics for paying this tax charge are beyond the scope of this book, but they will be driven by your tax return and the net result will be to cancel out any tax relief on excessive contributions. In some cases this tax charge can be paid by your pension scheme.

Contributions – recycling

HMRC has introduced rules to stop what is commonly known as 'recycling'. This is nothing to do with our battle against climate change, but is HMRC's attempt to stop people abusing the pensions tax relief system. Fuelled by aggressive marketing and press coverage in the financial pages of the broadsheets, elderly pension savers were being encouraged to pay a pension contribution, take benefits immediately in the form of a tax-free lump sum and take a pension income. They would then reinvest the tax-free lump sum as a further pension contribution, from which benefits would again be taken immediately – providing a further tax-free lump sum and pension income. And so on.

The key test is whether it is pre-planned or not. So if you don't plan it, you are not doing it. If you are interested in understanding this topic further then I would suggest HMRC's website as a good starting point. Just Google 'HMRC pension recycling' and you will get to the relevant section on the Revenue's website.

Contributions – salary sacrifice

A salary sacrifice arrangement can be a tax-efficient way in which to pay contributions to a SIPP, and its origins lie in the differing treatment of National Insurance between employer and personal contributions.

This option is only available for those who are an employee of a business and not for a partner or a sole trader.

A salary sacrifice arrangement involves an individual agreeing to give up some salary or bonus in exchange for their employer making a contribution to their SIPP.

This results in the individual being in receipt of lower taxable earnings, and so benefiting in two ways:

◼ They will pay less in National Insurance contributions.

◼ Compared with making an equivalent personal contribution to their SIPP, the payment of an equivalent employer contribution allows them to invest the full contribution amount immediately. A corresponding personal contribution would have been paid net of basic-rate tax relief and there would have been a delay in the tax element being paid by HMRC to the SIPP.

The employer will make a saving in the amount of employer's National Insurance contributions it pays. This can mean it is possible to negotiate with the employer to see whether it is prepared to pass on some or all of its saving in employer National Insurance contributions by way of an additional employer contribution to the SIPP.

Salary sacrifice involves a change to an individual's contract of employment, so will need to be properly documented. The employee and employer need to establish the arrangement properly, and take the appropriate advice in connection with it. If the arrangements are not established properly and in the right circumstances, they could be challenged by HMRC.

When considering salary sacrifice it is important to consider other possible consequences of the salary reduction. For example:

◼ It may affect the level of any other benefits (such as death-in-service benefits) provided by the employer if they are related to salary.

◼ It may affect the amount a mortgage lender is prepared to lend (as a multiple of salary).

◼ It will lower earnings, which may itself restrict the amount that can be paid as a personal contribution into a SIPP.

◼ Many state benefits are linked to salary and the National Insurance contributions an individual pays. If salary is reduced there can be changes to entitlement to a range of state benefits, including state pension, Statutory Paternity/Maternity Pay and Statutory Sick Pay.

Although most employees will still receive sufficient salary and pay sufficient National Insurance contributions to maintain proper entitlement to benefits, the individual's circumstances need to be carefully considered.

Salary sacrifice is normally only used by high earners or directors in conjunction with a bonus payment, and in these cases many of the above issues fall away.

Contributions – defined benefit accrual

This section is only relevant if you are a member of a defined benefits scheme, also referred to as a final or career average salary scheme. If you are not a member of one of these schemes, then you can safely skip this section.

A SIPP is a money purchase scheme, and the payment of contributions to it and their interrelationship with the annual allowance and the pension input period have already been outlined.

For members of a defined benefits scheme it is not the amount of any contributions paid that is taken into account. For annual allowance purposes, it is the increase in the level of benefits being provided that is taken into account instead.

The reason for this may not be obvious. If a defined benefits scheme is underfunded then contributions may be set at a temporarily high level to restore the funding position. Similarly, if a scheme is overfunded then contributions may have been temporarily reduced, or even suspended.

So, there is often a disconnect between the amount of contributions paid and the benefits accrued for an individual in a defined benefits scheme and hence it would not be equitable to test contributions against an annual allowance.

Instead, benefits under a defined benefit scheme are tested to see whether they have increased in value over the period concerned.

This involves creating a notional value of the increase in pension entitlement accrued during the period. After making an adjustment for inflation, crudely this involves multiplying the increase in accrued pension by 16 to get a notional value that can be tested against the annual allowance. This is best highlighted by an example.

> **example**
>
> Paula has been in her employer's defined benefits scheme since 1 April 2001. This scheme had a pension input period ending on 31 March 2012.
>
> The accrued pension rights at the start of the pension input period (1 April 2011) were 10/60ths of Paula's pensionable earnings of £60,000 p.a. (i.e. £10,000 p.a.).
>
> The accrued pension rights as at the end of the pension input period, one year later, were 11/60ths of Paula's pensionable earnings of £70,000 p.a. (i.e. £12,833 p.a.).
>
> The annual increase in the Consumer Price Index (CPI) for the year to September 2010 was 3.1 per cent. We use the increase in the CPI for the 12 months to the September before the start of the tax year in question.
>
> The pension input amount – the amount tested against the annual allowance – for the 2011/12 tax year for the defined benefits scheme would be calculated as follows:
>
> The closing value is 16 x £12,833 = £205,333
>
> The starting value is 16 x £10,000 x 1.031 = £164,960
>
> The pension input amount for the defined benefits scheme is the difference of £40,373, which is the amount for the tax year 2011/12.

There are many complications in connection with defined benefits scheme structures that go beyond the scope of this book, but hopefully this gives you a flavour of how defined benefits schemes are treated under the annual allowance regime.

Guidance will normally be available from the defined benefits scheme trustees/administrator who should be able to give information relevant to specific circumstances.

HMRC's website also has some useful guidance and a calculator to assist you. The calculator can be found at www.hmrc.gov.uk/tools/pension-allowance/index.htm.

6

Transferring existing pensions into, or out of, a SIPP

This is the moment, I am afraid, where you need to take a deep breath and dig out all of those old dusty files marked pensions, if you have any. Hopefully you may be pleasantly surprised at how much has accumulated in your various pensions over the years – or maybe not.

Transferring your various pensions into a SIPP can make sense for a number of reasons. The average person in the UK will have 11 employers through their working life, which means most people end up with lots of pension pots, none of which on their own is of any great value.

The paperwork that pensions can generate knows no bounds, so consolidating your plans into one place will help you to keep track of your retirement savings. Being able to see all of your investments in one place makes it easier to plan for your retirement. It also makes it easier to build a portfolio of investments that accurately reflect your retirement objectives and appetite for risk. With pension schemes littered all over the place, it is nigh on impossible to implement a coherent investment strategy to achieve these objectives.

You may want to transfer your existing pensions into a SIPP if they are invested in a pension with high annual management charges, or with limited investment options.

There are, however, several reasons not to transfer your existing pension benefits into a SIPP.

Unfortunately, there is unlikely to be a simple answer to the question of whether you should transfer or not. Search the internet and you will find plenty of conflicting messages on the issue of transfers, some of which are accurate but many of which are born out of a lack of understanding or an irrational fear that all transfers are bad.

Pension transfers – the rules

The transfer of benefits into or out of a SIPP is permitted as long as the benefits come from or go to another suitable pension arrangement.

Benefits can be transferred between any registered pension schemes. A registered pension scheme is one that registers with HMRC and agrees to follow UK pensions legislation. A transfer involves the transferring scheme paying a transfer value to the receiving scheme.

To effect a transfer of an existing pension into your SIPP, you need to tell your SIPP administrator the name, address and reference number of the pension to be transferred. There will then be a flurry of paperwork, with every pension provider having their own idiosyncratic ways of dealing with this.

Most transfers are made in the form of a cash transfer between the two schemes. But it is possible to transfer assets rather than cash – a process known as an in-specie transfer. This is normally only possible where both the transferring and receiving schemes are SIPPs.

While a cash transfer may take two to three weeks, an in-specie transfer is a more complicated process and can take several more weeks. The benefits of an in-specie transfer are similar to those of an ISA re-registration, which we covered in Chapter 3. The costs are lower because you don't have to sell then repurchase the investments, with the added advantage that you remain invested throughout the transfer process.

Types of pension scheme

Your first job is to find out what type of pension you have. The next job, which is rather more challenging, is to find out what the transfer value is and what benefits you will be giving up by transferring it to a SIPP.

The key types of pension scheme you will come across are as follows.

Company pension schemes

Occupational pension scheme – this is a pension scheme established by an employer. It typically takes one of two forms, either a **money purchase scheme**, sometimes referred to as a defined contribution scheme, or a **final salary scheme**, sometimes referred to as a defined benefits scheme.

■ **A money purchase scheme** would typically see both you and your employer contributing a percentage of your salary into the scheme. There are no guarantees as to the level of benefits you will receive at retirement. Basically, you accumulate a pot of money and, at retirement, see what that can provide in the form of a tax-free lump sum and a pension. In most occupational money purchase schemes, the pension is provided by buying an annuity.

■ **A final salary scheme** would typically see you accrue benefits for each year of service based on your final salary. This may be something like 1/80th of your final salary for each year of service. So, if you work for 40 years, you will get a pension of half of your final salary. There are variations on this theme where benefits may be based on the average of your salary near the end, or throughout the whole, of your career.

Due to the press coverage associated with final salary schemes – they are great if you are a member but terrible if you are the employer, due to the massive cost – you will probably know if you are a member of a final salary scheme.

An occupational pension scheme is typically established as a trust and has a board of trustees who look after the members' interests.

Personal pension schemes

Alternatively, your work-based pension scheme may be a **group personal pension scheme** or a **group stakeholder scheme.** Technically speaking, these pensions are simply groups of individual personal pension schemes (see below) that happen to be administered by the employer. These are also money purchase schemes, but the key difference is that, unlike occupational money purchase schemes, they do not have boards of trustees and are regulated by the Financial Conduct Authority (FCA), formerly known as the Financial Services Authority (FSA), rather than the Pensions Regulator.

Personal pension scheme – this is a pension scheme that is established by an individual with a pension provider. Contributions can be paid by the pension saver and their employer and there are typically no guarantees as to the benefits that will be available at retirement. Stakeholder pensions and SIPPs are both personal pensions.

Other – other schemes you may see reference to in your bundle of papers include Section 32 plans, executive pension plans, retirement annuities, AVCs (additional voluntary contributions), FSAVCs (free-standing additional voluntary contributions) and appropriate personal pensions. For all intents and purposes, these can all be treated as personal pensions.

Issues to consider before transferring your existing pension benefits into a SIPP

- **Charges** – Compare the charges under your old pension with the SIPP you are considering. This comparison is not always easy, but you should have a go. In most cases the cheaper option becomes apparent very quickly.

- **Transfer penalty** – Does your old pension have an exit or transfer penalty for leaving?

- **With-profits investments** – If your pension fund is invested in a with-profits fund and you are near to retirement age then there may be merit in staying invested in the plan until the end of the term. It is notoriously difficult to assess the merits, or otherwise, of a with-profits fund and, to do this properly, specialist financial advice is probably the only way forward.

- **Guaranteed annuity rates** – Does your plan entitle you to any attractive guaranteed annuity rates that would be lost on transfer?

- **Defined benefits** – Are you in a defined benefit scheme? If so, the decision whether or not to transfer is a lot more complicated.

- **Options at retirement** – Does your existing pension give you access to income drawdown, or must you buy an annuity in order to get a pension?

- **Protected tax-free lump sum or low retirement age** – Does your existing pension allow you to take more than 25 per cent of your pension fund as a tax-free lump sum or to take benefits before the age of 55? If so, this will normally be lost if you transfer.

- **Cash or in-specie transfer** – If you decide to transfer, will it be a transfer of cash or of assets?

- **Overseas transfers** – Take great care if you are considering transferring to an overseas scheme.

Let's explore each of the above issues in a bit more detail.

Charges and transfer penalties

What drove me out of working for an insurance company was spending my days designing long-term savings products with charging structures and exit penalties that should have meant nobody in their right mind would buy them. It didn't matter that these products were awful because they were sold by an in-house sales team who were well skilled in selling the sizzle of what were rotten sausages.

I am pleased to say that the sort of pension products I am describing here have now been outlawed, so any new policies you might take out will not have these problems. But there are many old-style pension policies out there that still carry these toxic features. When a pension policy was sold, it generated a big lump of commission to the salesperson. As well as the commission it paid, the insurance company also had expenses to cover in setting up the policy, such as IT, administration and marketing costs.

It didn't take a marketing genius to work out that selling a pension policy where the first few years' premiums are eaten up in charges would be as easy as selling Luis Suarez shirts outside Goodison Park.

To cover this massive cost of getting pension business on their books, insurance companies used a variety of very innovative solutions that masked the real impact of the product's charges. These charging structures enabled the insurance companies to recoup their expenses and earn a handsome profit over the lifetime of the policy. The real challenge came when the policy was transferred mid-term to another pension arrangement, as many were. A transfer penalty was needed to ensure that the insurance company was not out of pocket. This transfer penalty is best described as the difference between what is called the 'fund value' and the 'transfer value'.

The fund value is the headline figure you get on annual statements. It is the *Parkers* car guide 'showroom' value of the car on your drive. It is what the car is worth unless you actually want to sell it, when you need to look at the trade-in price.

Similarly, the real value of your pension policy is the transfer value, as this is what the insurance company will pay if you want to transfer to another pension arrangement.

What are the key messages here? First, only ever believe the transfer value. Any other valuation provided is an illusory one. Secondly, the transfer penalty is just a discounted value of charges that you would have paid in any event. That is, you will suffer these charges whether you stay or whether you go. Your only choice is whether you pay these charges on the drip over the lifetime of the pension policy or whether you pay them as a lump sum when you transfer your pension benefits to another pension scheme.

So, while it may sound a controversial statement, not transferring your pension benefits because you will suffer a transfer penalty is flawed logic.

With-profits investments

Special considerations apply if you have a pension that is invested in a with-profits fund. This type of investment was a popular option in the eighties and nineties, but rapidly fell out of favour in the early years of the new millennium.

With-profits policies were sold as low-risk funds, run by insurance companies, invested in a combination of shares, property, bonds and cash.

The deal between the with-profits policyholder and the insurance company goes something like this – the policyholder pays a premium that is invested in a broad spread of investments. Dependent upon the returns that these investments achieve, annual bonuses are declared each year by the insurance company. Terminal bonuses for those reaching maturity are also declared each year.

The idea is that with-profit funds provide a 'smoothed' investment return. Some of the investment return in the good years is held back to increase the investment return in the bad years. Some of the investment return is also held back to pay a terminal bonus on maturity or retirement, which is really a loyalty bonus for staying the term of the policy. In the case of a with-profits pension, this could be 30 or 40 years.

There are only two controls on the insurance company's decision as to the amount of annual and terminal bonus declared each year. The first is one imposed on the appointed actuary of the insurance company – the person responsible for declaring bonuses each year. The appointed actuary is duty-bound to ensure that the amount of bonuses declared each year meets with policyholders' reasonable expectations. No shortage of wriggle-room there then.

The second is a control driven by the insurance company's sales and marketing department and is now largely redundant. When with-profits were at their height, the rate of annual and terminal bonus declared in any year was key to winning new business in the following year. Once with-profits investments fell out of favour, this latter control ceased to be effective.

If you choose to transfer a with-profits pension to a SIPP, or indeed any other pension scheme, then the insurance company is likely to impose what is called a 'market value adjustment'. Basically, this means that even though they 'give' you those annual bonuses year after year, they aren't actually for keeps. Well they are, but only if you continue as a premium-paying policyholder for the full term of the policy. If you don't fulfil this obligation then, at the insurance company's discretion, they can and almost certainly will claw back some of the bonuses they have previously awarded. They may also make an adjustment to take account of investment conditions, again under the banner of a 'market value adjustment'.

While the return over recent years of most with-profits policies has been very poor, if you are very close to retirement there may be merit in sticking with the policy to get your full entitlement of annual and terminal bonuses. The further away you are from the retirement date set on the pension policy, the harder it is to justify sticking with what can be best described as an investment form of a bygone age.

Guaranteed annuity rates

Some pension policies, particularly old policies such as retirement annuities, contain valuable guaranteed annuity rates. These guaranteed annuity rates were inserted into policies when interest rates were a lot higher than they are today. They weren't intended to be particularly valuable, but they have proven to be. In fact, the cost of paying the valuable guaranteed annuity rates promised to some Equitable Life policy-holders was what tipped the organisation into insolvency.

If you have a pension policy with a guaranteed annuity rate, unless you are in poor health or are totally against buying an annuity then it is probably worth keeping that particular pension policy where it is.

Defined benefits

The widely accepted view is that it is rarely a good idea to transfer your rights from a defined benefit pension plan into a SIPP, and this should be your starting position. There is, of course, no debate if you are still working for the employer that runs the scheme – you should stay put – though if you have moved jobs then the position is not quite so clear cut.

If you seek professional advice on whether to transfer defined benefits into a SIPP, a key plank on which any advice will be based is the 'critical yield'. This critical yield is the rate of investment return you will need to earn on the fund you transfer to, in order to provide equivalent income to the income you are giving up. I do fear that at times this type of analysis misses the point.

There are professional guidelines imposed on the actuary who signs off a transfer value – the amount that the final salary scheme will pay to another pension scheme to extinguish their liability to pay you benefits. So, it is safe to assume that the transfer value represents fair value for money.

Comparing a defined benefits scheme to a personal pension is a bit like comparing apples with oranges. Anyone who is concerned that the critical yield they have been quoted is so high it is unachievable should not be transferring their defined benefits into a SIPP. But if the critical yield is too high then you should question whether the transfer value is fair value for money – or whether the critical yield analysis is correct.

The real decision you are making, when considering whether or not to transfer, is whether you value the certainty of the amount of pension benefits you will receive from the defined benefits scheme as compared to the unknown benefits you could get from a SIPP, if you manage the investments yourself.

There are a few special occasions when the pendulum will swing further towards justifying a transfer, assuming of course you have left the employment of the employer relating to the defined benefits scheme:

- If you are in poor health.
- If you are offered an enhanced transfer value to leave the defined benefits scheme – although my suspicious mind would tell me that there may be a catch.

■ If your defined benefits scheme is poorly funded with no prospect of improvement – this may be reflected in a reduced transfer value.

The FCA doesn't think there are many situations where a transfer can be justified as good advice. That means that you will find it difficult to find a financial adviser who will recommend such a course of action. Unfortunately, the regulator's nervousness has led to most DIY investment platforms refusing to accept transfers from defined benefit schemes unless professional advice has been obtained to support such a move. While not impossible, you will therefore find it very difficult to transfer final salary benefits into a SIPP, which can be very frustrating.

Options at retirement

Most personal pensions, and all self-respecting SIPPs, offer income drawdown. This allows you to take a tax-free lump sum and keep the residual monies invested, while drawing an income from your pension pot. More later on this, but if you decide that you are likely to opt for income drawdown in favour of buying an annuity then this may tip the balance in favour of you transferring an occupational money purchase pot into a SIPP.

Transfers – pensions in payment

It is possible to transfer a personal pension scheme, which of course includes a SIPP, even if benefits have commenced using income drawdown.

You should also note that you can't transfer benefits from a defined benefit scheme once you have started receiving your pension income.

And without wishing to state the obvious, once you have bought an annuity the option to transfer to a SIPP is lost.

Transitional protection and transfers

'Transitional protection' is the name given to certain exemptions and protections from the new pension limits and allowances introduced in April 2006. Some of these are lost on transfer. (Transitional protection is covered in greater detail in Chapter 8.)

Partial transfers

A transfer normally involves transferring benefits in their entirety. However, personal pensions, including SIPPs, are often structured as 1,000 or more identical arrangements. This allows you to transfer just part of your personal pension or SIPP to another provider. Why might you want to do this? Well, you probably wouldn't, but a couple of circumstances spring to mind where this may be relevant.

You may have a personal pension with half of your funds invested in an equity fund and half in a with-profits fund. For reasons described above, you may want to keep your with-profits investment intact and just transfer the part of your personal pension that is invested in the equity fund.

Or, you may have an online SIPP and want to invest your SIPP in an asset that your SIPP administrator won't allow, such as unquoted shares. You could transfer part of the assets in your low-cost online SIPP to a full SIPP, and then use the money to buy the unquoted shares.

Partial transfers cannot normally be made from a personal pension where you have started drawing benefits.

Transfers – in-specie transfers

Although most transfers are made in the form of a cash payment between the pension schemes, it is possible for the schemes to agree to an in-specie transfer of assets, in lieu of cash, as part of the overall transfer.

This may be useful where there is a desire to change your SIPP provider but not the underlying investments.

An in-specie transfer allows the existing investments, such as a portfolio of stocks and shares or a commercial property, to be retained without the need to realise them for cash, avoiding the risk of potentially being temporarily out of the investment markets at an inopportune time.

Not all investments can be transferred in-specie since they may not be assignable or be capable of being re-registered into the name of the new SIPP. Some investments, such as unquoted shares, may not be acceptable to the new SIPP administrator. This makes it important to check that your new SIPP provider will accept all the investments in your existing SIPP.

The in-specie transfer is also likely to take a significantly longer time to complete than a cash transfer between schemes. This can have practical implications on matters such as the payment of drawdown pension income, since the new scheme will not be able to commence income payments until the transfer of assets has been fully completed and documented.

Transfers – overseas schemes

Transfers from a UK-registered pension scheme can be made into a qualifying recognised overseas pension scheme (QROPS). Transferring to a QROPS may make sense if you are genuinely emigrating to another country, but there are situations where it makes more sense to keep your money in the UK, so it is worth taking advice before doing so. Beware any companies claiming to be able to liberate your pension through a QROPS, as these schemes have enormous hidden fees and some are in breach of HMRC's regulations.

What SIPPs can invest in

Much contained in the previous chapters on SIPPs is equally applicable to personal and stakeholder pensions. But it is in the area of investments that SIPPs really stand out from the pension crowd.

The current list of what SIPPs can invest in was fixed in 2006. But in the years running up to these new rules the government had consulted on whether it should radically open up what a SIPP can invest in.

The press printed story after story suggesting that holiday homes in the UK and abroad, racehorses, works of art, fine wine, luxury yachts, flats for your kids and many more eye-catching investments might all be allowable in your SIPP, enabling you to acquire these things with the assistance of tax relief.

Every week the stories became more outlandish, but the government seemed intent on maintaining their position that virtually anything would be acceptable when it came to investing in SIPPs.

This period of intensive press coverage just served to raise the profile of SIPPs in the eyes of pension savers and their advisers. People weren't interested in traditional personal pensions or stakeholder pensions anymore. Everyone wanted a SIPP.

I was quite vocal at the time – both in the press and in discussions with HMRC – saying that I thought this move was madness. I was taking phone calls from Spanish property agents seeing if we would run a branded SIPP for them. Just imagine the subsequent losses if UK pensions had been allowed to invest in Spanish holiday homes, considering the significant property slump in that country in recent times.

Anyway, good sense did eventually prevail. I am led to believe that two events in the run-up to the 2005 Pre-Budget Report, now called the Autumn Statement, caused ministers to change their mind. I was involved in both of these events.

The first involved a *Sunday Times* article, or, more specifically, its headline. One of the big Scottish insurance companies had put out a press release saying that approximately £10bn of pension money would be invested in residential property, come the day when the new rules would be introduced.

The journalist who wrote the story asked me to proofread her article to check it was technically correct. The article was fine, but I did have a problem with the headline. It read 'Residential property in SIPPs to cost Treasury £4 billion'. The simple logic applied by the headline writer was that tax relief at 40 per cent would be granted on this £10bn, so that was the cost to the Treasury. The point I made was that most of the money that would be used to buy residential property was already in SIPPs up and down the country and hence tax relief had already been granted. My point was ignored but apparently this headline acted as a wake-up call for ministers about the scale of what they were about to sanction.

While I can probably claim the moral high ground on the dodgy headline saga, I struggle to do so on the second part of this story. I received a call just before the 2005 October half-term from a BBC researcher, asking if I would be interviewed on *Newsnight* to discuss the impending pension rule changes. Their plan was do a feature on racehorses, boats, Spanish holiday homes and vintage cars. The thought of being on the wrong end of a Paxman grilling didn't appeal, but I did see the opportunity to put the voice of reason forward.

I checked my diary and realised I was in Spain that half-term week on holiday, so it was all academic. 'No problem', the researcher said, 'we will meet you in Puerto Banus when we are doing the boat piece and interview you then.' So I agreed and duly met up with the BBC presenter one Thursday morning in Puerto Banus. We boarded a luxury 65-foot Princess yacht that the BBC had chartered for the day and set out to sea.

In order to carry out a few soundchecks and take some background shots, they asked me to stand on the bow of the boat, gave me a glass of champagne and the filming began. You can probably see what is coming and, to be honest, as the first sip – no pun intended – went down, so could I.

When the interview was aired, my protestations for a government u-turn were replaced with some anodyne musings about pension simplification being welcome. What was evident to BBC viewers, however, was that the chief executive of this particular SIPP provider would be quids in if these changes went ahead. Look at him celebrate with champagne on what could well be his own boat, soon to be an asset of his SIPP, no doubt.

Apparently, ministers were apoplectic with rage and, very soon, I started hearing rumblings that a u-turn was on the cards. On 5 December 2005 it was announced, and at least the end result was the right one.

Some thought SIPPs would quietly slink back to their position as a niche savings product for the wealthy. But Pandora's box had been opened and pension savers had looked inside. The flexibility, transparency and low-cost nature of SIPPs had been well and truly aired during the many articles written on this topic. The traditional personal pension was dead. Long live the SIPP.

This u-turn introduced the concept of taxable property. It was not the outright ban I had hoped for, but, instead, tax charges would be imposed should a SIPP invest in any assets that HMRC deemed inappropriate. Residential property clearly fell the wrong side of the line, as did racehorses, vintage cars and most other esoteric assets at the heart of the press excitement. But the rules around some other investments, such as unquoted shares, were, and still are, horrendous and unworkable.

This was the start of a polarisation of SIPP providers who would become defined by which assets they would accept in the SIPPs they administered. The larger SIPP providers took a conservative view and broadly reverted to the pre-2006 permitted investment list. Some of the smaller SIPP operators decided to make investment flexibility their unique selling point.

This has led more recently to intervention by the Regulator, who realised that investments such as unquoted shares and some unregulated funds are illiquid and risky, thereby creating an unacceptable risk of customer detriment. This story has some way to go yet and, if I had my way, HMRC and the Regulator would put their heads together and agree a list of permitted investments applicable to SIPPs. Just like the one for ISAs!

Today's online SIPPs offer access to a wide range of investments from around the world, such as:

■ Shares quoted on a recognised stock exchange.

- Unit trusts and OEICS, also known as collective investments.
- Government bonds/gilts.
- Corporate bonds.
- Permanent interest-bearing shares (PIBS).
- Warrants.
- Investment trusts.
- Exchange-traded funds.
- Exchange-traded commodities.

Full SIPPs may also be able to hold:

- Commercial property.
- Unlisted shares.
- Unregulated collective investments.

Commercial property in SIPPs

It is possible to invest in commercial property through a SIPP, although you will not be able to do so through the online SIPPs typically used by DIY investors – you will need a full SIPP to take advantage of this. Your SIPP can borrow up to 50 per cent of the value of your SIPP to fund the purchase of the property.

It is possible for small business owners to use SIPPs to purchase their own premises. The tenant must pay a market rent, which is paid into the SIPP free of income tax, and growth in the value of the property is free of capital gains tax.

Borrowing

A SIPP is permitted to borrow money. The most common example is for borrowing to be used to assist with the purchase of a commercial property by a SIPP.

SIPP borrowing is restricted by HMRC rules and must not exceed 50 per cent of the net value of the SIPP. Net value means the value taking into account any existing borrowing.

Commercial property has worked well in SIPPs since their introduction back in 1989. It is not without its complications and, sadly, the borrowing rules introduced in 2006 have severely restricted flexibility on this front. Prior to 2006, SIPPs could borrow 75 per cent of the cost of a property. So, ignoring taxes and costs, a SIPP worth £25,000 could buy a property for £100,000, supported by £75,000 of borrowing.

Under the current rules, that same SIPP can only borrow 50 per cent of the fund value, namely £12,500, thereby facilitating the purchase of a property worth only £37,500. HMRC's response, normally off the record, has always been that if they had a blank sheet of paper they would not allow any gearing at all in tax-privileged products. An ISA can't borrow, so nor should a SIPP be able to. I sort of see their logic, but I have seen many small businesses survive and even flourish by using their SIPP to buy their commercial property and most of these purchases wouldn't have happened without some element of borrowing.

Care must be taken to include VAT in property and borrowing calculations as many commercial properties are subject to VAT. For example, in order to buy a property worth £150,000 plus VAT the SIPP will need to be worth at least £120,000, as the cost of the property is £180,000 including VAT, funded by £60,000 of borrowing. This is very unfair as in most cases the VAT on the property purchase is reclaimable by the SIPP, but those are the rules. This example makes no allowance for legal costs and stamp duty, which similarly need to be included.

Unlisted shares

It is possible to hold unlisted shares in a SIPP, although there are complex rules surrounding when it is permitted to do so. Many SIPP providers do not allow unquoted shares because of the complexities of ensuring these rules have not been breached.

Unlisted shares will trigger tax charges in SIPPs where:

■ The SIPP holder or a person connected to them has or will have in the future a 20-per-cent or more interest in the company. 'Connected person' means husband, wife, business partner, their partner, civil partner, brother, sister or child, or

■ The SIPP holder or a connected person is a 20-per-cent controlling director of the company or of any other company that holds an interest in that company, or

■ The transaction would enable the SIPP holder to occupy or use any property of the company at preferential rates.

Loans (not borrowing)

HMRC rules do not allow a SIPP to lend money to the SIPP holder (or to a person or company connected with the SIPP holder) without incurring significant tax charges, but they do allow loans to be made to third parties. Many SIPP administrators refuse to allow this due to the administrative complexities.

Investments – tax position

The tax rules on investments are the same as for a stocks and shares ISA, except that in a SIPP, interest on cash is received gross, with no deduction of tax. You will recall that for a stocks and shares ISA, tax is deducted at source on interest at 20 per cent.

The investments held within a SIPP are largely able to accumulate tax-free. It is the eventual benefits that are paid out from the SIPP that are subject to tax.

Interest on cash deposits or bonds/loan stock can be received gross by the SIPP, or the SIPP administrator can reclaim the tax deducted at source if the income is received net of UK income tax.

No capital gains tax is paid on the disposal of an investment in a SIPP (including shares and property).

Tax is deducted at source from dividend income and this cannot be recovered; however, there is no additional tax liability on receipt of dividend income.

Rental income from an investment property can also be received by the SIPP without any income tax liability.

The tax position on income and gains made on overseas investments will vary depending on the status of the SIPP holder and the country in which the investment is held. However, a variety of tax concessions can be available to UK pensions in respect of overseas investments.

8

Taking benefits from a SIPP

Overview

Unless you are in ill health or serious ill health, you cannot normally commence benefits from a SIPP until you have reached the age of 55.

When commencing benefits, you can normally take part of your benefits as a tax-free lump sum. The balance must normally be taken as a pension income, payable for the rest of your life.

If you have a SIPP, you can choose the way in which your pension income is provided from the following:

- A capped drawdown pension income.
- A lifetime annuity from an insurance company.
- A flexible drawdown income.

All payments are subject to PAYE income tax.

Normal minimum pension age

The normal minimum pension age is 55. Benefits can be taken from this age, or any time afterwards, irrespective of whether you are still working.

Lower retirement ages for specialist occupations are no longer allowed, other than for individuals who have a protected pension age – for example if they were a professional sportsperson or in a hazardous occupation prior to the new pension rules being introduced in April 2006. Where a protected pension age is held then it is possible to commence benefits before the age of 55.

The right to a protected pension age could be lost if the benefits are transferred out to another pension scheme.

Lifetime allowance

There is no absolute limit to the benefits that may be provided under a SIPP, or indeed any registered pension scheme. But if the total value of all benefits, under all registered pension schemes, exceeds the lifetime allowance then there will be an additional tax charge, called the 'lifetime allowance charge', payable on the excess.

The lifetime allowance for the 2013/14 tax year is £1.5m. The lifetime allowance has been on a similar journey to the annual allowance. At the outset, it was £1.5m for the 2006/07 tax year, with predetermined staged increases up to £1.8m for the 2010/11 tax year. It was then reduced to £1.5m for the 2011/12 and 2012/13 tax years and will further reduce to £1.25m from the 2014/15 tax year.

Where you exceed the lifetime allowance, if you leave the excess in your SIPP to be drawn as a taxable pension, the lifetime allowance charge is 25 per cent of the excess. You can, however, choose to draw the excess as a lump sum, which would be subject to a lifetime allowance charge at 55 per cent of the excess, with no further tax to pay.

Your SIPP administrator will deduct the lifetime allowance tax charge before the benefits are paid.

A simple example may help you understand how the lifetime allowance works. It relies on a concept of benefit crystallisation events – which normally refers to when benefits start to be taken from a particular pension scheme.

example

Fred has £150,000 in a personal pension and starts taking pension benefits in 2013/14. He takes this in the form of a £37,500 tax-free lump sum and £112,500 goes into capped drawdown. As the lifetime allowance is £1.5m, this benefit crystallisation event uses up 10 per cent of Fred's lifetime allowance.

If Fred has other pensions, then these will be tested against the lifetime allowance when they are crystallised. Once he has used up 100 per cent of the lifetime allowance, the lifetime allowance charge kicks in.

Tax-free lump sum

Once the decision has been made to take benefits, it is possible to opt to draw either a pension from the SIPP through drawdown, or to purchase an annuity from an insurance company.

Whichever of these options is chosen, it is usually also possible to receive a tax-free lump sum (properly known as a pension commencement lump sum) from your SIPP.

The tax-free lump sum will normally be the lower of:

- 25 per cent of the value of the fund used to provide the benefits, or
- 25 per cent of your unused lifetime allowance.

Higher lump-sum benefits may be available if you have a protected tax-free lump sum.

A tax-free lump sum cannot be taken with the intention of using some, or all, of it to fund a large increase in pension contributions. This is called 'recycling' and will result in significant tax charges.

Capped drawdown

After taking a tax-free lump sum from your SIPP, and assuming you don't buy an annuity, the funds remaining in the SIPP will be used to provide income drawdown benefits. These benefits will be provided as either a capped drawdown pension or flexible drawdown pension. Flexible drawdown is only available if certain eligibility requirements are met and, to this day, has only been used by a very small minority of pension savers.

In capped drawdown, also referred to as income withdrawal or income drawdown, the SIPP fund remains invested and a pension can be drawn up to a maximum level set by HMRC.

This maximum annual pension is calculated based on 120 per cent of what a notional annuity would pay, the precise amount fixed by the Government Actuary's Department (GAD). These notional annuity rates take into account the yield on government stock, namely 15-year gilts, and the SIPP member's age. But they do not reflect the enhanced annuity terms that might be available from an insurance company in the open market, which may take into account other factors such as the SIPP member's sex, postcode, state of health and smoking and drinking habits.

See Appendix 1 for a full table of GAD annuity factors.

example

Jo, who is aged 65 and has a £100,000 SIPP, commences benefits and takes a £25,000 tax-free lump sum. Assuming the relevant gilt interest rate at the time is 2.25 per cent, the GAD tables determine that Jo's GAD factor is 5.5 per cent. Jo's drawdown fund of £75,000 would allow her to take an initial capped drawdown income of £4,950 per year – this being £75,000 x 5.5 per cent x 120 per cent, although she can take less than that, and need take no income at all if she does not want to.

The capped drawdown limit is set at the date on which pension benefits are first taken, and applies for each 12-month period ending on the anniversary of that date. This period is sometimes referred to as the drawdown year.

Capped drawdown pension can be paid monthly, quarterly or as ad hoc single payments. But if you don't receive the maximum pension in any drawdown year, you can't carry any unused amount forward into subsequent years.

The capped drawdown pension limit is normally recalculated on the third anniversary of the benefit commencement date, until you reach the age of 75, after which it is recalculated annually. At a review date, the SIPP drawdown fund will be valued and the maximum pension calculated on a similar basis to that applicable when benefits commenced, but reflecting your age and the yield on gilts at that date.

The maximum pension will therefore be different at each review – reflecting a number of factors, including how your investments have performed, the annuity factors prescribed by HMRC at the time of the review and how much pension you have taken in between the review dates.

Before reaching 75 you can elect to have your maximum pension reviewed early at any anniversary of your benefit commencement date, but you must notify your SIPP administrator of an early review before the relevant anniversary.

Unlike a lifetime annuity, the drawdown pension level is not guaranteed and the maximum can reduce or increase significantly between drawdown pension reviews.

If drawdown pension benefits are transferred into your SIPP from another personal pension in drawdown, then these will be considered separately from other funds in your SIPP for drawdown purposes. They will retain their own maximum pension and review period. Frustratingly, HMRC rules do not permit these different review dates to be merged until after you have reached your 75th birthday.

Drawdown pension reviews are not necessary if you have registered for the flexible drawdown option, which is explained below.

Your SIPP can be used to purchase a lifetime annuity at any point, even after drawdown has been chosen.

Partial drawdown

Most SIPPs and personal pensions are structured as 1,000 individual arrangements to allow them to be divided and used in parts. One of the main reasons for this development was to allow partial drawdown, which allows investors who do not need all their tax-free cash or income straight away to take benefits from only part of their pension pot.

> ### example
>
> Assume Sally, age 60, has £200,000 in her SIPP. She needs £25,000 for a new car, but doesn't need to draw any income from her SIPP as she is still working. She elects to crystallise 50 per cent of her SIPP, being £100,000. This provides her with a £25,000 tax-free lump sum and she elects to take no income from her capped drawdown fund, which is worth £75,000. After she has taken her tax-free cash, 57 per cent of her total SIPP – £100,000 out of £175,000 – remains uncrystallised. This uncrystallised part of her pot could be paid as a lump sum free of tax to her beneficiaries if she died before the age of 75, whereas it would attract tax of 55 per cent if she had crystallised 100 per cent of her pot by taking all her tax-free cash out in one go. (This is covered in more detail in Chapter 17.)

Lifetime annuities

All or part of your SIPP can be used to purchase a lifetime annuity from an insurance company. This can be done either at the point benefits commence from the SIPP, or after a period during which a drawdown pension has been taken.

Purchasing a lifetime annuity involves passing your pension fund to an insurance company that, in return, agrees to provide you, the annuitant, with a pension income for the rest of your life. You can choose to have a pension income for your spouse or partner after your death.

HMRC does not set the level of pension that is taken each year. Instead, each insurance company decides what level of pension they are willing to provide, depending upon a number of factors. These include the individual's age, sex, personal circumstances, the amount used to purchase the annuity and the type of annuity selected. The annuity terms offered by insurance companies can vary considerably, so it is important to shop around to obtain the best deal.

A number of choices can be made regarding the type of annuity purchased. These will include:

- **Level or escalating pension income** – choosing an escalating annuity means that it can increase each year to help protect against inflation. But because the income will increase in the future, the starting level of an escalating annuity will be lower than that of a level annuity. This difference can be substantial. When considering this, it is important to balance the advantage of rising future long-term income against the disadvantage of a lower initial income level. This decision may be influenced by factors such as your health and life expectancy, any views on the long-term effects of inflation and an understanding of the fact that you will be more active in the early years of your retirement so are likely to want to be spending more money.

- **Type of escalating annuity** – the income can be increased by a fixed annual rate, such as 3 per cent per annum, or in line with some measure of inflation such as the Retail Prices Index (RPI) or limited price indexation, which provides inflation protection capped at an upper limit, again possibly 3 per cent per annum.

- **Investment-linked income** – some annuities offer the potential for income to increase if the underlying investments perform well. This is balanced against the risk that the annuity income may fall if the investments do not perform well.

- **Single life or joint life** – a proportion of an annuity can be paid after death to a surviving spouse/partner. This is called a joint life annuity. The level of the survivor's pension is usually expressed as a percentage of the annuitant's income, typically half or two-thirds. The income under a single life annuity ends on the annuitant's death. The income under a joint life annuity will continue for longer if the spouse/partner outlives the annuitant, and as a result the initial level of annuity income will be lower than for a single life annuity.

- **Guarantee periods** – provision of a guarantee period means that, if the annuitant dies during the period of the guarantee, the income due for the remainder of the guarantee period will be paid. In some circumstances this can be paid as a lump sum; if not, the income will be paid as a continuing pension.

- **Enhanced annuity** – depending upon your personal circumstances, it may be possible to receive an increased annuity. A number of factors will affect whether this is available. The most common are the health of the annuitant and their family and their lifestyle history, which is one of the few rewards for a lifetime of drinking, smoking and unhealthy eating.

- **Payment frequency and timing** – an annuity can be payable monthly, quarterly, half-yearly or annually in advance or in arrears. If the annual in-advance option is chosen, a lower income will be paid than if the annuity income is being paid monthly in arrears.

Taking benefits – flexible drawdown

Flexible drawdown is a relatively new form of income drawdown, intro-duced in 2011, that allows you to draw as much as you want from your SIPP provided you have enough secure income to persuade the government that you will never need to claim state benefits.

This secure income threshold is called the minimum income requirement (MIR). The MIR requires you to be able to demonstrate that you are guaranteed to receive secure retirement income of at least £20,000 per annum for the rest of your life.

Income from state pension and lifetime pension annuities counts towards the MIR requirement, as does a pension in payment from defined benefit pension schemes.

Income from non-pension sources, such as salary, investment income or rental income from a property, do not qualify; nor does income from a drawdown pension arrangement. Income from overseas pensions can qualify for the MIR, provided they are structured in a similar way to the various types of UK income that qualify.

Once you have elected to take flexible drawdown you are no longer able to claim tax relief on any future pension contributions.

While not many people use flexible drawdown, it is significant to the extent that it confirms the government's policy in this area. If you can guarantee that you won't fall back on state benefits, the official government policy is that you can cash in your pension, as long as you pay income tax. So why then do they penalise the vast majority of pension savers by imposing ridiculously low-capped drawdown limits on them?

Tax on pensions

When taking a pension income from your SIPP, the payments will be paid subject to income tax. This applies regardless of whether the benefits are being paid as capped drawdown, flexible drawdown or a lifetime annuity.

Where capped or flexible drawdown pension payments are being paid, your SIPP administrator will be responsible for the income tax deductions from the pension income. The insurance company providing the annuity will deduct this tax from annuity payments.

An emergency tax coding will normally be applied until your SIPP administrator or annuity provider has been provided with a tax coding by HMRC. Any under- or overpayment of income tax will then be dealt with via your self-assessment tax return.

Your SIPP administrator or annuity provider will issue a form P60 after the end of each tax year to help with completion of your self-assessment tax return.

Individuals who are resident abroad may live in a country that has agreed tax concessions with HMRC. This may allow your pension to be paid gross, with tax only being deducted in the relevant country of residence.

In order to benefit from any double taxation agreement with another country, you will need to negotiate a special tax coding with HMRC and may wish to take relevant advice to establish what is applicable for your chosen country of residence.

Which option to choose – capped drawdown, lifetime annuity or flexible drawdown?

The first question you should ask yourself before taking any benefits is, 'Should I take any at all?'.

Once you start drawing benefits, you will get a tax-free lump sum and can also take a pension income. If you spend this money, great. But if you just put it in the bank or in your Dealing Account, then this money is subject to income tax, capital gains tax and, in the event of your death, will form part of your estate for inheritance tax purposes.

That said, most people aren't fortunate enough to be able to afford to live without touching their pension once they have stopped working. So let us assume you have decided to start drawing benefits and now need to decide which of the three 'pension' options to choose – capped drawdown, lifetime annuity or flexible drawdown.

Let's look at flexible drawdown first. Few SIPP holders actually have sufficient guaranteed income to meet the minimum income requirement needed to be able to take advantage of flexible drawdown. Those who do are likely to be quite wealthy and may want to ask themselves the question again whether drawing any benefits is the most tax effective thing to do. Flexible drawdown may, however, prove attractive if the intention is to use the money to invest in an asset that can't be bought in a SIPP, for example a holiday home or unquoted shares in a family company.

Most people therefore are faced with a choice of capped drawdown or lifetime annuity. This is another of those apples and oranges comparisons and my advice would be: don't just focus on the numbers. I become infuriated when I hear people say they have chosen capped drawdown or a lifetime annuity because one or the other provided a higher initial level of income. This is totally missing the point.

The choice is, do you want certainty of income for the rest of your life or do you want an income that could be higher but might also be lower under capped drawdown? The price of the certainty of income throughout your life offered by a lifetime annuity is that you forego the capital, which stays with the insurance company when you die. The quid pro quo of the volatility of capped drawdown pension income is that you retain control of the capital, to invest how you choose and to pass on to your heirs after your death.

When you buy an annuity, you need to decide at the outset whether or not to include a spouse's pension. Should your spouse die before you, then paying more for the spouse's benefit has not paid off. As you will see in Chapter 17, if you die while in capped drawdown, the full fund is available to provide your spouse with benefits. If your spouse does die before you then the full fund, after tax, can be paid as a lump sum to your heirs.

Annuity rates are getting worse. People are living longer and the impact of this is magnified by the current low-interest environment. How sustainable annuities will be in years to come is anyone's guess, but for the time being there remains a competitive market, even if rates do look unattractive.

Income drawdown has grown in popularity in recent years as annuity rates have steadily declined, forced down by increases in longevity, lower interest rates and stricter rules governing how much capital insurance companies offering them have to hold.

The government's policy of quantitative easing – printing money – has accelerated the downward trend in annuity rates. In June 2008 a 65-year-old male with a £100,000 pension pot could have bought a level annuity paying over £7,800 a year for life. By September 2012 the same £100,000 pot would buy an income of less than £5,700 a year – a fall of over 26 per cent.

Pros of drawdown

- Can remain invested in stock market for longer, not tied to gilt returns for what could be a retirement of three decades or more. Equity investment has the potential to give protection against inflation.
- Able to pass on fund as a lump sum after death, subject to 55-per-cent tax.
- Can avoid cashing in entire fund when annuity rates seem poor or while you don't qualify for an enhanced annuity rate because of ill health.
- Can withdraw as much or as little as you choose, within limits, enabling you to remain invested for longer and to manage income flow to minimise income tax.

Cons of drawdown

- No guarantee that income will be sustained.
- Principal sum not guaranteed.
- You may end up buying an annuity later on; annuity rates could be even worse by then.

The decision between capped drawdown and a lifetime annuity boils down to a clear choice. If you want certainty, buy an annuity. If you are willing to accept the fact that your income may increase or decrease and that you will be exposed to the vagaries of the stock market, then capped drawdown is more likely to be suitable for you.

I make no apologies for the fact that I am pro capped drawdown. People save for their retirement in all sorts of ways, many of which are discussed in this book, and not all involving a pension. If someone suggested that you convert your ISA, which you have been using to save for your retirement, into an annuity when you retire, you would think they had gone mad.

People would never dream of converting personal savings and investments into an annuity, but it is quite normal to convert a personal pension pot that hitherto has had no guarantees, into a guaranteed income for life. Now that there is no legislative requirement to buy an annuity, my starting point is that there needs to be a compelling case to do so.

Incapacity/serious ill-health

Benefits can be taken before the age of 55 on the grounds of incapacity or serious ill-health, subject to satisfactory medical evidence.

Incapacity

To be eligible to take pension benefits on the grounds of incapacity, evidence must be provided that you are unable, and will continue to be unable, to carry on your occupation because of physical or mental impairment.

You will then be entitled to a tax-free lump sum from your SIPP and can use the balance to provide a retirement income in the same way as someone over 55 can.

Serious ill-health

To be eligible to draw benefits on the grounds of serious ill-health, evidence must be provided that you are expected to live for less than one year.

If this is the case, you are entitled to the full value of your SIPP as a tax-free lump sum, to the extent that you have sufficient unused lifetime allowance. For funds over the lifetime allowance a tax charge of 55 per cent will be deducted before the balance is paid out as a lump sum.

Incapacity or serious ill-health benefits are not available once you have started drawing pension benefits from your SIPP.

Withdrawing small funds

If the combined value of all your pension funds is less than a prescribed amount by the time you come to draw it, you can take the whole lot as a cash lump sum, a quarter of it tax free. This is known as 'trivial commutation'. The logic for allowing this is that the costs of providing a pension income for life from such a small pot would be disproportionately expensive.

To be eligible to take your pot as a lump sum under the trivial commutation rules you must meet the following conditions:

- You must be at least 60 years old and under the age of 75.
- The value of your benefits under all registered pension schemes cannot be more than £18,000.
- You must have sufficient lifetime allowance available.
- You cannot previously have taken any trivial commutation lump sums, subject to the exception below.
- Your entire entitlement to benefits under the SIPP must be commuted – it is all or nothing.

An additional type of 'small pot' commutation was introduced from 6 April 2012. This allows people with individual pots worth up to £2,000 to take the whole fund as a lump sum regardless of the value of other pension arrangements. Up to two of these small-pot lump sums can be taken by any individual.

Both the small-pot lump sums and trivial commutation lump sum are treated separately, meaning that if the small-pot lump sums are taken first, and they reduce the value of all remaining pensions to less than £18,000, an individual who previously did not qualify for trivial commutation can now do so.

Protection from the lifetime allowance

When the new 'simplified' pension structure introduced the concept of the lifetime allowance back in April 2006, some people already had pensions that exceeded the new £1.5m lifetime allowance by a considerable way, or had pensions that were likely to exceed this limit by the time they came to take lump sum and pension benefits.

To ensure that pension savers did not suffer any retrospective loss, a number of transitional protection measures were introduced. There was as much legislation, if not more, created to deal with protecting the lifetime allowances of those who had already built up big pension pots as there was to establish the new system itself.

Two forms of transitional protection against the new lifetime allowance were introduced – 'enhanced protection' and 'primary protection'.

The good news is that most people affected by this issue would have an adviser, so this is not normally an issue for DIY investors. And the time period to register for such protection expired on 5 April 2009, so if you haven't got this protection, there is nothing you can do about it.

A similar situation then arose when the lifetime allowance was reduced from £1.8m in 2011/12 to £1.5m from the start of the 2012/13 tax year, when people with pensions worth close to, or more than, £1.5m found themselves at risk of retrospective taxation under the new limit. To deal with this a further form of transitional protection was introduced, called 'fixed protection'.

Enhanced protection

If you have registered for enhanced protection, you are exempt from any tax charges should you exceed the lifetime allowance. The only condition is that you have had to permanently cease all pension contributions, including benefit accrual in a defined benefits scheme, since 6 April 2006.

Enhanced protection was relevant to pension savers who thought that their pension savings might in future exceed the lifetime allowance.

Enhanced protection is lost if an inadvertent contribution is made or benefit accrual arises after 6 April 2006.

Primary protection

Primary protection was an alternative to enhanced protection that was available only to people with pension benefits in excess of the £1.5m lifetime allowance on 5 April 2006. Contributions and benefit accrual in a defined benefit schemes can continue.

The value of pension benefits was protected by a factor calculated according to the amount by which they exceeded the lifetime allowance on 5 April 2006

So, someone with pension benefits worth £2.25m on 5 April 2006, amounting to one-and-a-half times the annual allowance at that time, would see their personal lifetime allowance increase by the same percentage rate as the actual lifetime allowance. By 2011/12, when the annual allowance had risen to £1.8m, their personal lifetime allowance would have risen to £2.7m.

Fortunately for those who have opted for primary protection, when the lifetime allowance was reduced to £1.5m in 2012/13, HMRC did not cut their personal lifetime allowances but instead allowed them to keep personal lifetime allowances based on a £1.8m lifetime allowance.

If someone with primary protection exceeds their personal lifetime allowance, then the rules apply in the same way as if a pension saver with no protection exceeds the standard lifetime allowance.

Fixed protection

This was introduced to protect pension savers when the lifetime allowance reduced from £1.8m to £1.5m on 6 April 2012. It was not available to those who had registered for enhanced or primary protection.

Put simply, you could register for a £1.8m lifetime allowance in return for ceasing future pension contributions and benefit accrual in a defined benefit scheme. You needed to have registered by 5 April 2012. As with enhanced protection, any contributions or benefit accrual would result in this protection being lost.

There are some exemptions where certain aspects of contributions or benefit accrual may continue, without jeopardising enhanced or fixed protection, including the indexing of benefits in line with an inflation index and payments for life cover.

A '2014' version of fixed protection is being introduced to protect those affected by the reduction in the lifetime allowance to £1.25m from 6 April 2014.

Auto-enrolment and the risk of losing enhanced or fixed protection

Anyone who has elected to take enhanced protection or fixed protection needs to make sure they do not inadvertently lose it by being automatically enrolled into a pension scheme through their workplace. This is because a single payment into a pension made on their behalf by an employer could invalidate their protection and potentially create a tax liability running into tens or even hundreds of thousands of pounds.

In October 2012 the government set in train a programme that will see in excess of 10m UK workers enrolled into workplace pensions without their consent, but giving them the right to opt out if they want to. The date employers are required to enrol staff is based on the size of the employer.

Individuals who have taken enhanced or fixed protection will have 30 days to opt out of their employer's pension scheme to avoid losing this protection.

And opting out once isn't the end of the story. Under auto-enrolment, anyone who opts out will be automatically put back into the scheme three years later, which quite frankly is an accident waiting to happen.

The Department for Work and Pensions says it will write to everybody with enhanced and fixed protection, warning them to ensure they remember to opt out of their workplace scheme in time, but experts are predicting some high-earners will neglect to do so, resulting in their being hit with potentially massive tax charges.

As if life isn't complicated enough.

Protected tax-free lump sum

There are various types of tax-free cash protection. Both primary and enhanced protection allowed you to protect the pension commencement lump sum provided it was in excess of £375,000 on 5 April 2006.

But tax-free cash protection is also available where a pension saver had accrued more than 25 per cent of their pension savings as a tax-free lump sum at 6 April 2006. You may not know if this applies to you, as there is no registration process required. It is a matter handled by pension scheme administrators.

If you are in a company scheme that is not a personal pension or stakeholder pension scheme, or have an executive pension plan or Section 32 plan, then it is worth asking your scheme administrator whether such tax-free cash protection applies to you.

If you have any tax-free cash protection, check with your provider or scheme administrator whether you stand to lose it before transferring.

part

three

The DIY investor's toolkit – the investments

9

Funds

The last few chapters have looked at the tax wrappers, or products, you can use as a DIY investor. While these may help you to save tax, they will never make you money. It is the underlying investments you put your money into that generate those spine-tingling financial wins and losses.

Different types of investment have different degrees of sophistication and complication. If you are new to DIY investing then you can achieve all of your investment goals without looking any further than funds, whatever your risk appetite.

If you want access to the stockmarket, but want to leave individual stock – another name for a share or an equity – selection to the experts, then funds could well be for you. By pooling your money into a fund with thousands of other investors you can get access to highly-skilled fund managers, while still staying in control of the sectors you invest in and the managers you use.

Competition between fund managers to deliver the best performance is fierce. The more successful they are, the more money they make, which means their interests and yours are very much aligned. If you do not see yourself having the time, energy or inclination to trade individual company shares, investing through funds can be an efficient way to get exposure to all sorts of markets – equities, bonds, commercial property and many other asset classes.

Or you may wish to invest some of your money through funds and some directly into equities and other investment types. Whichever way you want to construct your portfolio, getting exposure to the fund that is right for you has never been easier. These days, most investment platforms offer access to several thousand funds across a bewildering array of sectors, geographical regions, asset classes and investment strategies.

Even sophisticated DIY investors will often use funds in their portfolio, if only to access sectors or geographical regions that can be very difficult to gain exposure to by investing directly in equities. If you want exposure to a fast-growing emerging market, for example, then a fund is one of the best ways to do this.

You may not even want to use funds that pay fund managers large sums of money to manage your money. Many successful DIY investors ignore star fund managers and opt for the increasingly fashionable passive or tracker funds that have ultra-low charges and mimic the return that a particular sector of the market is delivering. Either way, investment platforms offer more funds than you will ever need.

Almost all of the funds available through investment platforms can be held in your SIPP, ISA or Dealing Account.

Some history

The first pooled investment funds were created in Holland in the 18th or 19th century, depending on which historian you believe. Similar funds soon emerged elsewhere in Europe, with the concept taking root in the USA in the 1890s.

The UK's first pooled investment funds were investment trusts, such as the Foreign & Colonial Investment Trust, which was founded in 1868 and is still going today. These first investment trusts were, and still are, closed-ended funds, which means that the number of shares in the investment trust is the same from one day to the next. We will cover investment trusts in Chapter 11 and see that this closed-end structure plays a significant role in how the price of an investment trust moves.

The open-ended funds that are the predecessors of today's unit trusts and open-ended investment companies (OEICs) were first developed in the USA in the 1920s. Open-ended funds were different from their closed-ended counterparts because they allowed new shares, or units, to be allocated to investors when they invested in the fund. OEICs (pronounced Oiks) are also known as ICVCs, standing for investment company with variable capital.

This ability to issue new units made these early open-ended funds less volatile than investment trusts, leading them to weather the Wall Street Crash of 1929 slightly better than their closed-end counterparts. Open-ended unit trusts emerged in the UK in the 1930s. The OEICs that are gradually becoming the dominant form of investment fund in the UK are a much more recent phenomenon, having only been around since 1997.

The main attraction of a fund being open-ended is that its price is not driven by supply and demand. New units/shares are created and existing units/shares are cancelled depending upon the demand for units/shares in the fund.

Investment trusts, as with most individual company shares, are closed-ended. If a company share is heavily tipped as a 'buy' in the financial press, the increase in demand drives the price up.

But open-ended funds aren't affected in this way by an increase in demand for their shares or units, as the supply of shares or units is altered daily to match the demand. So you can 'safely' follow a tip in the Sunday newspaper without fear of the price being artificially inflated – but there are, of course, other risks.

Think of it in a slightly different way. If you buy a company share, you give your money to the seller of the share and hence the price is subject to supply-and-demand economics. If you buy shares or units in an open-ended fund, you give the money to the fund manager to invest it on your behalf and new units or shares are created to meet this demand.

Different types of fund

The most common types of open-ended funds available in the UK are unit trusts and OEICs. Neither unit trusts nor OEICs are listed on the stock exchange, their price being reflected in the value of the underlying investments that they hold. The price is normally set once a day, this being called the valuation point.

There are structural differences between unit trusts and OEICs. When you put money into a unit trust you receive units, whereas in OEICs you receive shares. Investors in unit trusts are called unit-holders, while investors in OEICs are called shareholders.

Another key difference is the fact that unit trusts have a buy-or-offer price and a sell-or-bid price. OEICs have a single price and are the more modern structure for funds.

Prior to 31 December 2012, when RDR came in to force, the typical initial cost to buy both types of fund was 5 per cent of the amount invested, which was split 3 per cent for the adviser, if you used one, and 2 per cent for the fund manager. Where you buy the fund direct from the fund manager, they normally charge the full 5 per cent initial charge in any event.

For unit trusts, this charge is reflected in the difference between the bid and offer price. For OEICs, the charge is made by an explicit deduction at the point of investing.

You can usually avoid some or all of this initial cost by investing through an investment platform. You will be able to buy the vast majority of funds through an investment platform with no initial charge at all, though you may be charged a dealing commission, typically no more than £10.

Unit trusts

As the name suggests, a unit trust is a trust set up by a fund manager under a trust deed. The manager buys and sells assets that are held by the trust. New units are created when new investors pay money in, with units cancelled when investments are withdrawn.

Unit trusts are normally priced once a day, with their price depending on the value (referred to as the net asset value) of the investments held in the fund.

OEICs

The cleaner pricing structure of OEICs makes them the go-forward open-ended investment vehicle for UK investors. Run as companies, the fund manager issues and cancels shares, rather than units, when investors come and go.

Like unit trusts, the price of OEICs is determined by the net asset value of the assets held by them. Pricing is also normally fixed daily.

OEICs have always been able to offer investors different share classes, a flexibility that has only been granted to unit trusts in recent years. The reasons for having different share classes are explored later in this chapter.

As a DIY investor, the difference between a unit trust and an OEIC is largely academic.

UCITs and Newcits

When researching funds you may come across the term UCITS, which is a fund standard set up by the European Union. UCITS stands for the, not very memorable, undertakings for collective investments in transferable securities. The UCITS Kitemark means you have a certain level of investor protection and allows EU-based fund managers meeting its criteria to market their funds anywhere within the EU.

UCITS funds are designed for the retail investor as they are not considered complex. UCITS funds are not to be confused with the similarly labelled UCIS funds, which stands for unregulated collective investment scheme – typically riskier funds that are targeted at sophisticated and high net-worth investors.

UCITS funds have to be overseen by a regulator in an EU state, and are often based in Ireland or Luxembourg. This combination of regulatory oversight and investment flexibility has led many hedge fund managers to offer UCITS versions of their offshore hedge funds to a retail audience.

These products are sometimes referred to as Newcits. However, retail investors should handle anything looking like a hedge fund with care as these are complex funds and it is not always clear what is being invested in. In the absence of a UCITS Kitemark, it is likely that a hedge fund will be a UCIS.

Different share classes

OEICs can have sub-funds with different share classes, to reflect different charging structures, currencies or distribution. They often have different share classes for institutional and retail investors, with charges higher for the latter.

To make matters even more confusing, there is now also the added distinction between 'clean' and 'dirty' share classes of the same fund. Fund managers pay away part of their annual management charge on dirty share classes to advisers and investment platforms, meaning that their charges are higher than their clean counterparts, to allow for these payments.

In contrast, the fund manager retains all of the annual management fee it charges for 'clean' share classes. They are clean of any rebates to financial advisers or investment platforms and therefore the charges are lower.

Unit trusts and OEICs typically offer two main ways for shareholders to receive returns – the income class and the accumulation class.

Income

The income class of a fund pays, or distributes, dividends or interest depending upon the type of fund. These payments are made directly into a cash account with your investment platform. Payments are made shortly after the fund's distribution date.

Income class shares are more suitable if you are at a stage in your life where you need income from your investments, rather than growth.

Accumulation

The accumulation class rolls your dividends or other income back into your unit trust or OEIC, rather than pay it out to you. This has the effect of increasing the value of each unit or share held. Accumulation class shares are the ones to go for if your sole aim is to grow your portfolio. By opting for accumulation units or shares, your money gets reinvested in the fund without dealing costs, initial charges or bid/offer spreads.

The impact of the Retail Distribution Review

The abolition of commission payable to advisers on retail investment products from 31 December 2012 has caused a revolution in the way unit trusts and OEICs are distributed and priced. The commission ban was introduced under the Retail Distribution Review (RDR), a regulatory-driven initiative to remove product selection bias from the financial advice process and to improve the professional standards of advisers.

One of the consequences of the RDR is the creation of a whole new set of commission-free, or 'clean', unit or share classes of funds.

Before 2013 most retail unit trusts and OEICs carried an annual management charge of, typically, 1.5 per cent. The actual charge retained by the fund manager was typically 0.75 per cent, the other half being paid away, with 0.25 per cent usually going to the investment platform that held the fund and the remaining 0.5 per cent going to the independent financial adviser as trail or renewal commission.

This trail commission was designed to cover the cost of the adviser providing ongoing advice and assistance with the investment. Where there is no adviser,

DIY investment platforms have historically received the full 0.75 per cent. But, in recent years, competitive pressures have led to DIY platforms rebating some or all of this commission to clients, sometimes in return for an explicit custody or administration charge being imposed instead.

Any rebates paid to fund investors, either in the form of cash or units, are taxable from 6 April 2013 – rebates paid to a SIPP or an ISA continue to be exempt.

One of the advantages to DIY investors of using an investment platform provider has been that they can invest in funds with little or no initial charge. As the name suggests, DIY investment platforms operate on an execution-only basis, which means you have no comeback if you choose the wrong investments.

Now that commission has been abolished, fund managers have started to issue 'clean' RDR-compliant classes of units and OEIC shares, typically with a bare 0.75 per cent annual management charge.

From 6 April 2014, investment platforms will no longer be able to receive payments from fund managers with some exceptions for existing investments. Until that time, you may come across some share classes that are neither clean nor dirty. Let's call them 'off-white'. These will typically have a 1 per cent annual management charge and while they won't include a loading for adviser commission, they will include an annual loading, typically 0.25 per cent, which is paid to the investment platform.

RDR may not make investing in funds any cheaper. In fact it may have the opposite effect as it means advisers and investment platforms will charge for their services explicitly instead of living off payments from the fund managers.

Historically, the payments received from fund managers have been a lucrative source of income to DIY investment platforms, in many cases giving investment platforms enough revenue to enable them to have no charge for buying, selling and holding funds. But that is likely to end in 2014, so expect to see all DIY investment platforms levying explicit charges for these services.

More importantly, unless the fund management industry gets its act together and starts pricing for simplicity rather than complexity, they are in danger of finding their core customer base gravitating towards the simpler and cheaper passive tracker funds and ETFs covered in Chapter 10.

The mechanics of buying, holding and selling funds

Buying a unit trust or OEIC is easier than buying a flight on a discount airline. Once you have done your research and decided on the fund you want to buy, simply log into your investment platform, choose the account or tax wrapper you want to buy the fund through, identify the fund and then click on the buy button. It's that easy.

Settlement

Buying and selling funds is not as instantaneous as buying and selling equities, due to the fact that funds are normally only priced daily. For example, if you invest in a fund at 10.30am on a Tuesday, you will buy shares in the fund at the forward price, determined at the fund's valuation point, which is normally midday.

At some time after the valuation point, often overnight, the fund manager will confirm with your investment platform, the price and therefore the number of units or shares you have purchased. If you invest after the cut-off point, your order will be rolled forward to the following day's valuation point.

Switching funds

Why is the settlement process relevant? Well, you will hear talk of 'fund switches', where investors sell one fund and buy another. This process is not quite as slick as you may hope. When you sell a fund, you will normally need to wait at least until the following morning for your account to be credited with cash in order to go on and invest the proceeds in another fund or investment.

Before that point in time, your investment platform simply won't know how much money you are going to receive. In reality this means you will be out of the market for a day, and possibly even two, when you switch funds. It's not normally a major issue, unless you are very unlucky, but then again you may also be lucky enough for valuations to move in your favour.

This settlement period is only really relevant if you want to take your cash away from your investment platform immediately after selling the fund or funds. In these circumstances, your investment platform will wait until it has received the hard cash from the fund manager before it hands it over to you.

Research and fund selection

You are paying for a fund manager to do the stock selections precisely because you do not want to do it yourself. So when it comes to funds, the only research you have to do is around what fund to invest in. As with equity investments, it pays to spread your fund investments across several funds so you can even out the risk in your portfolio.

To decide what funds to go for you will first of all need to decide your investment objectives, your attitude to risk and the sort of portfolio you need to deliver these objectives within your risk appetite. Your portfolio might easily include funds covering UK, global and emerging market equities, corporate bonds and commercial property. These investment classes are considered in greater detail in later chapters.

Once you have worked out the type of asset allocation-split you think you will need, you will then have to find the right funds to meet these objectives. This will involve looking for funds, or individual fund managers, with a good track record in the areas of the market you are looking to invest in.

There are a number of places you can go to find fund recommendations. Some investment platforms will suggest their own lists of funds. These are often presented as model portfolios, or baskets of funds to meet different objectives and risk profiles. Historically, some model portfolios have been influenced by commercial relationships between the fund managers looking after the funds and the investment platform. Called 'shelf-space' deals, they are what the name suggests. Not all are bad, but you need to approach these fund lists with caution.

A simple test you can apply to check whether a model portfolio is largely independent from influence is by looking to see if the recommended funds are 'clean' funds with an annual management charge in the region of 0.75 per cent per annum. If they carry annual management charges nearer to 1.5 per cent, then you should approach these funds with a degree of scepticism.

The good news is that from 6 April 2014, investment platforms cannot receive payments from fund managers for new investments, so it will not be possible for model portfolios to be influenced by these payments.

I hope that the removal of these payments doesn't lead to this valuable model portfolio service being withdrawn, as model portfolios do make investing easier for the DIY investor.

Another approach is to look at independent research from organisations such as Morningstar, Digital Look, Hemscott, Trustnet, Motley Fool and Citywire, all of which have historic data, factsheets and other information on fund managers' performance. Specialist investment magazines such as *Investors' Chronicle, Shares Magazine, Money Week* and *Money Observer* will also have articles containing research and analysis of fund managers.

You can also easily see which sectors everyone else is investing in. The Investment Management Association (IMA) provides a lot of market data on its website, www.investmentfunds.org.uk, showing the most popular sectors.

Organisations such as Citywire and Trustnet also provide great market data, to give you a good starting point when looking at which funds to invest in.

Most weeks, the financial pages of the broadsheets cover which funds to buy and sometimes which to sell. As highlighted earlier, whereas a tip to buy an equity in the financial pages of your favourite national newspaper can send the price through the roof, this is not so for funds because their price is not influenced by the demand for shares or units in that fund.

You also need to understand what the fund is aiming to do and what it is allowed to invest in. Every fund has a set of investment objectives that the manager is required to follow. This is explained on the fund's factsheet, which you can find easily by searching the internet for the name of the fund and the word 'factsheet'. These are also available from your investment platform.

The factsheet will show how well the fund has performed against other funds in its sector over one, three and five years. It will also show the portfolio breakdown, dividends, fund size, top holdings and charges.

The cult of the star fund manager

No one is top of the tree forever, but some managers seem to have a knack for performing better than the pack through good times and bad. Whether this is down to skill or luck is a matter of debate in the investment industry. Some investors do not believe that there is any statistical likelihood of a particular fund manager outperforming the market over a long period. Others argue that the very best, most experienced managers will deliver the goods more often than not.

The archetypal star fund manager is Anthony Bolton, former manager of the Fidelity Special Situations fund. For 28 years Bolton was a money-making machine. Someone who invested £1,000 in his fund at launch in 1979 would have been sitting on £148,200 by the time he quit the fund in 2007. Bolton's record is a fabulous one, but he is one of thousands of managers, most of whom have come nowhere near achieving his returns.

The hard fact about fund management is that a substantial proportion of fund managers underperform the index or benchmark they are trying to beat.

Even Bolton managed to blot his copybook when he returned to the fray at the helm of the Fidelity China Special Situations fund in 2010, being forced to apologise to investors for below-benchmark returns at the end of 2011 when he admitted his bets on the Chinese economy decoupling from the West had been wrong. Bolton will step down from running this fund in April 2014.

Another problem with star fund managers is they can become victims of their own success. The most celebrated fund manager active in the UK today is Neil Woodford, who manages the £14bn Invesco Perpetual High Income fund and the £11bn Income fund, among others. Woodford has proved a dependable performer for over 20 years through all sorts of markets. But some experts argue he is powerless to make any significant market-beating returns because his funds are simply too big and unwieldy.

I like to keep an eye on what shares these star fund managers hold in their funds, if only to generate ideas for my own portfolio. While this path leads to investment in direct equities (see Chapter 12), it is sometimes as interesting to see what these star fund managers aren't investing in, as what they are.

Taking Woodford again as an example, if you analysed his holdings in the run-up to the bursting of the dot-com bubble you would not find any technology stocks. Similarly, in the run-up to the banking crash – he had no holdings in banks. With hindsight some call this genius, while others call it principled investing. But the truth is, in the run-up to both of these events, his significant underperformance against his peers led to many investors voting with their feet and no doubt ruing that decision.

Citywire allocates a star rating to fund managers, rather than to the funds that they manage. This probably says it all. Like premiership footballers, my view is that the great ones are handsomely paid and worth every penny. The rest make up the numbers.

Supporters of the concept of the star fund manager point to the big names that have delivered market-beating returns more or less consistently over a long period. And putting your faith in people who can demonstrate some level of success over a number of years surely feels more logical than giving your money to a fund manager whom you have picked at random.

Passive or active fund management

In the past, as a DIY investor you have had two clear choices – either choose your own equities, or leave a fund manager to invest your money on your behalf. This has been quite a stark choice, with no real middle ground.

But a new alternative to a fund manager actively managing investments on your behalf has emerged where funds are invested without active management – a process called passive fund management. Funds managed in this passive fashion are called *index trackers* and are covered in more detail in Chapter 10.

These passive funds are now proving to be a real alternative to the active fund-management industry and pose a real challenge to it. Best of all, the costs of passive funds are a fraction of active funds – not least because there are no star footballers to pay.

So, before trying to figure out which is the best fund or who is the best fund manager, there is a question to ask yourself first – do you even want to pay for active fund management?

While some passive funds do operate under the structure of an OEIC, the majority are structured in a different way, as *exchange-traded funds*. For this reason, passive or tracker funds are covered in more detail in Chapter 10.

Sectors

With thousands of funds for the DIY investor to choose from, it is important to know your way around the different sectors, regions, themes and strategies they are based upon.

Sectors are a way of arranging funds into groups that are invested using similar strategies or objectives.

The Investment Management Association (IMA) sector scheme divides

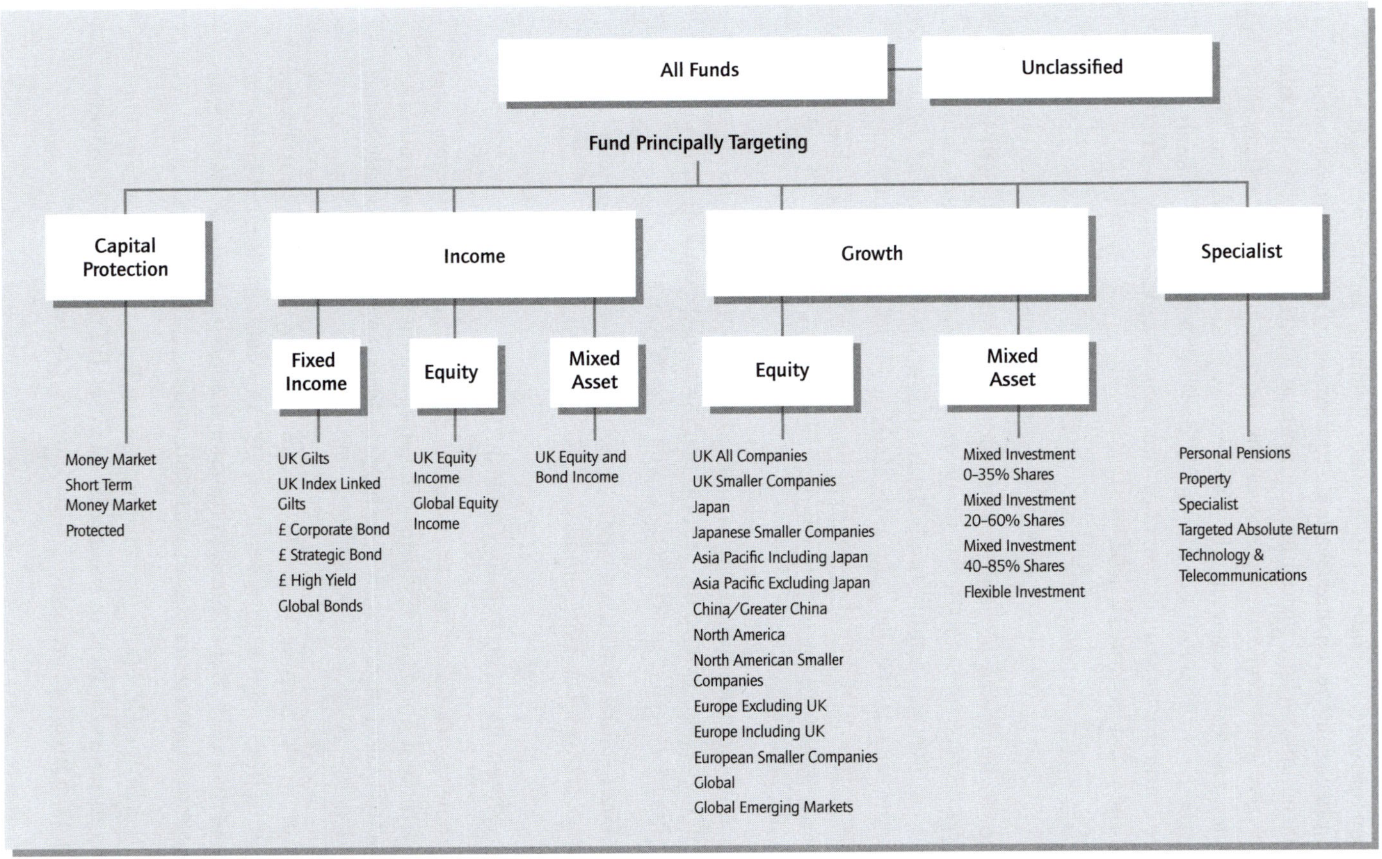

Fund Principally Targeting

All Funds

Unclassified

Capital Protection
- Money Market
- Short Term Money Market
- Protected

Income

Fixed Income
- UK Gilts
- UK Index Linked Gilts
- £ Corporate Bond
- £ Strategic Bond
- £ High Yield
- Global Bonds

Equity
- UK Equity Income
- Global Equity Income

Mixed Asset
- UK Equity and Bond Income

Growth

Equity
- UK All Companies
- UK Smaller Companies
- Japan
- Japanese Smaller Companies
- Asia Pacific Including Japan
- Asia Pacific Excluding Japan
- China/Greater China
- North America
- North American Smaller Companies
- Europe Excluding UK
- Europe Including UK
- European Smaller Companies
- Global
- Global Emerging Markets

Mixed Asset
- Mixed Investment 0–35% Shares
- Mixed Investment 20–60% Shares
- Mixed Investment 40–85% Shares
- Flexible Investment

Specialist
- Personal Pensions
- Property
- Specialist
- Targeted Absolute Return
- Technology & Telecommunications

figure 9.1 Fund sectors

Source: Investment Management Association

funds into 36 (including Unclassified) different sectors; it is one of a number of sector schemes available to investors. These 36 sectors can be divided into broader groupings, as shown in Figure 9.1. The IMA website will give you precise definitions of the aims of the funds within each sector and the parameters they are required to operate within. These parameters may be limits or minimum levels of certain types of assets, the size of the stocks held, i.e. small or large cap, or geographical restrictions on the investments they hold.

Growth

Growth funds can be equity or mixed asset in make-up. Growth funds cover sectors such as UK All Companies, UK Smaller Companies, and various overseas equity funds based on geographical region or on themes such as Global Emerging Markets. Mixed asset funds have set percentages that can be invested in different asset classes, typically equities and fixed income investments such as corporate and government bonds, and cash.

UK All Companies funds, for example, are defined by the IMA as 'funds which invest at least 80 per cent of their assets in UK equities which have a primary objective of achieving capital growth'.

However, funds within any IMA sector may have widely varying asset mixes, strategies and risk profiles.

Income – fixed income/equity/mixed asset

Income funds invest in fixed-income assets such as corporate and government bonds, in dividend-generating equities or a combination of the two. Fixed-income sectors include UK Gilts, Sterling Corporate Bonds and Sterling Strategic Bond funds.

Funds in the Sterling High Yield sector are riskier, with at least 80 per cent of their assets required to be in UK corporate bonds rated below, or more risky than, BBB–. Funds in the Global Bond sector are, as their name suggests, made up of overseas corporate bonds.

Funds in the UK Equity Income and Global Equity Income sectors must aim to achieve a yield of income in excess of 110 per cent of the yield of the FTSE All Share and MSCI World Index respectively.

Companies issue corporate bonds as a cheap way to raise finance, attracting investors with returns that are higher than cash on deposit. The coupon, or interest, is the amount paid each year by the company until the end of the bond's term, when the original capital is also repaid. If you hold corporate bonds until they expire you will know exactly what you will get out of them – the annual coupon for the number of years left on the bond plus the return of the amount that the company originally borrowed, provided the company does not go bust along the way.

But corporate bond funds buy and sell bonds before they expire, and their values change depending on how likely the market thinks it is that the company backing the bond is likely to go bust and default. The value of corporate bonds is also impacted by interest rates in the wider economy. Lower interest rates from banks means demand for high-yielding corporate bonds goes up and vice versa, meaning the value of the bond itself can also go down and up – an increase in interest rates normally means a fall in the value of a corporate bond fund, and vice versa.

Government bonds work in exactly the same way – UK government bonds are called gilts – with the market risk being that the country defaults on its debts. Government or 'sovereign' debt in developed countries had for decades been a relatively low-return, unexciting part of the economy. Returns are lower because of the lower perceived risk in a whole country not having the money to pay back what it owes.

Corporate bonds are generally perceived as being less risky than equities, and investing in corporate bonds through a corporate bond fund reduces your overall risk.

Capital protection

Funds in the capital protection grouping of IMA sectors include money market or cash funds and funds offering capital protection by locking in gains, or guaranteeing capital and linking returns to an index.

Some people refer to money market funds as cash funds, which is not strictly correct. Money market funds invest in cash, bonds with only a short term to maturity and other 'debt instruments'. There is some capital risk to these funds.

Specialist

The IMA's specialist sector grouping covers a range of sectors that do not fall into any of the others. Funds investing in specialist sectors, such as Technology & Telecommunications and Property, fall into this category. So do funds defined by a particular investment process such as Absolute Return funds, which aim to achieve an above-zero return at all points in the investment cycle. Targeted Absolute Return funds are supposed to smooth out returns by using derivatives and short-selling strategies, although many have delivered dismal performances in recent years.

Commercial property funds

Commercial property is a sensible component of a well-diversified investment portfolio, and the easiest way to get exposure to it is through a commercial property fund. The fund manager buys commercial properties with leases on shops, offices and other buildings and the rent it receives is paid out to investors as income. As with other income-generating funds, income can be withdrawn or accumulated into extra units or shares in the fund.

One advantage of having at least some exposure to commercial property is the fact that the sector theoretically performs in different cycles to other parts of the economy, thereby dampening risk in your overall portfolio. Commercial property funds are generally considered less risky than equity funds.

That said, commercial property funds performed terribly, along with virtually every other class, through the credit crunch, proving the theorists wrong when they fell around 40 per cent in around 15 months between 2007 and 2008. Asset values are yet to return to pre-2007 levels.

Analysts' views are split as to whether these lower valuations reflect a buying opportunity or a long-term negative trend as banks slowly unwind their debt mountains by drip-feeding commercial property back into the market. Most experts argue that high-quality commercial property in prime locations should continue to deliver, as securing quality tenants is easier. The prospects for lower-grade commercial properties are not as bright.

Information overload

One of the challenges that a DIY investor faces is information overload. There are now more funds than there are UK equities to invest in, and one of the main reasons for investing in funds is to make life simple.

Individual fund management firms can run many funds, each with different sub-classes and different charges. You need to make sure you invest in the right share class within a fund you have identified.

There are lots of good websites with information on funds listed at the end of the chapter and all DIY investment platforms have their own versions of these.

Let's use Invesco's incredibly popular High Income fund as an example (see Figure 9.2). By visiting the websites highlighted at the end of the chapter, or by looking on your investment platform's website, you can find all the key information you need about a particular fund. Once you have done it for one fund, you can do it for all funds.

You will see six different Invesco Perpetual funds, all called 'IP High Income', each followed by some letters. This is where you need to be careful. Each of these are sub-funds of Invesco's flagship High Income

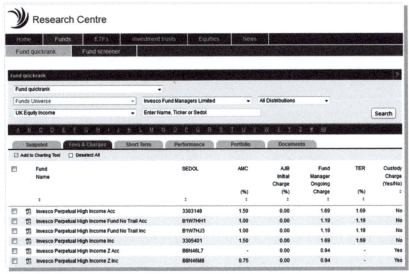

figure 9.2   **Example of website information for fund**   Source: AJ Bell Research Centre

fund, so while each sub-fund enjoys the investment return of the overall fund, the different sub-funds have different charges and prices.

You may be able to take a guess at what each suffix refers to:

table 9.1 Invesco Perpetual funds

Fund name	
IP High Income **Acc**	This is the most common share class, which includes a loading for adviser commission and/or the investment platform the fund is bought through. The 'Acc' means it is an accumulation share class, with all dividends reinvested in the fund. This share class has an annual management charge of 1.5 per cent. You will see that the total expense ratio, or TER, is 1.69 per cent. We will cover TERs later in this part of the book.
IP High Income **Inc**	Exactly the same share class as above, except that dividends are paid out rather than reinvested. The price of the Acc and Inc share classes will differ to reflect whether income is reinvested or paid out.
IP High Income **No Trail Acc**	This share class has no loading for commission payable to advisers, but does retain a loading of 0.25 per cent per annum for the investment platform that the fund is bought through. The annual management charge is 1 per cent and the TER is 1.19 per cent. The Acc bit again means that dividends are reinvested.
IP High Income **No Trail Inc**	Exactly the same as the Acc version, other than dividends are paid out rather than reinvested.
IP High Income **Z Acc**	This is the new breed of share class, introduced as a result of RDR. It doesn't include a loading for adviser commission or a payment to the investment platform. The annual management charge is 0.75 per cent and the TER is 0.94 per cent.
IP High Income **Z Inc**	Exactly the same as the Acc version, other than dividends are paid out rather than reinvested.

The first two share classes are 'dirty', the two No Trail share classes are 'off-white' and the two Z share classes are 'clean'.

Note the difference between the TER and the annual management charge is the same for all of the funds, as you may expect – in this case, 0.19 per cent.

As I take you on this journey I will show you a couple of other sites that may be useful if you are researching funds.

Search the internet for 'Invesco Perpetual High Income Fund' and you will find the relevant section of Invesco's own website (see Figure 9.3). All fund managers have their own website containing all their fund literature and information.

figure 9.3 Researching funds: literature and information
Source: Invesco Perpetual

Click on 'Related features and literature' and you will see Figure 9.4 appear (see overleaf).

You will find a factsheet for the whole fund, covering all sub-classes, that contains a whole host of information including an investment commentary, updated monthly in this case, dates when dividends are paid and the top ten holdings.

Each sub-class of the fund has its own KIID, which stands for key investor information document. Convention is still developing in this area and not all fund managers will produce a KIID for each share class. This can make it quite difficult to check you are actually investing in the clean share class, if indeed that is what you want to do.

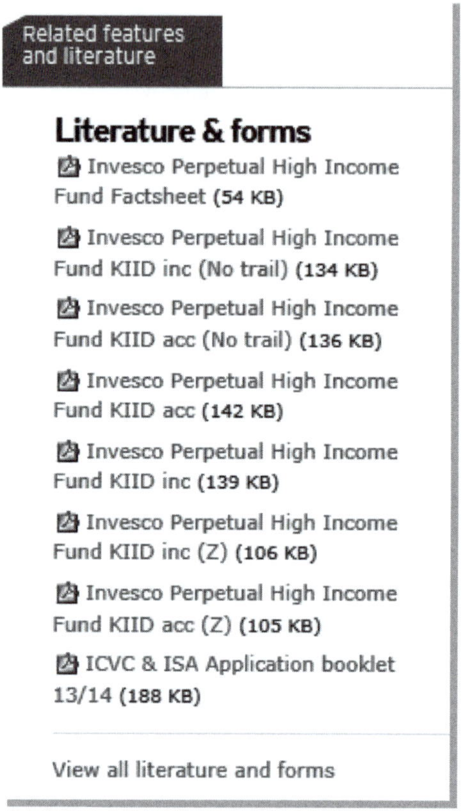

Related features
and literature

Literature & forms

📄 Invesco Perpetual High Income
Fund Factsheet (54 KB)

📄 Invesco Perpetual High Income
Fund KIID inc (No trail) (134 KB)

📄 Invesco Perpetual High Income
Fund KIID acc (No trail) (136 KB)

📄 Invesco Perpetual High Income
Fund KIID acc (142 KB)

📄 Invesco Perpetual High Income
Fund KIID inc (139 KB)

📄 Invesco Perpetual High Income
Fund KIID inc (Z) (106 KB)

📄 Invesco Perpetual High Income
Fund KIID acc (Z) (105 KB)

📄 ICVC & ISA Application booklet
13/14 (188 KB)

View all literature and forms

figure 9.4 **Researching funds: factsheet**   Source: Invesco Perpetual

If you click on the KIID for the Acc Z share class, this provides information such as the ISIN number (GB00B8N46L71), which is a unique identifier used when buying or selling a particular share class of any fund. Funds also have a SEDOL number, which is more commonly associated with shares. This fund has a SEDOL of B8N46L7, which you will see is a subset of the ISIN number. For acronym lovers, ISIN stands for international securities identification number and SEDOL stands for Stock Exchange Daily Official List.

In my opinion, Trustnet is a great website to confirm the SEDOL or ISIN of a particular fund, and while it is not intuitive, you can rely on it. All investment platforms I have ever used, and I have tried out most of them, show one or the other of these references at the point of investing a fund.

You will also find a risk and reward profile on the KIID, this fund being ranked 6 out of 7. You will also find details of the charges of the fund, but, as I mention above, not all fund managers have prepared KIIDs for each share class and as we know different share classes have different charges.

You will see from the KIID that the IP High Income Acc Z fund has an entry charge of 5 per cent (normally waived when buying through a DIY investment platform), no exit charge (very common), no performance fees (very common) and ongoing charges of 0.94 per cent. This is another little pothole in the road that can throw you off-course. Although not explicitly stated, this equates to an annual management charge of 0.75 per cent plus other charges that aren't included in the annual management charge – estimated at 0.19 per cent per annum. You can just about deduce from this information that this is the 'clean' share class you were looking for!

If you look further down the list of literature, you will see KIIDs for each share class. You will also find the interim report and annual report, in both short and long form. As I said, there can be too much information. It is there if you want it but I wouldn't advocate routinely reading fund managers' annual reports. The whole purpose of investing in funds is to make your life easy.

The final stop on this journey is www.trustnet.co.uk. Search 'Invesco High Income Fund' on Trustnet's home page and you will come across a pretty coloured page, with links to some of the documents referred to above (see Figure 9.5).

You will see the price of the shares in each of the six sub-classes. These sit in the middle of the Bid and Offer columns as this is an OEIC and hence has a single price, with no spread. This website gives you an idea of the income yield you will receive if you invest in this fund; this is particularly important if you are seeking income from your investments. If you scroll down the page you will see lots more information, including the fund type (OEIC), annual management charge and lots of other tools you can play with at your leisure.

These sites are all designed with the DIY investor in mind, so the best thing to do is have a play around on the various sites listed and see which one floats your boat.

While past performance is no guide to the future, nobody should invest in a fund without looking at a fund manager's past performance. All of

figure 9.5   Trustnet webpage

Source: Trustnet

the star fund manager ratings are pretty much predicated on this past performance. So, even if you don't want to spend hours analysing performance statistics, by following one of the star fund manager ratings, e.g. Citywire's, indirectly you are taking past performance into account.

Costs and charges

Fund managers charge for their services like anybody else, and as an investor it is important you find out what those charges are upfront. However, it is equally important to appreciate that the lowest and cheapest fund may not necessarily give you the best performance. Cost and charges are therefore one, but not the sole, factor in helping you decide which fund you choose.

table 9.2 ISA investment of £11,520, delivering a 5 per cent per annum gross return

	5 year	10 year	20 year	30 year
Gross return before charges	£14,703	£18,765	£30,566	£49,789
Net return with 1.6 per cent charges	£13,616	£16,094	£22,483	£31,410
Net return with 0.75 per cent charges	£14,185	£17,467	£26,483	£40,155
Net return with 0.25 per cent charges	£14,529	£18,323	£29,143	£46,353

Source: AJ Bell

Charges and costs can come in several different forms, and to make things more complicated, different people will refer to different parts of the costs involved in running a fund. Here are the key costs, charges and investment expenses you need to know about.

Initial charge

Many funds have an initial charge of 5 per cent, even if you buy direct from the provider. That said, these days most investment platforms rebate all of this back to you.

Annual management charge

The annual management charge, or AMC, is the fund manager's fee for running the portfolio on your behalf. Before the introduction of the RDR, it would typically have been 1.5 per cent, with half of this being retained by the fund manager. The remainder will have been used to pay your adviser and/or your investment platform. DIY investors typically will have received some or all of the 0.75 per cent per annum paid to their investment platform as a rebate.

Since the RDR came into effect at the end of 2012, fund charges have become unbundled from adviser charges and, in 2014, will become unbundled from investment platform charges as well. While the market is still settling down, you should not expect to pay an initial charge and a 0.75-per-cent per-annum management fee should be at the upper end of what you should be paying, unless it is a specialist fund.

Total expense ratio

The total expense ratio (TER) is a more accurate reflection of the actual cost of fund management on your investment returns. It includes not only the fund manager's annual management charge but also other costs of investing, such as legal expenses and yearly audit fees. You would normally expect a fund with an annual management charge of 1.5 per cent to have a TER of up to 2 per cent, but possibly higher.

The difference between the TER and the annual management charge for a 'clean' and 'dirty' fund should be the same.

But even the TER does not show the whole story. There are other costs involved in running funds, such as the 0.5-per-cent stamp duty on UK shares purchased and dealing costs. These will push total costs of investing even higher.

Fund managers would argue that these costs are hard to quantify as a fund manager has no way of knowing in advance how much trading they are going to do in any one year. The Investment Management Association is formulating a way to publish these costs in future. It is not clear how much use publishing this extra information will actually be to DIY investors. It is important, though, that you have a good idea of what the costs of investing in a fund will be – far more so than what these costs are for.

The number you are really interested in is the investment return net of charges – as we all know that the more weight a horse carries, the less likely it is to win the race.

table 9.3 What is included in fund managers' definitions of charges

Annual management charge (AMC)	Add additional items included in total expense ratio (TER) but not in AMC	Add additional items not included in AMC or TER
Running the fund management business	Legal and regulatory fees	Dealing costs
Profit	Custodian and registrar fees	Stamp duty
Commission (pre-1 January 2013)	Administration fees	Certain research costs
Payments to investment platforms (pre-6 April 2014)	Performance fees Audit fees	

More recently, the Ongoing Charges Figure (OCF) has become the industry standard for defining a fund's charges. This is broadly the same as the TER, but excludes performance fees.

Performance fees

Over one third of fund managers charge performance fees, but most only do this on a select number of their funds – in total only about 4 per cent of UK funds have a performance fee. Performance fees are often charged as a percentage of the returns achieved above either an index, interest rate measure or other benchmark. Typically these will be 15 to 20 per cent of a fund's gains.

Managers argue that you only pay more if the fund does well. Critics point out that fund managers can get an uplift even if they deliver average performance, provided returns are above the benchmark. Furthermore, fund managers are putting themselves in a no-lose position as they suffer no penalty when their funds underperform.

Those funds that charge performance fees do so because they think they are worth it. But they have some of the highest TERs in the entire fund management community. Avoiding or accepting them will be down to your view on the value of active fund management.

Share class conversions

If there is one call to action in this chapter it is this: look at any existing investments you have in funds and see if they are dirty funds. If you bought them before 31 December 2012, they almost certainly include a loading for a payment to the person who sold you the fund initially and to your investment platform.

You must consider whether to convert any dirty funds you have to a clean version, assuming one exists. You can switch from a share class charging 1.5 per cent to one charging 0.75 per cent per annum, while remaining in the same fund.

Some key points to consider:

- If you convert from one share class to another, HMRC has confirmed this will not be a disposal for capital gains tax purposes. This is only relevant if you hold the funds personally in a Dealing Account.

- You may already be getting a share of the payment that your investment platform gets from the fund manager. If so, the financial benefit of conversion, if there is one, won't be as stark. However, note that these rebates or loyalty bonuses are taxable – unless held in an ISA or SIPP.

- DIY investment platforms are not typically charging for share class conversions, but there is work involved and they may start doing so.

- If you invest in clean funds, your investment platform is likely to impose a charge for buying, selling and holding the fund for you. The cost of this needs to be factored in to any decision you make.

In simple terms, if you have £50,000 of funds charging an AMC of 1.5 per cent, you could save £375 a year (increasing as the value grows) by converting to a clean share class charging 0.75 per cent a year. So, unless your investment platform is going to charge you £375 a year for holding these funds, you are better off switching.

Changes to the structure of funds

You can occasionally find the fund you have invested in becomes merged with another fund. This can happen if it is unviably small and is not attracting the levels of investment the fund manager had hoped for, or if one fund manager buys another one and wants to consolidate similar funds.

You can also get the situation where funds that have become too big and unwieldy are split in two. That happened to the massively successful Fidelity Special Situations fund, which had become so big that in 2006 the manager decided to split it into two parts – a UK version and a global one.

Soft-closing of investment funds

Popular funds that generate big returns can attract floods of cash from hungry investors. But when funds get 'too big' they can become bloated and unwieldy, unable to make the nimble investment decisions that got them their stellar performance in the first place. To stop this happening, some fund management houses like to effectively close their doors to new entrants.

Rather than simply refuse to let any new investors in at all, some sought-after fund managers 'soft-close' their funds, which means they remain open but they deter new investors by putting in place punitively high initial charges to anyone wanting to come in.

The problem of access to top fund managers is particularly acute in the emerging markets sector, where many of the funds with the best track records have soft-closed in recent years. Emerging market top performers First State, Baillie Gifford and Lazard have all soft-closed some of their funds in recent years. But there are still several quality funds open to emerging market investors.

Multi-manager funds

If you like the idea of fund investing but do not want to have to work out which fund managers to go for, you can always choose a fund that does all of that for you. Multi-manager funds source what they believe are the very best managers in the market, hiring and firing them whenever they believe their performance merits it.

But while multi-manager funds sound a great idea in theory, they introduce a whole new layer of charges into your fund management costs. You end up having to pay the multi-managers' charges as well as the charges on the funds they select, which in turn can damage your returns.

Research carried out by *Money Management* magazine in November 2011 found that the average annual growth rate for multi-manager funds in the IMA Active Managed sector over five years was a dismal 1.6 per cent, compared to an average of 2.3 per cent for all of the funds in the sector. Average annual performance over a 10-year period was slightly better, at 5.3 per cent, compared to 5.2 per cent. Multi-manager funds in the All Companies sector did even worse, returning just 0.1 per cent over five years, against a sector average of 1.4 per cent, and underperforming over 10 years as well, with a 3.9 per cent return as against 4.5 per cent for the sector as a whole.

That said, multi-manager funds have seen increased inflows in recent years, partly because of the way they offer a one-stop shop for investors and their advisers who do not want to have to constantly revisit their fund manager selections.

Multi-manager funds come in two distinct flavours – 'fund of funds' and 'manager of managers'.

Fund of funds

A fund of funds manager invests in a range of whatever unit trusts or OEICs they think will give the best return, relative to the fund's objective. Funds of funds come in two types – 'fettered' and 'unfettered'.

Fettered funds of funds are those where the fund of funds manager can only invest in funds run by the same investment management house. This limiting of choice means the charges on fettered funds of funds are generally slightly lower, although critics say limiting the investable universe in this way goes against the grain of what a fund of funds is supposed to be all about. Unfettered funds of funds can invest in whatever funds the manager wants.

Manager of managers

Under a manager of managers structure the fund manager instructs different investment houses to run chunks of the fund's assets on their behalf. It is a structure that works in the same way as large pension funds. Manager of managers funds create even more suspicion among investment experts than funds of funds as they are perceived as being more cumbersome.

Tax considerations for funds

Investment funds held within ISAs and SIPPs enjoy tax benefits that are covered in more detail in Chapters 3 and 7 respectively. Funds not in ISAs or SIPPs, on the other hand, can be liable for tax in a number of different ways.

Income from a fund is either paid as a dividend or interest, depending upon the type of fund it is.

Where it is an equity-based fund, it will pay dividends. Where it predominantly invests in cash-type instruments or bonds, such as corporate bonds or government stock known as gilts, it will pay interest.

Tax on dividend income from funds

Most funds pay income as dividends, and when you receive it this has already been deemed to have suffered tax at 10 per cent at source, just like a dividend from an equity. If you are a basic rate taxpayer, or do not pay tax at all, this means you will have no further income tax liability.

The gross liability of higher rate taxpayers for dividend income is 32.5 per cent (see Table 9.4 below), meaning there is 22.5 per cent left to pay once the 10 per cent deducted at source is taken into account. Those paying tax at the top rate have a gross liability of 37.5 per cent, which falls to 27.5 per cent once the tax credit is taken into account.

table 9.4 Tax on dividend income from funds

Rate of tax	Higher rate @ 40 per cent	Additional rate @ 45 per cent
Net dividend received	£90	£90
Gross dividend equivalent (net dividend/0.9)	£100	£100
Tax rate	32.5 per cent	37.5 per cent
Tax due (tax rate × gross dividend)	£32.50	£37.50
Tax credit (gross dividend × 10 per cent)	£10	£10
Extra tax due (tax due minus tax credit)	£22.50	£27.50
Tax due as a percentage of the actual dividend paid (tax due/net dividend × 100 per cent)	25 per cent	30.56 per cent

This table is one we will refer back to when explaining how all dividend-paying investments are treated for tax.

Tax on interest income from funds

Interest income is paid by funds in one of two ways. Either it is paid after 20 per cent tax has been deducted at source or it can be paid gross, with no tax deducted. It is normally only paid gross to non-tax payers, which includes SIPPs and ISAs. Where this tax is deducted at source, your SIPP or ISA manager will reclaim this tax and credit it to your account.

Tax payers will have to pay tax, after allowing for the 20 per cent tax deducted at source.

Capital gains tax

Your fund manager doesn't pay capital gains tax on any gains made within the fund. Instead, you are taxed on any capital gains when you sell your shares or units in a fund. Capital gains tax is payable at the rate of either 18 per cent or 28 per cent, depending on your taxable income, although, as if you need any reminding, ISAs and SIPPs are exempt from capital gains tax.

For capital gains tax purposes, funds are treated exactly like an equity, unless they are a money market or corporate or government bond fund, when most are exempt from capital gains tax.

You only pay capital gains tax on gains above your annual allowance of £10,900.

Useful websites

www.citywire.co.uk

www.digitallook.com

www.fool.co.uk

www.investmentfunds.org.uk

www.londonstockexchange.com

www.morningstar.co.uk

www.trustnet.com

www.youinvest.co.uk

Tracker funds

Tracker funds, as their name suggests, track a particular investment market, usually a stockmarket index such as the FTSE 100, FTSE 250 or S&P 500. These funds deliver exposure to stockmarkets at very low cost because they do not pay fund managers to try to beat the market by picking stocks they think are going to go up in value.

The active versus passive debate

One of the fiercest debates in the investment industry is whether it is actually worth paying for active fund management. In the good old days when markets were regularly delivering double-digit returns, people were less concerned at the fund manager taking 1 or 2 per cent out of the pot for their costs.

But the difficult economic conditions of recent years, and a widespread acceptance that developed economies are set for restrained growth for years to come, have placed an increased emphasis on charges.

This, in turn, has fuelled a growth in interest in low-cost tracker funds that mirror an index, of which there are many.

Critics of active management also argue that there is so much information and analysis available on listed companies these days that we have a near-perfect market. The chances of fund managers beating the market are much slimmer than they used to be. Burden the fund manager's performance with charges and the task becomes Herculean.

Report after report has found that the majority of actively managed funds have failed to beat the index or benchmark they set themselves.

Supporters of active management say that while the average actively managed fund may underperform the index, high-calibre fund managers are more likely to beat it by a considerable margin. They also say that while certain markets may be so saturated with analysis that prices are near-perfect reflections of true value, there are areas in the world where this is not the case. Emerging markets and smaller companies are good examples, where local or specialist knowledge and understanding, it is argued, are needed to interpret the data.

Active management fans also argue that tracker funds overpay for companies that are new entrants into an index and are underpaid for those companies sold when they exit an index. By constantly rebalancing to an index, you are buying the risers and selling the fallers.

The active versus passive debate divides analysts, academics, advisers and investors to this day and is not likely to be settled any time soon.

A report by consumer group Which? ('Burying your true investment costs', *Which? Money,* published in 2011) pointed to funds with annual charges approaching 4 per cent a year. The 'worst' culprit in the report was the Neptune UK Mid Cap fund, which, despite an AMC of 1.6 per cent and a published TER of 2 per cent, in fact had a total cost of investing of 3.96 per cent a year when all the costs of investing were taken into account.

Ironically, the Neptune fund at the centre of the Which? report had in fact delivered absolutely stellar performance, up 150 per cent in the five years from its launch in December 2008 – more than three times the average return of 45 per cent for the IMA UK All Companies sector as a whole. If all high-cost funds delivered returns like that, there would be no debate over active versus passive fund management.

Indices

The best known index in the UK is the FTSE 100, or Footsie, which is reported daily in the national news and can be obtained from most investment platforms' websites – though often with a 15 minute delayed price. This index tracks the share price of the 100 largest companies by value listed on the London Stock Exchange (LSE). The FTSE 250 tracks the next 250 largest companies. The FTSE All-Share index seeks to track the top 98 per cent of companies, again by value, listed on the London Stock Exchange.

Currently the All-Share index tracks over 600 of the 3,000 or so companies listed in London – not as many as you might think, but this is due to a relatively small number of very large companies dominating this index based on market capitalisation.

There are hundreds of indices and more are now being created to cater for the demands of passive investors. They cover all the main IMA sectors that we looked at earlier (Chapter 9), including equities, corporate bonds, government bonds and property, across a wide range of geographies, be they developed or emerging markets.

The structure of tracker funds

Tracker funds can take the form of a unit trust or OIEC (described in Chapter 9). But a large number of the new generation of tracker funds are very different in their make-up, so are worthy of individual consideration.

The new breed of tracker funds are called exchange-traded funds (ETFs), with their cousins exchange-traded commodities (ETCs) and exchange-traded notes (ETNs) completing the suite of what are collectively called exchange-traded products (ETPs).

What are exchange-traded funds?

Exchange-traded funds, or ETFs as they are more commonly known, are very low-cost, passively managed funds that track indices. They have soared in popularity in recent years as canny investors have realised they can track exactly the same indices they were holding in the past for a fraction of the price, with greater trading flexibility than can be offered by traditional funds.

ETFs are traded on stock exchanges like any listed equity (see Chapter 12). The ETF holds a basket of equities or bonds that enable it to mimic the index it is tracking. As mentioned, ETFs are the best-known type of a group of investments known as exchange-traded products. Other ETPs include exchange-traded commodities, which track commodities, and exchange-traded notes, which track the bond markets, such as corporate bonds and gilts.

Charges on ETFs are low, often lower than those for an equivalent unit trust or OEIC tracker, and much cheaper than actively managed funds. They are tax efficient and they track their chosen indices pretty accurately, in fact more accurately than many unit trust or OEIC trackers. And they can be very liquid, meaning it is easy to get into and out of them at a fair price.

Similar to funds, they are open-ended in nature, so price is not driven by supply and demand. The number of shares in an ETF is adjusted daily to meet the supply and demand for them.

All these factors make ETFs an attractive way for DIY investors to access a broad range of markets.

ETFs are particularly suitable for charge-conscious passive investors as they keep costs down to an absolute minimum. As with funds, not all ETFs are UCITS funds aimed at the retail investor. Some are UCIS funds aimed at the sophisticated and high net-worth investor (see Chapter 9 to remind yourself of the difference).

There are two different structures of exchange-traded products – physical and synthetic.

Physical

A physical ETF mimics an index by holding the same investments that make up the index.

There are two main methods by which physical ETFs track an index – full replication and partial replication.

Full replication is where the ETF buys all of the assets in the index, and this is common for the more mainstream indices such as the FTSE 100. The holdings in the ETF aim to replicate exactly the holdings of the index.

Partial replication, often referred to as optimisation or sampling, is where the ETF buys the main components of an index, but not the whole of it. This may be used if the spread of the index is global, or the companies in the index are illiquid, or possibly if the ETF is small.

For an ETC tracking a commodity such as gold, physical replication would mean that the ETC physically owns the gold, albeit via a custodian. Physical replication is more common for hard commodities such as precious metals, as opposed to soft commodities such as coffee or grains such as wheat, where physical ownership of the commodity by the ETC provider is not practical.

In this instance, futures or swaps are used to gain synthetic exposure to the targeted commodity.

Synthetic

A synthetic ETF involves the ETF provider entering into a contract with a financial partner called a counterparty, which is often an investment bank. This contract involves the ETF provider investing in a basket of assets, as stipulated by the counterparty, which acts as collateral.

Although this collateral must typically adhere to regulatory guidelines, it may have varying levels of correlation to the index being tracked by the ETF. The ETF provider and the counterparty then 'swap' the return on the basket of assets for the return of the index: this allows the ETF provider to offer to provide the return on the index to its investors. This is why synthetic ETFs are sometimes called 'swap-based' ETFs.

Synthetic ETFs are considered riskier than physical-backed ETFs because of the counterparty risk.

They are also less likely to be a UCITS investment and hence may not be readily available to the retail DIY investor.

Tracking error

This is one of the key considerations when looking at a tracker fund, along with financial security and charges. The tracking error is the deviation from the index it is tracking.

Tracking difference, or performance variation, between the fund and index is caused by charges – an index makes no allowance for charges – and also by the fact that the holdings in the tracker fund may not be identical to the index it is tracking.

Synthetic ETFs normally have the lowest tracking errors – the tracking error of a synthetic ETF reflects the costs associated with the underlying swap agreements. Fully replicated ETFs are the next most efficient trackers of an index and, as you may expect, partially replicated ETFs tend to have the largest deviation from their index.

The history of ETFs

The prototype for today's ETFs was the launch in the USA back in 1989 of Index Participation Shares for the S&P 500. The idea for these structures emerged from the post-mortem of the stock market crash of 1987. Investment managers worked out that they would have been able to deal with the crash more effectively if they had been able to trade large amounts of stocks quickly, preferably instantaneously. The idea was that stocks could be grouped together in a basket and traded as a unit on an exchange.

But their growth wasn't straightforward. Index Participation Shares were put on pause for several years when the Chicago Mercantile Exchange sued to stop them, although the Toronto Index Participation Shares started tracking the Toronto Stock Exchange 35 shortly afterwards in 1990.

The first actual ETF started trading a few years later in January 1993. It was called the S&P 500 Depository Receipt, which was abbreviated to SPDR and given the nickname 'the Spider'. It remains popular with US investors to this day.

Barclays joined the fray with its iShares series of ETFs in 1996, State Street followed in 1998 and Vanguard launched its first ETF in 2001.

The growth from the launch of that very first ETF back in 1993 has been explosive, with over 1,400 funds in existence at the end of 2011, across literally dozens of issuers. Fund inflows into ETFs in the USA overtook those into mutual funds (the US name for OEICs and unit trusts) for the first time in 2003, although since then mutual funds have tended to attract bigger inflows in the years when markets have performed positively.

The Spider, which is run by State Street, is still the biggest ETF in the world, holding assets of £70bn. Its size and the efficiency of the ETF structure mean it has a gross expense ratio of 0.1 per cent. To put that in context, the HSBC FTSE 100 tracker that was, until the arrival of cheaper ETFs in 2012, one of the cheapest OEIC tracker funds available in the UK, has a total expense ratio of 0.27 per cent.

The second biggest ETF in the world at the beginning of 2012, the £45bn SPDR Gold Shares ETF, is said to be the sixth-largest holder of gold in the world, holding more of the shiny stuff than the governments of many developed nations.

The introduction of ETFs has not only seen cost pressure on active fund managers, but also on the early entrants to passive fund management. A 10 basis points annual management charge for a mainstream index is, if not the average, where the market seems to be heading.

The UK was relatively late to the party with ETFs, but with investors on the other side of the Atlantic getting access to passive investments so much more cheaply it was only a matter of time before they hit these shores.

The first launch on the LSE did not happen until April 2000, when iShares brought its FTSE 100 ETF to market. ETFs soon picked up momentum in the UK and 2002 saw the creation of a dedicated ETF trading segment on the LSE, while Chinese, Japanese and European ETFs were launched in London in 2004 and energy, metals and agricultural sectors were added the following year.

Suddenly providers everywhere wanted a piece of the ETF action, with new market entrants popping up overnight. In a three-week period in November 2005 the number of ETFs available on the LSE doubled, with launches targeting Asia, South America and Eastern Europe all coming to market. The scrapping of stamp duty on non-resident ETFs in 2006 made it considerably more attractive for international ETF issuers to list their products on the LSE, bringing UK investors even more choice of these low-cost instruments.

A couple of years ago the rapid increase in the number of ETF providers launching synthetic ETFs using swaps to track indices started to set off alarm bells with authorities. The regulator was, and remains, concerned that with ETFs becoming increasingly complex in their structures, investors could lose out in the event that a counterparty to a swap goes bust.

In 2011 the FSA fired a warning shot across the bows of the industry, cautioning providers against marketing synthetic ETFs as simple alternatives to trackers.

However, many wise heads in the investment community have questioned whether synthetic ETFs are quite as risky as they have been made out to be. And the FSA's warning has not stopped ETFs from continuing to form a key part of many investors' portfolios.

Talk to top independent financial advisers and most will recommend ETFs for at least part of an individual's overall holdings. However, with physical

ETFs just as able to cover most of the areas of the market that the DIY investor is likely to want to invest in, you may want to take the sleep-easy-at-night option and err on the side of caution.

The major players

There is safety in size with ETFs. Not only is a larger ETF more cost-efficient than a smaller one, but there are simply too many ETFs in the market at the moment. It does seem that professional and DIY investors have an increasing appetite for ETFs, but, nevertheless, there will be ETF closures to come, which are best avoided.

The big players are Blackrock, with its popular iShares ETFs – bought from Barclays Capital in 2009, Deutsche Bank with their db X-trackers, Société Générale with their Lyxor range, State Street and their SPDR ETFs and Vanguard, the US giant whose presence in the UK is increasing rapidly.

Cost

The number one attraction of ETFs and their kind is their low cost, making them a perfect way for the cost-conscious DIY investor to get access to equity and other markets.

Costs are very low indeed. It is not only the giant US Spider ETF that has got a total expense ratio of 0.1 per cent. These ultra-low charges are available for UK markets too.

Vanguard offers a FTSE 100 with a total expense ratio of 0.1 per cent. Some physical-backed ETFs, like the Vanguard fund, charge an explicit 0.5 per cent initial charge to cover the cost of stamp duty paid by the fund.

The impact of your investment platform's costs on the total cost of ETF investing

The arrival of ultra-low-cost ETF managers in the UK has caused a bit of a stir in investment platforms. With the ETF's annual management charge having no loading for a payment to investment platforms, or indeed advisers, ETFs truly are cleanly and keenly priced.

Investment platforms have faced something of a dilemma figuring out how to charge for them. By the very nature of an ETF, it can be traded many times a day due to the large liquidity and small spreads. But equally it can be bought as a long-term hold. In the former scenario, the investment platform will earn its money from dealing commissions as it is treated like any other equity.

Where the ETF is held for a long time, the investment platform has the holding cost of the investment but no dealing income, so some level of holding or custody charge may be unavoidable.

With the advent of the RDR, this asset class may be lumped in with clean funds for charging purposes, but it should go without saying, if ETFs are to be the cornerstone of your portfolio then check out the charges.

Tax

ETF holdings are simply shares and so can be held within your SIPP, ISA or Dealing Account. They are generally treated in exactly the same way as unit trusts and OEICs for tax purposes.

You will recall (in Chapter 4) that I pointed out that 'bed and breakfast', where you sell a share and then buy it back again immediately to minimise your capital gains tax bill, is no longer effective.

HMRC has introduced a '30-day rule', whereby if you sell and then repurchase the same investment the transaction is ignored for capital gains tax purposes. One way around this is to hold two tracker funds in your portfolio that track the same index.

If you need to crystallise a gain or a loss, you can sell out of one tracker fund and buy the other, meaning you are not 'out of the market' for any time and you can still manage your tax position effectively.

Investment returns on ETCs and ETNs is normally by way of capital gain, for tax purposes.

If you buy an ETF domiciled outside of the UK – the majority of ETPs listed on the London Stock Exchange are domiciled in Ireland – there is no stamp duty. The ETF itself pays stamp duty when it buys shares, so this is consistent with how stamp duty is applied to funds.

Dividend income

Dividend income from ETFs is treated in exactly the same way as from equities and other equity funds, with 10 per cent taxed at source. (This is covered more fully on page 117.)

Capital gains

When you sell a UK-based ETF that has increased in value it will be considered in the same way as any other share or fund for capital gains tax purposes. (Capital gains tax is covered in detail on pages 35 and 118.)

'Reporting status'

You will find some ETFs are domiciled in countries outside the UK, such as Ireland or Luxembourg.

Virtually all UCITS ETFs you come across as a retail investor will have a 'reporting status' in the UK.

You can check this out on the ETF's factsheet. If the fund does have a UK reporting status its gains will be treated under capital gains tax rules. But if it does not, you might find gains are treated as income, which could lead to a far higher tax bill.

The risks associated with ETFs

The most obvious risk with an ETF is the possibility that the index or assets it is tracking will fall in value. The risk of this will reflect the underlying risk inherent in the market that the index is tracking.

As you would expect, equity ETFs will be far riskier than gilt and other fixed-interest ETFs.

Tracking error occurs when an ETF doesn't accurately track its index. I would suggest that for most ETFs that a DIY investor will use, this is unlikely to be a major issue. However, recent European Securities and Markets Association (ESMA) guidelines will require that expected tracking error is published by fund issuers starting in 2013, providing greater due diligence information for DIY investors.

Counterparty risk is an issue that the regulator is concerned about. This is most relevant for synthetic ETFs, which are normally the preserve of the sophisticated and professional investor.

Plenty of expert investors use both sorts of ETF, but unless you feel very adventurous, stick with physical ETFs – check the factsheet before you buy to find out what the ETF is backed by. Providers whose ETF range is principally made up of physical ETFs include Credit Suisse, Blackrock, Invesco, UBS and Vanguard.

Small ETFs carry the risk of closure, so the answer is if you want to be on the safe side, make sure any ETF you invest in is reasonably well established and of a substantial size – I use £100m as my threshold, but the bigger the better.

Other kinds of exchange-traded products (ETPs)

Exchange-traded products all track indices with low-cost fees, although they have slight structural differences.

Exchange-traded commodities (ETCs)

While ETFs typically track equity, bond or gilt indices, ETCs typically track commodity indices such as energy resources, metals such as gold, silver, copper and platinum, agricultural produce and livestock. Directly accessing the investment return associated with commodities in your portfolio was very difficult for DIY investors before ETCs came along. The arrival of ETCs has allowed a new generation of investors to get access to the increases in commodity prices that have been fuelled by demand for resources from emerging markets.

Because it is impractical to actually hold perishable commodities such as foodstuffs for any length of time, there are a large number of synthetic ETCs in this area. As explained above, these carry some extra risks, but there is no way for a fund to track these assets other than through synthetic structures.

Exposure to commodities can be a good diversifier in an overall investment portfolio and ETCs offer an easy way to achieve this.

Similarly, if you want to play particular themes such as oil or metals, you can do so quickly, easily and cheaply with ETCs with exposure to these parts of the market.

Exchange-traded notes (ETNs)

First created by Barclays Bank back in 2006, ETNs are structured in a way that means they operate more like corporate or government bonds. They are not collateralised, so the investor is subject to the risk that the issuer, usually an investment bank, goes bust. This means their value is also affected by the credit rating of the bank that has issued them. The bank does not have to go bust for the investor to lose out – if the issuing bank is merely downgraded the value of an ETN can go down, even when the index they are tracking does not move at all.

With so many more straightforward trackers available on the market, DIY investors are unlikely to need to use ETNs.

The mechanics of buying and selling ETFs

Price

One advantage of ETFs over unit trusts and OEIC trackers is that they are priced continuously through the day. Unit trusts and OEICs are typically priced once a day and once you have placed an order you are never sure exactly how much you are going to pay for them. While OEICS and unit trusts are purchased at net asset value, or NAV, ETFs are typically bought and sold at a 'market price'. Because ETFs are shares in companies, they are tradable whenever the market they are listed on is open.

Spread

Spreads on ETFs – the difference between the sell and the buy price – are very tight indeed. The ETFs that DIY investors are likely to want to access are massive and demand for them is never going to be a problem, which means you buy and sell for a price that is very close to the index's actual price.

Settlement

As with equities and funds, the settlement period is the time from the point the ETF is bought to the time the payment must be made to the selling party. The standard settlement period for ETFs is three days – this described as T+3, T being the trading day. For the DIY investor using an investment platform, this will be largely academic as the purchase or sale of an ETF will show up on your account instantaneously.

Income

Most ETFs pay dividends, which will be paid in the same way as for other funds, whether quarterly or half-yearly. Details of income payments will be on the ETF's factsheet.

One area where a unit trust or OEIC tracker may have an advantage over an ETF is dividend reinvestment. As we saw earlier (Chapter 9), OEICs and unit trusts often have a sub-class that reinvests dividends automatically. ETFs may track an index with dividends reinvested and, if so, your dividends will be reinvested automatically. If the ETF is paying dividends to you then you may incur additional dealing and spread costs to reinvest this cash back into the market.

Stop losses and sell orders

It is possible to protect your ETF investments falling below a certain level, or bank gains once they reach a certain level, by setting up stop losses and sell orders. These are automated instructions placed through your investment platform to sell out of an ETF if its price falls to or below a certain level. These are not available for funds. (Stop losses and sell orders are covered on page 167.)

Research

ETFs are most likely to be used as a simple answer to a straightforward part of an investor's portfolio requirements – low-cost exposure to key equity and bond markets. Part of the beauty of ETFs is the fact that because they are passively managed, researching them is far less complicated than researching funds.

Once you have worked out the portfolio you want to build and decided the index or indices you want exposure to, research need not go beyond comparing the charges on different ETFs tracking that index. You may also want to check the domicile and reporting status of the ETF and decide whether to go for a synthetic or physical structure. In reality, if you are seeking to track one of the major indices, it will come down to a choice between one of the major providers, probably based on price.

Useful websites for ETFs

www.etfdb.com

www.etf.db.com/uk

www.ft.com

www.indexuniverse.eu

www.lyxoretf.co.uk

www.morningstar.co.uk

www.spdrs.com

www.trustnet.com

http://uk.ishares.com

www.vanguard.co.uk

Investment trusts

D escribed by some as the City's best-kept secret, but attacked by critics as complex and risky, the truth about investment trusts probably lies somewhere between the two.

They are collective investments that give you access to active management at lower management charges than you typically pay for unit trusts and OEICs. Supporters argue that their refusal to pay commission to financial advisers is one of the main reasons why they are less common than OEICs and unit trusts.

But these closed-ended investment vehicles do come with a level of complexity and risk that is simply not an issue for their open-ended counterparts. That said, on the whole their performance has been better than comparable unit trusts and OEICs, making them a viable alternative for money you are looking to have professionally managed, whether for growth or income, over the medium or long term.

History

Investment trusts are the great-great grandparents of modern OEICs and ETFs. Investment trusts you can still invest in today were among the very first collective investments the world ever saw. The first investment trust was the Foreign & Colonial Investment Trust, set up in 1868 'to give the investor of moderate means the same advantages as the large capitalists in diminishing the risk of spreading the investment over a number of stocks'. Today it is still going strong and has assets of £2.2bn, giving thousands of investors access to a blend of UK and overseas equities.

Five years after the F&C Investment Trust was established, the Scottish American Investment Company started operating in Dundee, investing in railroads and government stocks. As well as being the birthplace of both *The Dandy* and *The Beano*, Dundee also gave us Alliance Trust – founded in 1878 and, more than a century later, the largest investment trust in the UK with assets of over £2.5bn. It is still headquartered in the city.

These early investment trusts set up in London and Scotland started life as a means for Victorian industrialists to raise cash to finance many of the great development projects of the 19th century. Funds from these early investment trusts went towards building American railroads, establishing Malaysian rubber plantations, exploiting cattle ranches across North America and laying undersea telegraph cables between continents.

There was, however, a blot on the otherwise clean copybook of the investment industry in the early noughties, when investment trusts were very naughty. Investment trusts were split into two share classes, one would receive the income and one the capital – a structure known as split-capital trusts or 'splits' for short.

Add in the fact that these splits borrowed to 'gear up' their return, while also investing in each other, and it will come as no surprise to find that disaster was just around the corner. Around 50,000 investors lost over £600m when a series of splits collapsed. But the investment trust sector is in far better shape now and controls are in place to ensure this will never be repeated.

Having survived depressions, recessions, world wars, a cold war and a scandal, some are predicting that the abolition of commission on unit trusts and OEICs, which happened as a result of the introduction of the Retail Distribution Review in January 2013, will lead to a new golden age for investment trusts in the UK.

This is a perspective I would have agreed with if commission had been abolished a decade ago. But I can't help thinking that the arrival of ultra-low-cost ETFs (covered in Chapter 10) in the UK will attract many of those investors for whom cost is the top priority.

What investment trusts can invest in

You will certainly not be stuck for choice if you want to put your money into an investment trust. There are currently more than 400 investment trusts, from generalist trusts targeting mainstream sectors for either growth or income, to niche ones targeting discrete industries such as litigation, reinsurance and media.

Some investment trusts are set up with a remit of targeting specific geographical areas, from core areas such as the UK, Europe, the US and Asia Pacific to less developed markets like those in Africa. You can also find investment trusts targeting property and cash, and at the riskier end of the spectrum those investing in hedge funds and private equity projects.

Structure

The term 'trust' is confusing as investment trusts are limited companies, typically listed companies, whose business is to manage investments.

Investment trusts are collective investments that invest in different parts of the market, in the same way that unit trusts and OEICs do, with a manager making the selections on your behalf. But the difference is that there are only a fixed number of shares in each investment trust, so price changes are reflected by demand for those shares. They are closed-ended, unlike unit trusts, OEICs and ETFs, which are all open-ended.

Investment trusts are curious things. The majority of them are valued by the market as being worth less than the total value of the assets that they hold. If you have ever seen an article in the personal finance section of a newspaper about how to buy £100 worth of shares for £90, it is bound to be about investment trusts.

There are explanations aplenty for this, but none is particularly satisfactory. Why should a company with £100m of assets be valued at £90m? This is not just a temporary state of affairs – discounts have been around for nigh on 150 years.

One explanation of this difference between an investment trust's share price and the total value of its assets is that the share price is also influenced by the market's perception of the way the trust's assets are likely to perform in the future. This, in turn, is influenced by the perceived skill of the management team and the value the market believes this team can add to the trust's future performance.

To understand investment trusts, if you ever truly can, you need to understand three key factors – share price, net asset value and discount/premium.

Share price

Investment trusts, like all listed shares, have an offer price and a bid price, depending on whether you are buying or selling. The offer price is the price you pay when you buy the share and the bid price is the price you receive when you sell it.

Investment trusts are closed-ended vehicles, which means that the amount of shares in existence remains the same from one day to the next. Shares are normally issued only once, when an investment trust is set up, though it is possible for new shares to be issued. Like with all listed shares, the price is dictated by supply and demand.

In the case of unit trusts and OEICs, whenever you pay money to the fund manager it simply issues more units or shares and buys more assets with your cash. With investment trusts, if you buy a share in an investment trust it is not the fund manager who receives your money, but the person selling the share – exactly the same as if you bought a share in a company such as Tesco.

As Tesco's business performance improves, so does its share price. Investment trusts don't sell food, they manage investments; and the better they do, the higher their share price.

The market capitalisation of an investment trust is the number of shares in existence multiplied by the price.

Net asset value (NAV)

The net asset value of an investment trust is the value of all of the assets held by the trust, less any borrowings. The net asset value per share of the trust is the net asset value divided by the number of shares in issue; 'net asset value per share' is also often abbreviated to 'NAV per share'.

Discount

This is the odd bit. Logic should dictate that an investment trust's market capitalisation is the same as its net asset value. This is the same as saying the share price should be broadly equal to its net asset value per share. But this isn't the case, and the difference between the two is known as the discount or premium.

In most cases, investment trusts' share prices are lower than their net asset value per share. If this is the case, the trust is said to be trading at a discount. If a trust has a share price of 90p and its NAV per share is 100p, it is said to be trading at a 10 per cent discount.

In early 2013, approximately 75 per cent of investment trusts were trading at a discount to NAV.

Movements in discounts, which can narrow or widen significantly, can have a greater influence on the investment return you get from your investment trust holding than the actual performance of the underlying investments.

Some people argue that if you are investing for a long time you can ignore the discount because the difference it will make to the overall total return will be marginal. If you buy at a 10 per cent discount and sell later at a 10 per cent discount, then the fact there was a discount has had no effect on your return. The quality of the fund manager and the consistency of its performance will be more important.

But discounts can be very volatile over the short term and may undergo a structural shift over the long term. Take the F&C Commercial Property Trust. It was trading at a 40 per cent discount in late 2008. Theoretically that meant by investing in it you were buying £100 worth of UK commercial property for £60. That suggests that the market did not believe the investment trust's valuation of its assets. Within a year, it was trading at a 15 per cent premium.

It is not hard to accept a discount or premium on a commercial property investment trust as the valuations of commercial property are open to judgement and can often lag the market. But these discounts also exist on equity-based investment trusts that do not face the same liquidity and valuation challenges.

One conclusion you may reach when looking at a discount for an investment trust is that the market is ascribing a negative value to the fund management team that is managing the fund. The market is saying that the investment trust is worth more wound up than it is if it carries on.

So why aren't all investment trusts that trade at a discount wound up? Good question. In reality, if the market thought that an investment trust had a realistic prospect of winding up, its discount would narrow. What typically happens is that the managers of an investment trust can narrow its discount by buying its own shares in the market, and many investment trusts do this.

Some will argue that a large discount on an investment trust is a buying opportunity, but I would suggest that, in itself, the level of a discount shouldn't be a sufficient justification to buy. There will be a reason why the market has placed a high discount on an investment trust and the market will always know more than you. Until you know why a discount exists, you cannot make a call as to whether it will widen or narrow.

These fluctuations in discounts can give investors either fabulous or terrible returns depending on which side of the deal they are on. They also show just how heavily dependent on market sentiment investment trusts are. If things go well, you do very well, but if markets turn sour, you can get the double whammy of a falling NAV compounded by a widening discount.

Discounts are a barrier to new investment trusts being launched. Why would you subscribe to a new share offer in an investment trust, if you thought that in a week's time it would be trading at a 10 per cent discount? You would just wait and buy it in a week's time. While it has been a difficult time for new investment trust issues over the last couple of years, sweeteners in the form of warrants are offered to persuade investors to invest in a new issue of shares in an investment trust. I will explain this in more detail in the section on warrants below (see page 148).

Premium

While the majority of investment trusts trade at a discount, some actually trade at a premium, which means the investment trust is valued at more than the total value of the assets it owns.

This is the flip side of a discount. It may represent the high demand for the services of the management team, it may reflect the fact that an investment trust is investing in an area that investors want exposure to but that is very difficult to get access to, or it may be that the net asset value understates how much the investment trust is really worth.

I would urge extreme caution if you are buying an investment trust at a premium. As with buying one at a discount, you should try and understand why the premium exists before investing.

In October 2012 Nick Train, manager of the top-performing Lindsell Train Investment Trust, told investors not to buy his investment trust because it was too expensive. At the time of his warning it was trading at a massive 21 per cent premium to its assets. You have to admire Train's honesty – he pointed out that the last time the premium on the trust was so high, which was back in 2011, it had fallen to a discount of 15 per cent within two years. Sure enough, four weeks after he warned investors off, the investment trust's premium was down to around 5 per cent.

Borrowing/gearing

Unlike unit trusts and OEICs, investment trusts are allowed to borrow money to gear their investments. The amount of borrowing, or 'gearing', that an investment trust is allowed is prescribed by the investment trust itself. Usually they allow borrowing of around 10 per cent of the investment trust's market capital. This amplifies returns, either good or bad, which is why investment trusts often perform better than unit trusts and OEICs in rising markets and worse in falling ones.

You can find out how much gearing an investment trust has at the Association of Investment Companies website. Like other types of fund, you will find that investment trusts have factsheets that contain key information about them and these can be obtained from websites such as Morningstar or Trustnet.

The idea is that the investment trust manager will gear up the investment trust when they think there are good opportunities and reduce borrowing in more difficult times. It's a way for the manager to be able to put their foot on the gas if they think there are fantastic opportunities out in the market.

Risks

Investment trusts are risky investments in the same way that most unit trusts, OEICs and ETFs are risky – they invest in equities, property and other assets whose price can go down as well as up. The fact that collective investments invest in lots of different assets means risk is lower than direct investment into single company shares.

Investment trusts are riskier than unit trusts and OEICs in part because they are able to borrow money to increase potential returns.

But demand for the investment trust itself can also fluctuate. For example, around the time of the split-cap investment trust debacle, sentiment towards investment trusts was relatively negative, and was reflected in wider discounts. As it happened, this presented investors with a great investment opportunity – as faith was subsequently restored to the market and discounts narrowed.

But their risks should not be overstated. They are still a viable alternative to actively managed unit trusts and OEICs and have, over most sectors and criteria, performed better than them.

Split-cap trusts, warrants, real estate investment trusts and venture capital trusts all carry their own special risks, which are explained in their various subsections below.

Performance

A report from *Money Management* in July 2012 found that the average investment trust outperformed its open-ended counterparts in all sectors except for UK smaller companies over the previous 10 years.

Investment trusts have been beating their open-ended counterparts for years, in part because of their lower management costs. This makes them an attractive alternative to actively managed unit trusts and OEICs for those willing to accept the additional risks associated with gearing and discounts.

Charges

For years the investment trust community has trumpeted the lower charges levied by closed-ended funds compared to unit trusts and OEICs, and rightly so.

Research by Lipper from 2010 found the average TER on an investment trust to be 1.2 per cent, compared to 1.65 per cent on unit trusts and OEICs. That said, it will be interesting to see a similar comparison done once all investment managers have moved their products into commission-free clean share classes that comply with the Retail Distribution Review.

Performance fees are more common among investment trusts than they are in the unit trust and OEIC world, with more than half of investment trusts charging performance fees of up to 20 per cent of outperformance of a predetermined benchmark.

If low cost is your primary objective then it may be that passive funds such as ETFs may be more suitable. But if you want actively managed pooled investments, investment trusts are an affordable option.

It is not quite as easy to get hold of an annual management charge, TER or estimate of the fund's total expenses for an investment trust as it is for a unit trust or an OEIC. But if you dig hard enough, possibly by looking on the investment trust's own website, you should be able to find most of the information you need in order to carry out a comparison of charges.

Research

There are plenty of specialist investment trust teams within broker organisations that produce reams of material on whom they think the good and bad managers are – see the websites at the end of the chapter.

Both Trustnet and Morningstar have a lot of easy-to-access information on investment trusts, including historic data on share price, net asset value, structure and analytics, allowing you to compare different investment trusts across a range of criteria. Morningstar's weekly *Investment Trust Times* newsletter gives regular comment on what is going on in the investment trust sector.

When researching investment trust managers, you should take a similar approach as researching unit trust and OEIC fund managers – look at independent sources such as *Shares* magazine and *Investors Chronicle*, look at Trustnet and Morningstar, read the financial press and look at the investment trust's own website.

You want to look for managers with a track record of at least three years' decent performance. Always consider the NAV per share as much as the share price and – for income-generating trusts – make sure the trust has not had to eat into its capital to maintain its dividend.

Given so much of the value of an investment trust is down to sentiment, it is also very much worth gauging the mood for or against a particular trust around the various internet sites commenting on the sector, as this will ultimately be reflected in discounts and premiums. And avoid anything trading at a huge premium or discount unless you are absolutely convinced of the fundamentals – it may be trading at such a large discount because the market knows something about it that you don't.

If you have any questions, The Motley Fool has a board on 'investment trusts and unit trusts'. You can ask any sensible question you like and there will be no shortage of willing helpers.

Corporate actions

Occasionally you will get mergers or takeovers of investment trusts, particularly where small operations are failing to achieve critical mass and can benefit from the economies of scale that being part of a bigger organisation will offer.

If you are a shareholder in a small investment trust the likelihood is you will be a target if the management is not doing very well or because costs make up a disproportionately large part of the fund's assets, so being acquired by a bigger player is probably no bad thing.

If you hold shares in the investment trust making the acquisition, chances are you will not be offered anything as part of the deal. Beyond exercising your shareholder vote, you will have little say in what happens.

While the number of investment trust shares in existence does not change from day to day, new shares can be issued, just as for any limited company, which has the impact of raising new funds for the company to manage.

Dividends

Investment trusts can be used for growth or income, in the same way that other investment funds can. Some income investment trusts have very high yields indeed.

Unlike unit trusts and OEICs, investment trusts have the ability to retain income in revenue reserves, which means they can hold money back in good years so they can maintain their dividend payment in leaner ones. Unit trusts and OEICs are obliged to distribute the income they receive.

Growth investment trusts will hope to use this mechanism to steadily grow their dividend year after year. The Murray International Trust has increased or at least maintained its dividend in real terms every year from 1973 to 2012.

The mechanics of buying and selling investment trusts

As previously stated, despite their name, investment trusts are not trusts but limited companies. As such, when you buy or sell your holding, you are simply buying or selling an amount of shares in a company. The mechanics of doing this are the same as buying and selling any other shares through your investment platform, although it is worth noting that some investment trust shares can have liquidity problems.

As with the purchase of other shares, you will have to pay stamp duty of 0.5 per cent on the purchase of shares in an investment trust. If the purchase is over £10,000 in value you have to pay the £1 Panel of Mergers and Takeovers levy as well – this levy applies to all equity purchases.

In addition to stamp duty you will also have to pay your investment platform's dealing commission when you buy and sell.

You will recall that when you buy a unit trust, an OEIC or an ETF, you don't pay stamp duty as the fund pays stamp duty on all the shares it buys. There is no such exemption for investment trusts. You pay stamp duty when you buy a share in an investment trust and the investment trust also pays stamp duty when it buys shares as an investment, which seems somewhat inconsistent, but that's the way it is.

Unit trusts and OEICs have grown with the retail investor in mind, particularly those who don't have much money to invest. Hence we have seen the growth of income and accumulation units – regular premium investing is part of their DNA.

Investment trusts, like ETFs, are more akin to equities in that they are slightly more grown up and you may not find it quite as easy, or cost-effective, to reinvest dividends from an ETF or investment trust as you would from an OEIC or a unit trust.

Spread/liquidity

As with any other traded share, the spread on the share price of an investment trust is the difference between the bid price and the offer price. Spreads are set by market makers and their size will depend on liquidity.

This liquidity issue is not a problem for unit trusts and OEICs, where units are created or cancelled to meet demand. When you come to sell a small stake in an investment trust then there will usually be a market there waiting to take them off your hands. But large orders may face liquidity problems. What amounts to 'large' will depend on the trust. There is usually no trouble offloading £50,000 stakes in the bigger investment trusts, but for some smaller ones, £5,000- or £10,000-worth can be problematic.

You can check how much the market says it will take off your hands at more or less the price being quoted on the screens by looking at the exchange market size (EMS) – which is quoted under 'trading information' on the London Stock Exchange website (www.londonstockexchange.com).

The EMS is the number of shares in the investment trust that you can safely expect to be able to trade without the spread widening significantly. You can normally trade up to three times the EMS figure without facing any problems, although in volatile market conditions only the EMS may be available.

Attempt to buy or sell even £10,000-worth of shares in a less well known investment trust automatically through your investment platform and it is unlikely you will be able to place the deal online. You will be asked to ring up your investment platform to place the deal and it is likely that you will get a less favourable price than the price on your screen.

Settlement period

We discussed the challenges of switching between funds earlier (Chapter 9), in particular the problem with the fact that you will be out of the market for a day or more if you want to sell a fund and then use the proceeds to buy another fund. You don't have this problem with investment trusts, as your account will be credited immediately when you sell an investment trust and you can use these funds to buy another, there and then. As with most equities, settlement is normally T+3.

Special types of investment trust holdings

Split-capital trusts

Split-capital trusts, also referred to as 'split-cap trusts' or 'splits', are a special sort of investment trust that issue different classes of shares that pay out returns to their different classes of shareholders in different ways. They also differ from mainstream investment trusts in that most have a set winding-up date.

Investment trusts, on the other hand, normally only have one class of share and the performance of the trust is only reflected in the dividends and the share price.

The idea behind creating different classes of shares is that it enables the trust to better meet the needs of different types of shareholders. For example, a simple split-capital trust might issue income shares and growth or 'zero' shares, with the income shareholders getting all of the income and capital shareholders getting all the capital growth.

The split-cap debacle

Just because zero dividend preference shares are supposed to pay out a fixed sum does not mean they always do – as 50,000 investors found out to their cost back in 2000 and 2001 when a whole raft of split-cap trusts collapsed, leaving zero holders with next to nothing.

As is so often the case, the problem stemmed from a lack of understanding of the risks the products held, which in the case of the split-cap debacle was compounded by aggressive marketing that skated over these risks. At the end of the 1990s some brokers were pushing zeros as low-risk investments that had never failed in the past.

When markets then plummeted in 2000 many split-cap trusts collapsed, leaving zero and income shares worth just a few pence in the pound, or in some cases nothing at all. Investors suffered combined losses in the region of £650m. It emerged that split-cap trusts had been investing in each other, a revelation that sparked allegations of a magic circle of managers buying each other's trusts to keep their asset prices from falling.

The regulatory bodies intervened and investigated, although never published their findings of exactly what had gone on. But fund managers and brokers were forced to pay hundreds of millions of pounds in compensation. Since then, split-cap trusts' reputation has slowly recovered and respectable names have continued to launch new ones since then. But splits remain a niche product for real experts, and DIY investors will want to treat them with care.

Subscription shares and warrants

Subscription shares and warrants give you the option to buy new shares in an investment trust, but there is no obligation. They will come with a conversion price and an expiry or conversion date. These are often issued by established investment trusts as a way of raising new capital and were initially created as a sweetener as part of an initial fund-raising for a new investment trust, to offset the likelihood of an investment trust going to an immediate discount, as explained earlier.

Subscription shares can be held in an ISA whereas a warrant cannot; both can be held in a SIPP or a Dealing Account.

Warrants and subscription shares are volatile and, I would suggest, are only for the expert DIY investor. But you may find that you receive some free as part of an investment trust holding you have, so it is worth knowing the basics.

Real estate investment trusts (REITs)

A real estate investment trust (REIT) is a company listed on the stock exchange that makes money by buying, selling and renting properties. A REIT, which is pronounced 'reet', has the same structure as an investment trust in that it is closed-ended, so does not issue new shares to match supply and demand for its shares. Instead, as with other investment trusts, the price of the shares goes up or down depending on the demand for them, in turn reflecting both the value of the underlying asset and the market's perception of the prospects for the sector.

REITs can invest in both commercial and residential property. Until the launch of a brace of residential property funds in 2012, REITs have also been the only way to be able to hold residential property assets in your SIPP.

REITs originated in the USA in 1960 when they were introduced as a structure that would reduce or eliminate corporation tax in real estate investment companies. But they were not introduced in the UK until 2007, at which time nine UK property companies, including British Land, Land Securities and Liberty International, converted to REIT status.

To qualify as a REIT, the company has to distribute 90 per cent of its income as dividends.

Liquidity

Spreads on REITs will widen at times in the economic cycle when the property they hold, be it commercial or residential or a combination of both, is out of favour. But at least you will always be able to sell your stake in a REIT for whatever the market really thinks it is worth. This is not always the case with open-ended vehicles such as commercial property unit trusts and OEICs, which have the power to close their doors in the event that prices fall, so they do not have to offload their property holdings in a fire sale if investors demand their money.

Investment trusts – tax rules and considerations

These are broadly the same as for equities.

Investment trusts can be held within ISAs, SIPPs and Dealing Accounts, though note that warrants cannot be held in an ISA.

UK dividends from investment trusts are taxable and are received with 10 per cent dividend tax deducted at source. This tax credit is not reclaimable by ISA or SIPP investors, but no further tax on dividend income or capital gains will be payable if held in these wrappers.

Nil rate and basic rate taxpayers will not pay any further dividend tax, but 40 per cent taxpayers will pay 22.5 per cent of the gross dividend, being the special higher dividend tax rate of 32.5 per cent less the credit for the 10 per cent taxed at source. Where income tax rates are 45 per cent, the dividend tax is also 5 percentage points higher.

Non-UK dividend income is normally received net of local withholding taxes. Some credit may be given for tax already paid if the UK has a double taxation agreement in place with the country where that dividend income is generated.

Many REITs pay out property income dividends, which are more tax-efficient than ordinary dividends for the retail investor. They are paid out gross and for all intents and purposes are taxed as rental income – as if you had invested directly in property.

Investment trusts do not pay capital gains tax, similar to unit trusts and OEICs. Instead the gains are taxed in the hands of the investor, after their capital gains tax allowance has been used up.

Venture capital trusts

Tax-free income, tax-free capital growth and 30-per-cent tax relief on the way in are the bait used to try and get you to take on the risk of investing in early-stage companies. To access these attractive benefits you have to put your faith in venture capital trusts (VCTs).

With the lower limits on contributions into pensions starting to bite in the next few years and the top rate of tax at 45 per cent, interest in VCTs amongst wealthier investors is expected to grow. For less wealthy DIY investors, on the other hand, VCTs are likely to remain off the spectrum.

VCTs are a specialist form of investment trust given generous tax advantages to encourage investment in small businesses at an early stage in their expansion. You invest in the VCT and the VCT invests in the underlying start-up companies. They are a way for companies not big enough to be listed on a stock exchange to get access to funds.

For investors to be able to claim tax breaks, the VCT's assets have to be invested in qualifying companies – small companies that carry out a qualifying trade. 'Small' in this case is a company with less than £15m of gross assets on its balance sheet and it may be unquoted or possibly listed on one of the junior stock exchanges, such as the Alternative Investment Market (AIM). Non-qualifying trades include farming, property development, professional services and several others.

Some of the tax reliefs are only available to those who subscribe for the initial shares. But the shares in the VCT are then typically listed on a stock exchange, so there is a secondary market. Discounts are quite high for VCTs, as there isn't that much secondary trading for these shares.

Without the tax advantages, most DIY investors would probably not want to invest in the companies that a VCT invests in. A large degree of faith in the expertise of the managers who run them is needed. But the generous tax advantages they offer can make them a useful tax-planning tool. And if you are an experienced DIY investor, understand the risks and wait for opportunities to materialise, you can find corners of the VCT market that offer good value and that will deliver decent returns.

Tax relief on VCTs

The tax relief you get on VCTs depends on whether you are an original investor or you bought the shares on the secondary market via the stock exchange.

Relief on newly issued VCT shares:

■ Exemption from income tax on dividends on ordinary shares.

■ Exemption from capital gains tax on disposal of shares.

■ You can invest up to £200,000 each year with income tax relief at 30 per cent for subscriptions of new shares, provided the shares are held for at least five years – tax relief is limited to the amount of income tax you pay.

Relief on VCT shares bought on the secondary market:

■ Exemption from income tax on dividends on ordinary shares.

■ Exemption from capital gains tax on disposal of shares.

If you buy VCTs on the secondary market, there is no income tax relief on your investment but this counts towards your £200,000 limit.

VCTs for income

The tax-free income from VCTs can make them attractive for DIY investors paying tax at 40 or 45 per cent, provided of course you find the right ones. For a 40 per cent taxpayer, a 6 per cent yield from a VCT is equivalent to a 10 per cent yield from income not getting any tax relief.

When looking for VCTs for income, focus on past net asset value returns more than share price. You should also look out for VCTs that have shown they can maintain payouts at a decent level without eating into their net asset value per share.

You do not get the 30 per cent tax relief on the secondary market, but that does not mean there are not bargains to be found, and you do not have to worry about holding them for five years to benefit from the tax-free income and gains.

In fact, with a steady supply of investors getting rid of their shares after the five-year holding period into a market generally considered beyond the pale for most mainstream investors, the secondary market in VCTs can throw up good opportunities when shares trade on large discounts.

Allenbridge produces a very useful *Tax Shelter Report*, which has a large amount of information on VCTs (see websites on page 152).

VCTs can be specialist, meaning they target a particular sector such as healthcare and biotech, technology or environment, or generalist, meaning managers can invest in a broad range of companies.

'Early bird' discounts on VCT shares

It is worth getting in early if you are going for new VCT shares. Most people invest in VCTs as the end of the tax year approaches, in February or March, yet launches usually start in January, with some open for subscription in November.

To help build momentum behind their launch many VCTs offer 'early bird' incentives, normally some extra shares. There is always the risk that the VCT won't achieve critical mass and the launch doesn't go ahead, in which case your money is returned to you. On the other hand, leave it too late and you can find the VCT you want reaches capacity early and closes before you get in.

But VCTs are by no means plain sailing. The companies they invest in are notoriously risky and charges are much higher than other investment trusts and funds – often well in excess of 2 per cent.

What's more, when you come to sell, liquidity can be poor, meaning you may struggle to find someone to buy your shares. For this reason, when buying and selling VCT shares, however big or small the holding, it is always worth getting on the phone to your investment platform to get them to see how the land lies. Try to sell them online and you may get a poor deal.

Useful websites

www.fool.co.uk

www.investorschronicle.co.uk

www.londonstockexchange.com

www.morningstar.co.uk

www.reita.org

www.sharesmagazine.co.uk

www.taxshelterreport.co.uk

www.theaic.co.uk

www.theitlist.co.uk

www.trustnet.com

12

Equities

E quities are likely to be the driving force behind many DIY investors' portfolios. They can be held directly through an ISA, SIPP or Dealing Account or indirectly through funds run by professional managers.

Yes their value can go down as well as up, but since the 19th century equities have outperformed pretty much every other regularly traded asset class by a country mile.

The word 'equities' is interchangeable with 'stocks' and 'shares', and covers all the different types of shares in a company that an investor can buy, hold and sell. A limited company's owners are its shareholders, so when you buy shares you become a part-owner of the company.

Investors can profit from holding shares in two ways – when the company pays a dividend and when the value of its shares increases.

The history of equities

The rise of equities over the last few centuries pretty much tracks the growth of the capitalist economic system. The concept of ownership of a profit-making organisation being divided up into tradable shares, however, first appeared back in Roman times.

Arguably the first recognisable limited company was the East India Company, set up in 1600 under a charter granted by Elizabeth I that gave it trading privileges in India. Two years later the Dutch East India Company issued shares on the newly created Amsterdam Stock Exchange. The concept of the limited company, with individuals' legal liability for any debts or other losses created by the company limited to their investment in the shares, coupled with the ability to pool thousands of investors into a single project, fuelled much of the economic growth in Europe and the United States through the following centuries.

Until 30 years ago, share ownership was pretty much the preserve of wealthy individuals. But the privatisations and demutualisations of the 1980s and 1990s saw millions of individuals become shareholders for the very first time. Schemes offering employees shares in the company they work for have also increased share ownership, while the growth of the internet has seen the cost of buying equities fall, cutting out the need for an old-school stockbroker.

A bumpy ride

Europe and America's economies have been on an upward trend for many decades now and equity investors have benefited from the ride. But it hasn't all been plain sailing. In fact, history shows us stock markets have crashed with depressing regularity.

One of economic historians' favourite crashes, if you can have such a thing, is the so-called South Sea Bubble of 1720. Stock in the South Sea Company, a British company with the rights to exploit parts of South and Central America, started a seemingly inexorable rise from £100 a share to almost £1,000 in a matter of just a few months. Blinded by greed, investors rich and poor ploughed their savings into what they believed was a one-way bet, without regard to the fact that the territories the company held the rights to exploit were all controlled by Spain, with whom Britain was at war.

When promised dividends didn't materialise, investors started running for the door and the shares were decimated, falling back down to £100 again by the end of the year. And it wasn't just stupid people who lost money – the very clever Sir Isaac Newton is said to have lost today's equivalent of £2.4m in the company.

The 19th and 20th centuries have also had their fair share of market collapses, with the Wall Street Crash of 1929 perhaps the most famous of them all, kicking off the Great Depression of the 1930s.

Within living memory for anyone over the age of 50 is the crash of 1973 and 1974, which was caused by the devaluation of the US dollar and a spike in the price of oil. The UK fared worse than most in that crash, with the FT30, then the leading index in this country, falling 73 per cent top to bottom.

Since then we have lived through 1987's Black Monday, 1992's Black Wednesday, 1997's Asian Crisis, 1998's Russian Crisis, 2000's dot.com bubble, the 9/11 market falls and the 2002 downturn, among others. Then, of course, there was the credit crunch of 2008, kicked off by the collapse of Lehman Brothers, which triggered the global financial crisis that developed economies are still struggling to extricate themselves from to this day. And it is fairly certain there will be more along in the future.

But don't let that put you off.

Easy to say, you might think, but with all that bad news, why would anyone want to invest in equities? Because equities are still expected to do what they have done for long-term investors ever since the 19th century – perform better than other asset classes.

Barclays Capital has been comparing the performance of equities, cash on deposit and gilts for over half a century, with performance comparisons going back to 1899. The 2012 edition of its annual *Equity Gilt Study* showed that equities have outperformed gilts and cash on deposit consistently for over 110 years. The sum of £100 invested in equities back in 1899 would, with dividends reinvested, have grown to £1,639,368 by 2012. If you had put your money into cash, it would have grown to just £20,228.

The compounding effect of reinvested dividends

Reinvesting your income, dividends or otherwise, has a massive influence on your long-term investment returns, as these figures from the Barclays *Equity Gilt Study* show.

table 12.1 Value in 2012 of £100 invested at the end of 1899 without reinvesting income

	Nominal	Inflation adjusted
Equities	£11,808	£160

Source: Barclays Capital

table 12.2 Value in 2012 of £100 invested at the end of 1899, income reinvested gross

	Nominal	Inflation adjusted
Equities	£1,639,368	£22,239
Cash	£20,228	£274

Source: Barclays Capital

Equities can have sustained periods when they do not deliver – the first decade of the new millennium has been described as the 'lost decade for equities' because returns were lower than bonds and cash over the period. However, equities have almost always delivered the goods over the long term. Of the 91 21-year periods between 1899 and 2012, equities have outperformed gilts and bonds in 90 of them.

Of course equities can be volatile, which is why you might not want your whole portfolio in them. And there is no guarantee that equities are going to make you rich quickly. But over the long term they can deliver returns that you will not be able to get down at the bank or building society.

The different types of equity

Ordinary shares

These are the mainstream shares typically held by equity investors. An ordinary share is anything that is not a preference or convertible share.

Preference shares

Preference shares are a special class of share that pay investors a fixed dividend, making them typically of interest to investors looking for steady returns. That said, they are considerably less common today than they were a decade ago.

Dividends on ordinary shares are not guaranteed, as investors in BP found in 2010 when the oil giant cut its dividend altogether following the Gulf of Mexico disaster. Dividends on preference shares, on the other hand, are fixed. But if the company does not have the cash to pay it in any one year, they accrue until it does.

Unlike ordinary shares, preference shares do not normally entitle the holder to a vote, unless the dividend has not been paid.

Preference shares rank higher than ordinary shares in the event that a company goes into liquidation but they rank behind bank creditors on the winding-up of a company. In practice this protection should not be overstated, as preference shareholders often get little or no money back in the event of a company's insolvency.

Convertibles

Convertible preference shares are a form of preference share that also gives the investor a predetermined dividend with the option to convert them into ordinary shares in the event their price reaches a fixed price at a later date.

Companies use them as a way to raise cash more cheaply than bonds because the option to convert later is deemed to be of value, meaning they can offer investors a bit less income up front. The option price is usually set considerably higher than the share's current price.

The benefit for the investor is that they have the security of knowing they will get a certain dividend come what may, with the added flexibility that if the company starts to do really well and pays an even higher dividend than that paid by the convertible, the holder can convert and benefit from it, provided the share price has risen to the option price.

If the convertible never makes up that ground on the option price it is known as a 'busted convertible' and will be valued in a similar way to a bond. However, as it approaches or exceeds the conversion price, its value will increasingly correlate with the value of the stock itself, because the chance of conversion becomes more likely.

Where to invest – markets, sectors and indices

Modern investment platforms and brokers give you ready access to a bewildering array of investment markets around the globe. But unless you are an experienced stock picker, most of the stocks you are likely to hold will be listed in the UK.

Companies can be classified on basis of size, the index under which they are listed, the sector or industry they operate in or the geographical region in which they trade. With so many companies out there, filtering companies on this basis can guide you towards the sorts of stocks that are right for you.

The London Stock Exchange (LSE)

The London Stock Exchange is the fourth-largest stock exchange in the world, and the largest in Europe. Founded in 1801 and now based in new premises near St Paul's Cathedral, it is open for trading between 8.00 and

16.30, Monday to Friday, excluding bank holidays. Its main market lists the shares of over 1,300 companies from around the world.

The LSE also houses the Alternative Investment Market, called AIM for short. AIM shares can be held in your SIPP, ISA or Dealing Account.

FTSE 100

Everyone has heard of the FTSE. Pronounced 'Footsie', originally it stood for Financial Times Stock Exchange.

The FTSE 100 index is the one you constantly hear referred to on the news and in the papers. It reflects the average weighted share price of the 100 largest stocks on the LSE. If the FTSE is up, the average price of those shares has risen. If it falls, their price has fallen.

These companies are the giants of the UK economy, dominating the stock-market – their combined share value representing more than four-fifths of the entire value of all the quoted shares in the UK.

The FTSE 100 was established in 1984, with a base price of 1,000. It peaked at 6,950 on the penultimate trading day of the last millennium, 30 December 1999. The post-credit crunch gloom took it to below 3,500 in March 2009.

It is worth remembering that all the FTSE indices reflect only the value of the companies' shares and not the income generated through the payment of dividends. So if, for example, the FTSE 100 stayed at 5,000 for a year, that does not mean investors would have made nothing at all over that period, as they would have received the dividends paid. The average dividend yield of the FTSE 100 through 2012 was around 3.6 per cent.

FTSE 100 companies are generally mature companies that should be less volatile than smaller companies. Some pay dividends well in excess of this average.

The index includes household names such as Vodafone, Tesco and Unilever, as well as banks, tobacco and pharmaceutical companies and oil producers. But just because FTSE 100 companies are listed on the LSE, it doesn't mean they are British companies through and through.

Companies do not have to be based in the UK to get a listing on the LSE, they just need to trade their shares in London. Fifteen years ago the FTSE

100 pretty much reflected the UK economy and its trading overseas. Today things are very different. Kazak copper company Kazakhyms and Evraz, the mining business with large operations in Russia and the Ukraine, are just two examples of the numerous companies whose businesses are conducted almost entirely outside the UK, but which are included in the FTSE 100.

Overseas companies listed on the LSE can give you great returns, but they are largely commodity plays and you should not think they are similar in profile to steady consumer goods or utilities stocks just because they are in the FTSE 100.

These overseas companies like being listed on the LSE because it gives them kudos and demonstrates a certain level of governance. It also means that once they become a FTSE 100 constituent, a certain level of demand for their shares will be supported by investment houses running index trackers following the index unless, that is, their price falls so sharply that they drop out of the index.

FTSE 250/mid-cap stocks

If you want to go for growth in your portfolio and are comfortable with some risk, a good place to start is the FTSE 250.

The FTSE 250 is the next tier below the FTSE 100, covering the 101st to 350th largest companies quoted in the UK. For most mainstream indices, size means market capitalisation, or value.

Stocks in the FTSE 250 are generally described as mid-cap companies, which generally means between £3bn and £400m in a raging bull market and £1.2bn and £250m in a bear, or depressed, market. Promotion and demotion between higher and lower indices happens on a quarterly basis, so recently ejected former FTSE 100 stocks find their way into this index.

Because they are smaller than FTSE 100 companies, they tend to have more scope for growth – Domino's Pizza was the FTSE 250 success story of the last decade, its shares growing in value 19 times.

It goes without saying that it is a lot easier for a company with a market cap of £400m to double in size than, say, HSBC with a market cap of £115bn.

But these companies can also be less stable than FTSE 100 companies. Income seekers will generally do better with FTSE 100 shares as FTSE 250 companies tend to pay lower dividends, although there are some exceptions.

Mid-cap stocks theoretically reflect the UK economy more closely than the FTSE 100, which has a large global bias through its constituent companies. That said, FTSE 250 companies are themselves becoming increasingly global, with around half having overseas revenues. The FTSE 250 also contains several investment trusts, which are basically funds set up as limited companies that invest in other shares.

Supporters of mid-cap investments argue that they offer a greater choice than large-cap companies, which are dominated by whatever the theme of the moment is – banks and insurance companies one year and oil, gas and mining companies the next. Less risky than small-cap stocks and more nimble than blue-chips, the FTSE 250 should be the ideal hunting ground for the experienced stock-picker.

Recent history has actually turned the conventional wisdom that large-caps do better in tough market conditions on its head. Between September 2000 and September 2012, the FTSE 100 rose just 45 per cent. The FTSE 250, meanwhile, rose 150 per cent. That said, in times of market stress, mid-caps are likely to be more volatile.

FTSE 350

Rarely followed as an index, the FTSE 350 is simply the 350 largest companies on the LSE, and is an amalgamation of the FTSE 100 and FTSE 250.

FTSE SmallCap

Companies listed on the FTSE that are not in the FTSE 100 or FTSE 250, but are not on AIM, are listed on the FTSE SmallCap index. They are typically companies with a market cap of less than £200m.

Small-cap companies are, by their very nature, more volatile than bigger ones, meaning you should only invest in them if you can afford to lose some or all of your money. On the other hand, they can deliver spectacular growth if, of course, you choose the right ones.

Their very volatility can make small-cap companies an attractive target if you are looking to deal regularly. If a company performs badly for a long period of time, unhappy investors will tend to sell out of the stock. Management should eventually take note of this and make positive changes, and provided the company's basic proposition has not been undermined by external factors, canny investors can eke out decent returns.

That said, spreads (explained in more detail below) can be wide, making high turnover of shares an expensive business.

Studies have suggested that small-cap companies tend to perform better coming out of an economic downturn, but lag at other times. However, the wide variety of companies that make up the FTSE SmallCap means that some will do the exact opposite.

There are also a lot of investment trusts in the index – both Henderson and JP Morgan have nine investment trusts apiece listed in the FTSE SmallCap.

The Alternative Investment Market (AIM)

AIM is the LSE's market for smaller companies, including early-stage businesses and those backed by venture capital. It now lists around 3,000 small companies.

AIM has less rigorous reporting standards than the main LSE market, allowing smaller companies the flexibility to float on a recognised exchange, but without the high accountancy and legal costs associated with a full listing. There are also no capital requirements for companies and they come with tax breaks for investors. This is why, in recent years, considerably more small companies have moved from a listing on the main LSE index to an AIM listing. Many stocks listed on AIM are overseas companies.

Tax breaks for AIM shares

A large number of shares held on AIM become exempt from inheritance tax once they have been held for two years, making them a potential estate-planning tool, although the downside is that the volatility associated with them makes them generally less suitable for investors approaching the end of their life. From 6 April 2014, AIM shares are exempt from stamp duty when they are purchased.

Investing in AIM companies

AIM companies are all about growth – not dividends – and liquidity is even more of an issue in AIM than it is in the FTSE SmallCap. They are more volatile and hence riskier than main-market-listed companies.

Overseas stock markets

You can invest in most of the major stock exchanges around the world through your investment platform, with most overseas blue chip companies eligible for ISA and SIPP investment. The majority of mainstream shares can be traded online, provided the market is open in that country, although some will need to be done over the telephone.

There is no 0.5 per cent stamp duty on overseas equities, although some markets may have their own levies.

When you buy overseas equities, your investment platform will convert the sterling in your account into the currency of the country in which you are buying the shares.

Why buy overseas equities?

DIY investors tend to stick with UK equities, in part because it is a market we are closer to and understand better. But there is nothing wrong with putting your money in overseas equities, whether it is well known names such as Apple, BMW or Coca Cola, or fast-maturing companies in developing nations.

In fact, investing overseas will not only give you access to some of the world's dynamic manufacturing and commodity-based economies, it will also help dampen down volatility in your overall portfolio. This is because different economies around the world are rarely at the same place in the investment cycle at exactly the same time.

But there are risks to investing overseas, the most obvious one being currency risk. If your US shares rise by 20 per cent, but the dollar depreciates 20 per cent against sterling, then you have made nothing. Worse still is if both your US shares and the dollar fall 20 per cent, in which case you can end up seriously out of pocket.

When it comes to emerging markets, while they may be more volatile in the short term, the conventional wisdom is that developing economies' currencies are likely to strengthen against sterling in the coming decades, meaning UK investors will get an exchange rate kicker on their equity returns.

It should also be pointed out that investing directly into less developed markets overseas also carries political and regulatory risk. You can never be sure how politicians or other pressure groups are going to change the terms under which companies are allowed to operate in less developed economies.

Tax considerations for overseas equities

While UK share purchases attract stamp duty of 0.5 per cent of the transaction cost, overseas equities do not. That said, France has introduced a transaction tax, and with governments around the world looking for new ways to raise cash, there is no guarantee others won't follow suit, so check online what the rules are in the country you are planning to invest in before making too many trades, as these dealing costs will hit your returns.

Before investing in US equities you should make sure your investment platform gets you to fill in a W-8BEN form, which is a Certificate of Foreign Status of Beneficial Owner for United States Tax Withholding. This basically allows you to pay less withholding tax on income from shares in these countries. A similar reduction in withholding tax is available for Canadian shares by completing their equivalent – an NR301 form.

Investing beyond the world's established economies into emerging and developing economies should be approached with the same caution as buying AIM-listed stocks, although doing so is relatively straightforward through your investment platform.

In practice, many DIY investors seeking to access overseas markets do so by investing in collective funds, such as unit trusts, OEICs, ETFs and investment trusts.

Who's who in the share trading process – stockbrokers, market makers and nominees

Understanding how the stock market actually works is essential if you are going to buy and sell shares with any regularity. Trading blue chip shares is not problematic, but the smaller the company you want, or the larger the volume you are looking to buy, the greater the risk you can find your own actions pushing up the price. That is why it is important to understand the mechanics of the stock market.

The key players are investment platforms or stockbrokers, retail service providers (formerly called market makers), nominees and you, the share-buying customers.

Everyone has heard of a stockbroker. Back in the 1960s and 1970s the image of the bowler-hatted gent on the 7.23 into London Bridge from Tunbridge Wells wasn't that far from the truth. Before the rise of the internet, if you wanted to buy or sell shares, bonds or other securities you had to go through a stockbroker, who would arrange your deals over the phone.

These old-style stockbrokers have been largely replaced by investment platforms that, while still being stockbrokers, offer fast, cheap and easy-to-use web-based platforms giving you access to markets around the world. If you want an old-style stockbroker to do everything for you, there are still some around. But it will cost you.

Less famous than stockbrokers are retail service providers, yet they are equally vital to the functioning of the stock market. As their more traditional name of market maker suggests, these people are the ones who actually make the market. They are standalone speculators that make the link between buyers and sellers. They play a key role in establishing the price you ultimately pay for your shares or the amount you receive when you sell them, but perhaps of equal importance is the liquidity they provide.

A nominee is the name for the company that is the legal owner of your investments and this company is typically owned by your investment platform or stockbroker. It will be a dormant company and will do nothing other than hold shares. In the event of your investment platform or stockbroker going bust, your investments are segregated and cannot be used by the liquidator or administrator to pay off your investment platform's debts.

Price

The price of something is only what someone else will pay for it. This is as true for shares as for anything else. It is worth remembering that if you see a company tipped in a Sunday newspaper for £1.00, you can be sure the market maker will have read the same article, so you may find the price has gone up to £1.05 by the time you try to buy it. Prices are all about supply and demand, and if there is no demand, the price will fall.

Investment platforms' systems usually plug into around 30 different market makers and, when you want to buy a share, offer you the one quoting the best price. When you are buying a share online, the price quoted will be held for up to 15 seconds. If you accept the price within that period, the deal is completed. If not, you have to refresh the process and start again, by which time the price may have gone up or down.

It would be a bit of a coincidence if every time someone wanted to sell some shares there was someone else wanting to buy exactly the same amount of stock. The reason there is always a price quoted for pretty much every share on every stock market in the world is because market makers are prepared to buy or sell those shares.

The spread

The spread is more precisely the difference between the best sell price offered by the most competitive market maker and the best buy price. It is also referred to as the 'bid offer spread'.

When it comes to selling stocks in larger companies, the likelihood is the market maker will be able to offload the shares they have bought without much problem and the spread is often no more than 0.5 per cent.

But for smaller companies, you can find the spread can exceed 2 per cent of the share price. This is because these shares are less liquid, because the market maker is less confident of being able to sell them on.

Liquidity issues and exchange market size (EMS)

For very small companies, such as those listed on AIM, you can find that there is little or no market in these shares. Your investment platform may find it only receives quotes from two or three market makers interested in the stock.

Try to buy or sell a big stake in a small company online and that handful of market makers will raise or drop their price to flush out interest in moving the stock on. In this situation, rather than dealing online, you will need to phone up your investment platform and they will need to call the market makers to place the deal.

Understanding how much of a market there will be is as important when you come to sell shares as when buying them. You can check how much liquidity there is in the market by checking the stock's exchange market size (EMS). EMS for every company traded in the UK is available through the London Stock Exchange website, under 'trading information'.

The number given is the number of shares you can safely trade without the spread widening significantly. You can normally trade three times the EMS figure, although if the market goes into freefall, the market makers can turn you away and only offer you quotes at the EMS level. This can cause a problem if you build up a holding in a particular company that far exceeds the EMS level, if you have to sell them all quickly. If this happens, you can end up having to sell at a much lower price.

Settlement period

The settlement period is the time from the point the trade is made to the time the payment must be made to the selling party. The standard settlement period for shares is three days. This is sometimes described as T+3, T being the trading day.

For the DIY investor buying shares this has little relevance – you cannot actually buy the share unless there are sufficient funds lodged in your trading account with your investment platform. It is the investment platform who has three days to hand over the money. If you have sold shares, your investment platform will credit your account with the proceeds of a sale immediately and you can use these funds to buy another investment. However, you won't be able to withdraw your funds until your investment platform has received the hard cash, which should be available for withdrawal by you on the fourth working day after sale.

Stop loss and limit orders

Stop loss and limit orders are some of the most useful tools for the DIY share investor, allowing you to get in or out of the market at predetermined levels. They are automated instructions to buy or sell shares in the event they reach a particular price. You can use them to make sure you do not suffer heavy losses or to bank gains, making them a useful way of instilling discipline into your investment process. They also liberate you from having to stare at a screen all day.

All modern investment platforms' systems are capable of setting up stop losses and limit orders on your behalf through a simple online process.

Stop loss

Also known as a 'stop order', a stop loss is an order to sell a stock if and when the bid or sell price falls to or below a predetermined price. The stop loss is a way to protect yourself from incurring heavy losses if a share price goes into freefall.

There is plenty of research showing that successful investing is more about doing less badly on the downside than punching the lights out on the way up. Setting stop losses is a sensible way to insure yourself against taking a complete hammering on a stock, because when a stock starts diving it does not always come back up.

A 'trailing stop loss' is a stop loss that rises in the event that the share it is linked to rises. So if you set a 15p trailing stop loss on a stock you buy for 100p, your shares are sold if the price falls to 85p. But if the share price rises to 150p, your trailing stop loss rises with it and is fixed at 135p.

Buy limit

A buy limit is an instruction to buy a stock if the offer price drops to or below a predetermined price. This allows you to buy a stock if it hits a price you are willing to pay for it, without you having to keep watching the markets to see if it gets there.

Sell limit

A sell limit is an order to sell a stock if the bid price rises to or above a price set by you in advance. You can use sell limits to bank gains in the event that shares hit what you think is a good price. Without setting a sell limit you could find yourself missing out on a profit if a share price spikes but then falls back again by the time you next check into your account to see how it is doing.

Where to set stop losses

The economic uncertainty of recent years has seen extreme volatility become a normal part of investing. With markets falling and then bouncing back on a regular basis, setting stop losses too tightly can see you simply getting out of the market at the bottom, only to see it rise up again the following day. This will lose you money.

Some shares will be more volatile than others – you can check the historic range of prices of shares through any number of online data sources. So for steady mature companies you may want to set a stop loss at a fall of somewhere around 10 or 15 per cent of the share price, whereas you may want to go a little higher for more volatile companies.

Problems with stop losses and limit orders

Fast-falling shares, particularly those with poor liquidity, can sometimes fall past your stop loss limit before the investment platform has time to sell it. For example, if your stop loss is for 150p and the share price falls from 155p to 145p without actually hitting 150p, your shares will be sold at 145p – a lower price than you specified.

Most brokers allow you to set a two-stage stop loss order to mitigate this risk, so the order will have a 'trigger' price that, as the names suggests, will trigger the system to try and execute the stop loss because the price has fallen below the limit you set, but there will also be a 'bottom' price, the level that you are not prepared to sell below. So, if the share price falls dramatically, possibly on news but equally possibly on rumour, then you would not be sold out unnecessarily.

Due to fast-moving markets you need to be aware that while investment platforms will try to undertake your deal, this isn't always possible – so be careful.

Research

The internet is awash with information about the tens of thousands of companies trading on the world's stock exchanges. There is so much information out there that making sense of it all can be a challenge.

But if you are going to invest in a company and you want to satisfy yourself that it is fundamentally sound, the internet gives you the tools to do it. Company reports, sector research, financial news alerts, share tips and much more are all out there if you have the time and inclination to read them.

Remember that any tips posted on bulletin boards or in the media will already be out of date by the time you come to read them. And be alert to the fact that people promising the world on some website are probably trying to pump up the share price of a stock they hold or dump the price of one they don't in the hope of getting in at a lower price. These anonymous posters are becoming more common on the various online bulletin boards and are often referred to as 'rampers' and 'de-rampers'.

The phrase DYOR or do your own research is widely used by genuine posters on the bulletin boards but often ignored by newcomers to the market: it's an important discipline for the DIY investor to follow.

One source of data that you will receive at the same time as everyone else in the market is the Regulatory News Service (RNS) updates, which are formal company announcements to the market. Your investment platform should have a facility allowing you to sign up for RNS alerts by email or text.

One way to get ideas for companies to invest in is to look at the holdings of top fund managers in that sector. Unit trusts all publish their top holdings and there is nothing to stop you piggybacking on the research of well-resourced professional fund management houses by simply buying what they hold.

If you want to keep a general eye on markets, MoneyAM's 'High Noon' and 'Market Roundup' emails provide a succinct summary of market movements and company announcements at midday and close of play respectively. Registration for these emails is free.

Level 2 market data

If you are serious about trading on a regular basis, you will need access to more information than is freely available on the internet. By paying for what is known as 'Level 2' information, you gain access to comprehensive and in-depth data on trading activity. Level 2 information is provided by some investment platforms, usually for a fixed subscription fee, or you can access it direct from information providers such as MoneyAM, ADVFN, AlphaTrade, Digital Look, Interactive Data, the London Stock Exchange, Proquote, ShareScope, Tenfore or Thomson.

Accessing Level 2 data will give you a greater picture of the factors and trends underlying share price movements at exactly the same time as professional dealers. Charges can range between £50 and £200 a quarter, depending on the amount of data you want to source.

Level 2 market data gives information on:

- Orders awaiting execution on the buy and sell side of the order book.
- Analysis of movements in prices.
- Factors that can help identify automated trading patterns.

Financial ratios

Financial ratios are ways of measuring the value and profitability of companies. Understanding them is important if you are planning to actively trade equities on a regular basis. Financial ratios cover liquidity (the availability of cash to pay debt or dividends), activity (converting non-cash assets into cash), debt (the company's ability to pay down their debts) and profitability.

You will see many financial ratios published in a company's accounts, and there is lots more information available online. Research and analysis of companies is a massive subject and there are many great books out there that can tell you how to do it, so I will not go into it in a massive way here.

I will, however, mention two of the most important ones – the P/E ratio and the dividend yield ratio.

P/E ratio

The price-to-earnings ratio, or P/E ratio, is the price of the share divided by the earnings per share. This is one of the most widely used valuations of companies. If a company has a P/E ratio of, say, 12 it means its earnings are a twelfth of its market cap. Looked at another way, that means on current after-tax earnings it would take 12 years for the company to generate the shareholder's investment in it.

P/E ratios are often used to compare companies within an industry, sector or market. If similar businesses have very different P/E ratios then those companies with lower ones may be perceived as being undervalued or may not have as good growth prospects as the company with the higher ratio.

A thumbnail guide to P/E ratios

Negative: A company making a loss has an undefined P/E ratio.

P/E 0–10: The company may be undervalued or its stock may be in decline.

P/E 10–18: Considered fair value in historical terms for companies in mature markets.

P/E 18–25: Could be a growth stock with good prospects, or could be overvalued.

P/E 25+: As with many emerging market stocks, high P/E ratios indicate a strong belief in the market that a company will deliver high returns in the future.

Dividends

Dividends are payments companies make to their shareholders to pass on some of their profits. They are the investor's reward for risking their capital in the company.

Shares yielding high dividends have been favourites of both income and growth investors in recent years as cash-rich companies have made record payouts to shareholders.

If it is income you are after, high-yielding blue-chip stocks will usually give you more than cash on deposit, and can act as a hedge – or protection – against inflation as share prices generally go up with inflation.

But dividends are also valuable for growth-seekers. By reinvesting your dividends in the company you can potentially get the compounded effect of both the income from the shares and any increase in share price.

How dividends are paid

The dividend is a fixed amount per share, typically paid twice a year but sometimes quarterly. Some companies also pay one-off dividends out of the blue, which are called 'special dividends'.

Not all of the profits a company makes are paid as dividends, with some cash usually being held back to reinvest in the business.

Any dividends you receive from your investments will be paid into your cash account with your investment platform. You can leave it in there to invest in other assets at a later date, set up an instruction for it to be automatically reinvested or have it paid into your nominated bank or building society account.

Dividend payments are treated as a form of income and so they are subject to income tax. Non-tax payers and basic rate tax payers have no further tax to pay, whereas higher rate and additional rate tax payers pay tax as explained earlier (see Chapter 9 on funds).

In case you wondered what happens to a share price around dividend payment time, I will explain. A company's dividend is not automatically paid to the person that owns the shares on dividend pay day. Instead, each company has an 'ex-dividend' date, often several weeks before the dividend is paid. If you buy shares on or after the ex-dividend date, you won't receive the forthcoming dividend payment. The person who owned the stock when it went ex-dividend gets that chunk of change. You will see the share price drop by the value of the dividend as it goes ex-dividend.

You can often tell which stocks are trading ex-dividend because they'll have a special designation in stock listings, such as an 'xd' next to their name.

A 'scrip' dividend is a dividend paid out in the form of extra shares in the company.

Understanding dividends – dividend yield ratio

A share's dividend yield, also known as its dividend-price ratio is, technically speaking, the company's total annual dividend payments divided by its market capitalisation. It can more simply be calculated by dividing the dividend per share by the price of the share. So if a share costs 200p and it pays an 8p dividend, it has a 4 per cent dividend yield. An historic dividend yield is calculated using dividends that have been paid, whereas a forward dividend yield is calculated using the market's estimates of future dividends. In both cases the current price is used.

As explained above, preference shares pay predetermined dividends. All other dividends are payable at the discretion of the company's board and are therefore not guaranteed. If they think they have not got enough cash in the bank to pay them, dividends can be cut or suspended altogether.

The backward-looking nature of dividend yields – a cautionary note

It is worth stressing that dividend yields are normally backward-looking statistics, and are as much a function of the share price as of the amount that will be paid in future.

For example, at the end of 2007, Lloyds TSB had been paying a dividend of around 7.4 per cent and its share price was in the 450p bracket. The week before Lehman Brothers collapsed in 2008, its share price had fallen to 289p and, on the basis of the historic dividend paid, divided by its now shrunken share price, its dividend yield had soared well into double figures.

An income-seeking investor looking solely at the company's dividend yield would have thought Lloyds TSB a great bet. Unfortunately, the following Monday Lehmans collapsed and within four months the stock tanked to almost a tenth of its 2007 value. It is now paying no dividend at all and its share price has struggled to get above 70p ever since.

Payout ratio

Arguably a more accurate way of assessing a company's dividend is its payout ratio. This is calculated by dividing the dividend by the earnings per share. If the payout ratio is greater than 1, the company is paying out more in dividends than it is earning. Unlike dividend yield, a company's payout ratio is not, therefore, affected by market sentiment towards the company's share price.

Choosing good dividend-paying stocks

UK blue chips are among the best dividend payers in the world. The average yield on the FTSE 100 stood at around 3.6 per cent in October 2012, compared to 2.09 for the S&P 500. Within the FTSE 100 there are lots of mature companies that paid dividends way in excess of returns for cash on deposit. In 2012 National Grid paid a dividend of 5.9 per cent net of basic rate tax, equivalent to 7.4 per cent gross, while Vodafone paid 5.6 per cent and GlaxoSmithKline paid back 4.9 per cent to shareholders.

Demand for income has also pushed up the price of high-dividend-yielding companies, giving investors in them a double boost. UK PLC is sitting on a cash pile of around £750bn, in part because it is holding back on reinvesting because of the economic uncertainty, and is returning some of this capital back to shareholders through dividends. A record year for dividend payments in the UK was 2012, with dividends for the year approaching £80bn, and even more are expected to be paid in 2013, according to research from Capita.

The website www.topyields.nl/Top-dividend-yields-of-FTSE100.php is a good source of information on the best dividend-paying companies in the UK.

Of course there are risks in holding equities – neither share price nor dividends are guaranteed. But they do offer some protection against inflation – unlike cash on deposit – as equities tend to rise when prices rise. And by buying a basket of high-income equities you can spread the risk of one of them going bad.

People who buy and hold equities long term are often investment platforms' least profitable customers. That is why some investment platforms charge a custody fee or a quarterly inactivity fee for investors who are not actively trading. If you want to buy and hold income shares, make sure you use an investment platform that is not going to penalise you for doing so.

Corporate actions – rights issues, open offers and takeovers

Corporate actions are changes to the structure of a company that affect the shares you hold. The key corporate actions for DIY investors are takeovers, rights issues and consolidations, although there are less of these than there were a decade ago. Some require shareholder votes, while others are determined by management.

Rights issues

A rights issue is a way for a company to raise more cash by issuing more shares. Under a rights issue the company offers existing shareholders the right to buy the new shares before anyone else. The price offered, known as the 'call cost', is usually lower than the current market price and shareholders are all offered new shares at the same ratio – for example, you can buy one new share for every two shares you already hold.

You can either take up a rights issue, allow it to lapse (which means the company will sell the 'nil paid rights' and pay you the proceeds) or sell the 'nil paid rights' in the market. This is not likely, and is only worthwhile if you have a large position.

Rights issues are commission-free and also free of stamp duty.

Companies have rights issues for a number of reasons – it could be they need to refinance their business or want to invest in new markets, or they may want cash to fund an acquisition of another company. Deciding whether to accept a rights issue will involve considering what you think of the management's reasoning behind the rights issue. You should be able to get a feel for what the experts think through commentary in the media.

Any shares not taken up by shareholders are then offered to the market or taken by the underwriter of the rights issue.

Open offer

An open offer is a cash-raising exercise like a rights issue, except the shareholder does not have the opportunity to sell the right to exercise the right to buy the shares to a third party. It is a 'take it or leave it' offer.

Another difference is that although the ratio of shares you are offered guarantees you a minimum number of shares, you can often apply for more. This is called an 'excess application'.

Takeover

If a company you hold becomes the target of a takeover it is usually good news for its share price. The takeover has to be approved by a proportion of the shareholders, although if the bidding company acquires 90 per cent of the shares of the target company then it can force the acquisition of the remaining target company's shares.

The bidding company usually pays for the shares in either cash or shares in itself. Accepting a share offer does not crystallise gains for capital gains tax purposes.

Some bidding companies offer 'loan notes' instead of cash. This, too, can help an individual defer a capital gains tax liability, while giving them the security of fixing a price for offloading their shares.

Shareholder perks

Being a part-owner of a company by virtue of holding its shares can, in some cases, bring with it special shareholder perks which are tax-free. Some companies require you to have a set amount of shares before you get access to the perks. Some companies will not pay shareholder perks if the shares are held in nominee, and some investment platforms take the view that the administration of dealing with these perks is too much trouble. I would urge you not to buy a share just for the perks and if they are important to you, check out whether your chosen investment platform will pass them on to you.

Either way, shareholder perks are not as generous as they were years ago, and fewer and fewer companies are offering them.

Shareholder perks – some of the best

Aga Rangemaster Group – 10 per cent off purchases over £500; minimum holding 5,000 shares.

Bellway – £2,000 discount off price of a home per £25,000 of shares held.

Marks & Spencer – discount vouchers sent out with January dividend.

Moss Bross – 20 per cent off full-price merchandise.

Mulberry Group – 20 per cent off full-price merchandise; minimum holding 250 shares.

Tax considerations for equities

Hopefully you are getting the drift of tax considerations, as equities are taxed broadly as funds (see pages 117–19).

Returns from equities come in two ways – dividends and growth in share price.

Dividends are treated as income and therefore your dividend income is added to your other income on your tax return and you pay tax on it at your marginal rate. Dividends are paid with a 10 per cent tax credit, to reflect the fact that the company has paid corporation tax on its profits.

Growth in the value of your shares is subject to capital gains tax at the time you sell them, if the increase in value exceeds your annual allowance.

For equities held within an ISA or a SIPP you do not need to think about tax when deciding to go for equities that will give you growth or income. But for any equities outside a tax-advantaged wrapper, it can make sense to go for whichever will give you the lowest tax bill – though saving tax should not be the sole motivation for making an investment.

The risks of equities

Equities are at the riskier end of the investment spectrum and should be handled with care. Invest in them only if you fully understand them. And that means understanding that you may not get all, or indeed any, of your money back if the company performs badly. Share prices may fall, dividends may be reduced or stopped altogether, companies may even go bust, leaving investors completely out of pocket.

It would be foolish to suggest that buying and selling equities like a day trader is going to make you a million. But, despite their risks, a well diversified portfolio of shares is likely, in the long term, to generate higher returns than you would get from most other asset classes.

Top websites

www.advfn.com

www.fool.co.uk

www.investorschronicle.co.uk

www.londonstockexchange.com

www.moneyam.com

www.sharesmagazine.co.uk

chapter

13

Corporate bonds and gilts

L
ess risky than equities but usually returning more than a bank or
building society, bonds aim to give a steady income through good
times and bad. Understanding bonds is all about understanding risk,
and, as with investments across the board, the more of it you are prepared
to take, the greater the returns you can hope to get.

Before the credit crunch and the Eurozone crisis that followed it many
people hadn't a clue what a corporate or government bond was. Today we
are all too familiar with the idea that nations and other organisations see
their borrowing costs go up if the bond markets don't trust in their ability
to pay their debts.

Bonds are issued by governments and companies to raise capital to pay
for high-cost projects, from wars to railways to housing projects, and, in
the case of many debt-ridden nations these days, to pay the interest on
existing liabilities. They are promises to pay an annual sum, the 'coupon',
for a fixed term, in return for the bond-holder lending the issuing organisation a lump sum of money, known as the 'principal'. The principal is
also refunded to the bond-holder at the maturity date.

By investing in a bond you effectively become a lender to the country,
company or other organisation issuing it. Once you have handed over
your cash to the bond-issuer you have nothing other than a piece of
paper containing a promise to pay you back. If that bond-issuer then
goes bust you are out of pocket. So to reward you for taking on the risk
of their bonds, issuers pay you an annual or six-monthly coupon – the
more likely a company or country is to go bust, the higher the coupon
they pay.

Bonds issued by the UK government are called 'gilts', short for 'gilt-edged security', which is precisely what Bank of England bonds were until the last century. The bonds issued by the Bank of England were large pieces of paper with gold-leaf edges that were divided into sections. Each section was a coupon that reflected a payment due to the holder, and would be ripped off and given back to the issuer upon receipt of the sum due. When all of the coupons had been ripped off, the bond expired and the principal sum was repaid.

While there are no gold-leaf-edged parchments any more, the principle behind today's bonds is exactly the same.

Gilts are among the safest investments in the world and the returns they offer are low on account of this. In November 2012 the return on 10-year gilts stood at 1.7 per cent. To reflect its rather higher risk profile, anyone prepared to invest in 10-year bonds issued by the Greek government at that time earned a return of 17 per cent.

Corporate bonds range from the very secure, offered by cash-rich blue chip companies, right up the risk scale to the very insecure, known as *junk bonds*, offered by struggling companies facing financial headwinds or early-stage companies whose prospects are unclear.

Bonds had, until the turn of the century, traditionally been accessed through stockbrokers, or through unit trusts and OEICs investing in baskets of them. But the advent of online investment platforms has brought them to a wider audience of investors who are looking to beat miserable cash-on-deposit rates by taking on a little extra risk.

For years, investors wanting to take a DIY approach to the bond market have only really been able to do so if they had very large portfolios. That was because the minimum threshold for investing in bonds was between £10,000 and £50,000. You could access bonds for less than this in the past, but not as a retail investor.

But since the start of this decade we have seen a trend of companies offering retail bonds direct to consumers, knowing they can beat the cash rates on deposit and still raise funds more cheaply than going to a bank by themselves.

This market took a massive step forward when the London Stock Exchange launched its Order Book for Retail Bonds in 2010 (ORB). This created a market for the trading of bonds aimed at retail investors wanting to invest far smaller sums. Since then a string of household-name companies, from National Grid to Tesco, have offered bonds to retail investors, with a minimum investment threshold of just £1,000.

ORB has created a more efficient market for the DIY investor, with far tighter bid/offer spreads on the buying and selling of corporate bonds. With around 180 corporate bonds and gilts now available to the public, and with many more through the main stock market, access to this asset class has never been easier.

The history of corporate bonds and gilts

People have been using bonds to raise money for literally thousands of years. Archaeologists tell us the oldest surety bond that has ever been found dates back to 2400BC and is from Mesopotamia, modern-day Iraq. It is a piece of stone with carved letters guaranteeing the payment of grain.

Governments have been issuing bonds to pay for wars for centuries. In fact, the ability of nations and political groups to raise money for wars through bonds has been one of the key driving forces of the history of the world. These have usually been big-ticket bonds issued to institutions and wealthy families, but cash-strapped countries have also regularly appealed to the nationalist fervour of their populations to issue war bonds available to the man or woman in the street.

Rothschild, bonds and the Battle of Waterloo

Nathan Mayer Rothschild was one of the most celebrated bond dealers history has ever known. Not only did he help defeat Napoleon by bankrolling Wellington's troops, he also knew a thing or two about how to play the bond markets.

Fully understanding the value of up-to-date information to financial markets, Rothschild placed an agent near the Battle of Waterloo, knowing a victory for Napoleon would be a terrible blow to the British economy that would wipe millions off the value of his massive holding of British government bonds.

Rothschild's agent arrived in London a day before Wellington's courier and delivered the momentous news to his boss. The story goes that Rothschild went to the stock exchange where he stood hanging his head and selling large amounts of British government bonds. Falling for his bluff, all the other traders started selling their bonds too and prices fell to the floor. Rothschild's agents duly hoovered them up at rock-bottom prices, only to see their value bounce back up again when the actual result of the battle came through.

Corporate bonds have been in existence for almost as long as there have been companies, with the East India Company and the Dutch East India Company both issuing bonds early in the 17th century.

The first decades of the 20th century saw an increase in the issue of corporate bonds. These early issues were mainly investment-grade bonds, with appetite for junk bonds verging on the non-existent.

The modern market in non-investment grade, or high-yield bonds, really took off after the financial crisis of the 1970s, when falling asset prices led to banks lending only to those companies with a strong credit rating.

The 1980s saw high-yield bonds delivering excellent returns without the increased levels of defaults their yields suggested, attracting increasing numbers of investors to the asset class. In the USA, yields through the 1980s averaged 14.5 per cent, while default rates averaged just 2.2 per cent.

Yes, there have been collapses as long as there have been companies issuing them, but corporate bonds have continued to deliver steady returns more often than not. On rare occasions, canny investors (such as Rothschild two centuries ago) have been able to make money out of overreactions to negative sentiment about corporations. But most investors prefer it when bonds do what they are supposed to, which is give boring but reliable returns, year in, year out.

That said, be in no doubt that companies can and will go bust. The recent clamour for retail corporate bonds – most recent issues have been heavily oversubscribed – partly reflects the low returns on offer from banks. But it also reflects a tendency for people to think that because there is a household name attached to a bond that they are protected in some way, when they are not.

Most will come good, but there is a risk that if people come to perceive these bonds as akin to cash on deposit with a bank, one day someone, or more accurately several thousand investors, are going to wake up to a nasty surprise.

The financial crisis, the Eurozone and corporate bonds

Back at the height of the credit crunch in 2008, investors were staring into the abyss and fearing the worst. Fear of corporate collapse meant bond prices fell off a cliff, meaning the income you got for buying them soared. Don't get me wrong – the doom and gloom at the time was very real – who would have thought that Lehman Brothers, Bear Stearns and many more household-name companies at home and abroad would be consigned to history? But bond managers knew that valuations had fallen far further than the fundamentals justified.

Back in October 2008 corporate bond prices had fallen so far that, for anyone holding a basket of stocks, at least a third of investment-grade issuers would have had to go bust over the next five years before investing in government bonds would have delivered a better return. In other words, one in three major companies in the UK would have had to be wiped out in a financial collapse greater than the Wall Street Crash of 1929.

The fear that stalked investors back in 2008 meant that the Investment Management Association sterling high-yield bond sector, which tracks riskier bonds, saw an average fall of 25 per cent in 2008. But when the world didn't completely melt down, the rebound in 2009 was 48 per cent.

Concerns over corporate bond defaults became much more muted as corporate Britain accumulated stockpiles of cash having pulled in its horns and trimmed its operating expenses. Instead, the focus switched to sovereign debt – the bonds issued by nation states.

The financial crisis suddenly woke up the markets to the fact that some countries in southern Europe might actually go bust and not repay the loans they had taken from the world's banks. The so-called PIIGS – Portugal, Ireland, Italy, Greece and Spain – all found themselves on the critical list, with even France seeing its cost of borrowing soar as Germany persisted in its refusal to share these other countries' liabilities by issuing Eurobonds. Events in Cyprus in early 2013 acted as a reminder that problems remain.

Outside the Eurozone, meanwhile, the UK's budget-trimming measures and its ability to print money and devalue its currency earned it safe-haven status around the world. With foreign cash rushing from the Continent into gilts, their prices have soared, pushing gilt yields down to historic lows, leaving them struggling to beat inflation, and punishing annuities and savers' interest rates.

The last few years have shown us that the textbooks can be wrong. Government and corporate bonds are meant to be steady, solid investments. And it is true that if you hold a bond until maturity, you know exactly what return you will get – provided the issuer remains solvent.

But it is worth bearing in mind that, not just in the extraordinary circumstances we have seen in the last few years, bonds can default.

Bond terminology

You should be able to access market data on bonds through your investment platform or from a number of other sources across the industry (see below). So it is important to understand what the various pieces of jargon from the world of bonds actually mean, and how they all piece together.

Conventional gilts

These are the simplest form of gilts. They pay a fixed coupon, usually twice a year, and mature on a fixed date. They can last for a few months or several decades. Some have 'calls' that allow the government to pay them off early. Always check the small print of what you are buying before completing your purchase. The gilts most commonly used by individuals are those with between two and ten years left to run.

Index-linked gilts

Like index-linked bonds, these pay a coupon that is indexed to the Retail Prices Index. The principal is also indexed in a similar way. They offer the investor a protection against inflation.

Maturity date

As it sounds – the maturity date is the date the bond expires and the principal is repaid to the bond-holder. The date or year of maturity is usually contained in the name of the bond, for example 5 per cent Treasury Gilt 2018 or Tesco plc 6 per cent 2029.

Gilts are categorised in relation to their maturity, with short defined as 0–7 years, medium as 7–15 years and long anything 15 years or more.

'Ultra short' gilts have a maturity of less than 3 years, while those issued since 2005 with a maturity of 50 years are 'ultra long'.

Some gilts are undated, meaning they have no maturity date. There are only eight of these in existence and typically the coupon is very low. The government can redeem these at their discretion and up until recently there has been no reason to do so – as new borrowing would be at a higher rate.

But questions have been asked recently as to whether the government should redeem some of these gilts, for example War Loan stock. This undated gilt was issued by Lloyd George's government to raise £2bn, which translates as over £50bn in today's money, to cover the cost of the First World War. It carries a 3.5 per cent coupon – it started out with a 5 per cent coupon but was reduced in 1932 by Prime Minister Ramsay Macdonald.

Corporate bonds don't have a formal short, medium and long naming convention but a rule of thumb is short is anything between 0 and 5 years, medium is 5 to 12 years and long is anything over 12 years.

Coupon

This is the rate of interest the bond agreed to pay at the outset. The coupon rate will normally also be in the name of the bond.

Issue date

The date the bond was first issued.

Income yield

The income yield, also known as the current yield or running yield, is the percentage return the bond is delivering at a particular point in time. Put another way, it is the annual coupon divided by the price. It therefore only reflects the annual interest payment and the price paid.

So, a bond with a face value of £100 that pays out £5 has an income yield of 5 per cent. If the price of the bond goes down, to say £50, the income yield goes up to 10 per cent.

Par value and price

When bonds are issued, they are at 'par value', which means face value. If any of the risk factors that influence bond values reduce their value below this level, they are described as 'below par', while if their value rises above the par value they are said to be 'above par'.

The issue price for bonds issued on the London Stock Exchange is '100', which is par value. The figure shown as 'price' on its website reflects the percentage of par at which the bond is currently trading. So if its price is shown as 90, that means the price of the bond has fallen by 10 per cent since the issue date.

Gross redemption yield

The gross redemption yield, also known as the yield to maturity, is arguably the most important yield for investors. It is a measure that reflects the overall rate of return of the bond. It is the effective rate of return the investor will get if they buy a bond and hold it until it matures. It is a useful figure because it gives you a clear view of the extra return you are getting compared to other more secure interest rates available on the market.

The figure not only assumes all coupons will be paid and the principal redeemed, but also that you will be able to reinvest the coupon payments and earn the same return, which may not in fact be possible. It also reflects the repayment of the principal at the end of the term. So if you have bought a bond at less than par, your gross redemption yield will include the capital gain you will make.

You should note that the gross redemption yield makes no allowance for tax.

The risks of bonds and how these affect their value

A company's bonds are less risky than its equities because in the event the entity goes bust, bond-holders rank higher in priority when it comes to paying out what remains of the company's assets than shareholders.

But that does not mean they do not carry any risk. The key risk to a bond is that the company goes bust and is unable to pay. If that happens, the company is wound up and once other creditors have been paid out, bond-holders may or may not get a certain number of pennies in the pound of their investment back, although it could take years.

If you hold the bond until redemption, and it remains solvent, then you will get precisely the return you are expecting – namely the coupons for the remainder of the term of the bond, plus the return of the principal.

If you sell the bond before maturity, however, then there are other risk factors that can make the value of the bond you hold fluctuate up or down. These are the length of time until redemption, changes to the company's fundamental strength or lack of it and the interest rate environment. The manner and extent to which these factors impact your bond-holding's value will also depend on whether you purchased it at, above or below par.

Another less tangible risk to holding bonds is inflation, which in the case of government bonds can be mitigated by investing in index-linked bonds.

Bonds approaching maturity

As the bond's redemption date approaches, the greater certainty you will have that the issuer is going to be able to pay back the principal. This means its value will, all other things being equal, approach par.

Issuer credit risk

The company or government that issued the bond may have been in rude financial health when you took out the bond, but since then it may have run into financial difficulties. Bond markets ultimately match the payoff between the return being offered by the bond against the risk of the issuer defaulting.

So if the analysts think your bond issuer's prospects have declined since you bought it, it will negatively affect the bond's value. If you have taken a bet on a junk bond with a risky company that has subsequently turned a corner towards financial strength, and the ratings agencies have upgraded its credit rating, the value of your bond will go up.

If you hold the bond to maturity and the issuer does not go bust, then the changes in the value of the bond will not affect you as you will have received precisely the coupons and maturity proceeds you envisaged when you invested.

The effect of interest rates

Changes to the market's expectations of future interest rates have a big impact on the value of bonds. At its most simple level, if something happens to lead the market to expect interest rates to rise then the value of a bond will fall. The longer a bond has to maturity, the more sensitive its price is likely to be to a change in interest-rate expectations.

These two statements oversimplify what is a complex interaction between market expectations of interest rates and the price of a bond, which is also influenced by inflation, wider views of the economy and many other factors.

People often mistakenly believe that because bond investments are promoted as being safer than equity investments, that they carry some form of capital protection. They don't, unless you hold them to maturity.

Inflation-linked bonds

High inflation erodes the value of fixed-income bonds, which is what most conventional gilt and corporate bonds are.

If you are concerned about inflation you can opt for bonds that increase their payout in line with inflation. National Grid issued the first inflation-linked corporate bond ever to be made available to retail investors in 2011, paying 1.25 per cent above the Retail Price Index. Since then Tesco has launched one paying 1 per cent above RPI.

Index-linked gilts have been around for years – since 1981 to be precise, when the very first one was issued by the then chancellor, Geoffrey Howe.

No compensation

Corporate bonds must be distinguished from the sorts of bonds issued by banks and building societies. Bonds issued by financial organisations of this sort, often described as 'fixed-rate bonds', benefit from the protection of the Financial Services Compensation Scheme, which guarantees to pay up to £85,000 of losses incurred in the event that a bank or building society bond issuer goes bust.

Corporate bonds and gilts, on the other hand, do not benefit from Financial Services Compensation Scheme protection if the issuer goes bust.

You need to read the small print to make sure you fully understand which type of bond you are investing in. The line between the two types of bond can become blurred when a financial services organisation issues a retail corporate bond. For example, Tesco Bank has issued a number of corporate bonds that do not come with Financial Services Compensation Scheme protection. But it also offers a range of fixed-rate savings accounts that might also be described as bonds, which do come with investor protection.

How bonds are risk-rated

There are several ratings agencies that assess bond issuers' ability to pay back their debts. Ratings agencies have many different gradations of risk, but corporate bonds are generally divided into two clearly defined sectors – investment-grade and high-yield or junk bonds.

As a DIY investor, if you are going to make direct investments into bonds, you should only touch investment grade ones, unless you really know what you are doing. If you want to access high-yield bonds, it is best to do it through a fund.

Before buying a bond you should check where the issuer stands in the league table of risk. Standard & Poor's, Moody's and other ratings agencies give free access to their ratings of thousands of companies and governments around the world, provided you register with them. Ratings for companies are provided, as well as the agency's view on the outlook for them and other research on them.

Investment-grade bonds

Also known as high-grade corporate bonds, investment-grade bonds are those issued by companies perceived by the ratings agencies to be the most secure. Each ratings agency has their own way of ranking companies. For Standard & Poor's, a company with a credit rating of BBB– and higher is considered investment grade. Under Moody's ratings, companies must be Baa3 or higher to qualify as investment grade.

These ratings apply equally to countries – the downgrade of a country's investment rating can be politically and economically damaging.

High-yield/junk bonds

Anything rated below these levels is considered a high-yield or junk bond. These bonds, as you might have guessed, pay higher yields, but the chance of them going bust is also far higher. Furthermore, ratings agencies can downgrade high-yield bonds further, meaning their resale value will fall. The only way you should be investing in junk bonds as a DIY investor is through a high-yield bond fund, unless you really know what you are doing.

table 13.1 Understanding ratings agency classifications

Moody's Long term	Moody's Short term	S&P Long term	S&P Short term	Fitch Long term	Fitch Short term		
Aaa	P-1	AAA	A-1+	AAA	F1+	Prime	Investment
Aa1		AA+		AA+		High grade	
Aa2		AA		AA			
Aa3		AA-		AA-			
A1		A+	A-1	A+	F1	Upper medium grade	
A2	P-2	A		A			
A3		A-	A-2	A-	F2		
Baa1		BBB+		BBB+		Lower medium grade	
Baa2	P-3	BBB	A-3	BBB	F3		
Baa3		BBB-		BBB-			
Ba1	Not prime	BB+	B	BB+	B	Non-investment grade speculative	
Ba2		BB		BB			
Ba3		BB-		BB-			
B1 '	B+	B+	B+	BB+		Highly speculative	
B2 '	B	BB	B	BB			
B3 '	B-	BB-	B-	BB-			
Caa1		CCC+	C	CCC	C	Substantial risks	Junk
Caa2		CCC				Extremely speculative	
Caa3		CCC-				Default imminent with little prospect for recovery	
Ca		CC					
		C					
C		D	/	DDD	/	In default	
/				DD			
/				D			

Gilts

In the more than 300 years since it was established, the Bank of England has never defaulted on any of its liabilities. That does not mean it is the most secure bank in the world today. In the 1930s Germans needed wheelbarrows of Deutschmarks to buy a loaf of bread, so bad was the hyperinflation in the country at the time. Today bond markets clearly think the German central bank offers investors more security, which is why its cost of borrowing is lower than the UK government's.

But while they might not quite beat the Bundesbank when it comes to security, gilts – bonds issued by the Bank of England – are still among the most rock-steady investments in the world. Despite the massive deficit the UK carries, it had until recently maintained its AAA rating with all the major ratings agencies. Even the mighty USA saw its rating cut by Standard & Poor's in 2011 to AA+ over its budget concerns. France saw its S&P downgraded by the same degree at the beginning of 2012. The UK suffered a politically embarrassing single notch downgrade to its Moodys' AAA rating in February 2013, the first time since 1978. Standard & Poor's has put the UK on a negative outlook.

The mechanics of buying, holding and selling corporate bonds and gilts

DIY investors can either buy bonds through a bond fund or hold them directly. Both ways of holding bonds can be achieved through an investment platform.

Bond and gilt funds

If you buy a bond fund, the fund manager will endeavour to buy and sell bonds as their value changes, attempting to deliver you a return from the coupon paid on the bond and also on the bonds themselves hopefully rising in value.

There are two main types of bond fund – those that simply target a part of the market, for example investment-grade or high-yield, or 'strategic' bond funds that allow the fund manager to move from one type to the other as and when they feel fit.

Bond funds give you access to an expert managing your purchases and sales on your behalf, and your risk is spread by virtue of the fact you are investing in a basket of many different bonds. But you will also pay an annual management charge for the privilege. In normal conditions, investment returns from bond funds will be modest, at best, so you need to ensure that fund management charges are not disproportionately high.

That said, in the extraordinary markets of recent years, most of the top bond managers have proved their worth and justified their annual management charges.

However, if you are passionate about cutting charges to a minimum, there is less scope to do so in the world of corporate bonds. While it is relatively easy for DIY investors to cut out the cost of the fund manager and create their own equity portfolio, this strategy is harder for corporate bonds. This is because you can't always get good liquidity in the market with small amounts of a corporate bond. Unless you have a very large amount of money to invest, this makes getting a diversified corporate bond portfolio prohibitively expensive.

If the relatively high costs proportionate to the returns on the bond fund make it unappealing then you have two alternatives – get exposure to the whole of your chosen part of the bond market (most likely UK investment-grade) through a low-cost bond ETF or OEIC tracker, or build your own portfolio of directly held gilts and retail corporate bonds from the 180 or so that are available through the London Stock Exchange's ORB service.

If you want to invest in bonds via an ETF or tracker OEIC then there are many indices that track the UK and overseas gilt and corporate bond markets.

Buying a bond fund or ETF is done in exactly the same way as any other form of collective investment.

Buying and selling bonds

You can buy your retail corporate bond either at the time it is issued, known as the 'primary market', or second-hand in the secondary market. You can check what retail bonds are either available for subscription or about to come to market by keeping an eye on the 'New and recent issues onto ORB' page in the bonds section of the London Stock Exchange website.

There you will find a list of the stockbrokers that are sponsoring the bond issue, as well as the prospectus and other information about the bond. Minimum investments are either £1,000 or £2,000, depending on the issuer, with increments going up in steps of £100 thereafter.

Some but not all investment platforms have a direct link to the London Stock Exchange's ORB service. If one does, then the cost of buying existing retail corporate bonds will typically be similar to any other trade, usually around £10. There is normally no explicit charge for investing in a new issue as your investment platform will receive between 0.5 per cent and 1 per cent of the investment as commission.

You can buy and sell gilts through the government's Debt Management Office, but it will be easier, quicker and probably cheaper to do this through your investment platform. Dealing charges for gilts are likely to be the same as for corporate bonds.

There is no stamp duty payable on purchases of gilts or corporate bonds.

Spreads and settlement period

As for equities, there is a spread on both corporate bonds and gilts – the difference between the price at which you buy and the price at which you sell. The more liquid the bond, the lower the spread, so typically you will find that gilts have a smaller spread than corporate bonds, and the bigger the issue, the smaller the spread.

The settlement period for corporate bonds is the time from the point the trade is made to the time the payment must be made to the selling party. The conventional settlement period for gilts is one day, also described as T+1, with T being the trading day, although many providers nowadays settle on T+3, in line with equities. For corporate bonds the settlement period is T+3.

Research

One of the best websites for gilts is the Debt Management Office's website, www.dmo.gov.uk.

You will find a full list of all gilts in existence with the key information for each of them.

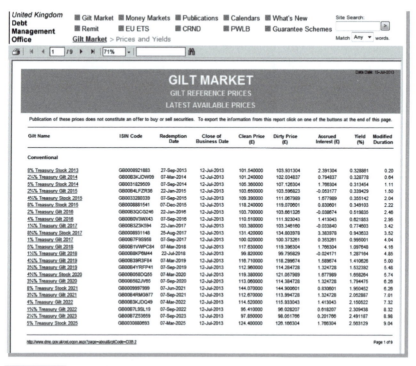

figure 13.1 Key information on gilts   Source: UK Debt Management Office (DMO)

Taking '5% Treasury Gilt 2018', you can see the ISIN code – the unique identifier of this gilt. The redemption date is 7 March 2018 and you will see a clean and dirty price. The clean price excludes, whereas the dirty price includes, accrued interest. Both prices are well above 100, so this gilt is trading above par. This is, as you may expect as the coupon is 5 per cent, far higher than the market is paying for new issues.

So, in very simple terms, by buying this gilt for just under £120 you will get £5 a year, payable half-yearly, until 2018, when you will get £100 returned. The gross redemption yield on this gilt is just over 1 per cent per annum.

Digital Look also has good basic information on gilts.

Before you buy corporate bonds you need to research the companies issuing them. You can:

■ Check RNS announcements to see if there have been any warnings given that would raise concerns about the company's financial position.

■ Check the company's accounts to see if it is profitable and also check its interest cover. This is the ratio that shows how easily a firm will be able to meet its debt interest repayments. This is calculated by dividing earnings before interest and taxes (EBIT) by interest payments.

■ Check what the bond debt is secured against, and where it stands in the priority order in the event of insolvency. This information should be available in the prospectus.

■ Check the company's rating with any of the big ratings agencies. Compare the relationship between the rating and the return being offered with other similar companies to see if you are taking more risk than you need to for the return you are getting.

Tax rules and considerations

Coupon payments on bonds and gilts are taxable as income at your marginal rate.

You can hold bonds and gilts in an ISA if they have five or more years left to run at the time you buy them. Once they are within your ISA you can hold them to maturity.

Unlike dividends, where there is a deduction of tax at source, income received from bonds and gilts is normally paid gross.

The good news is there is no capital gains tax on gilts or on 'qualifying' corporate bonds if their value increases for whatever reason, including indexation increases to the principal for index-linked gilts. Most corporate bonds you can buy will qualify for this relief; only those with special features, such as the ability to be turned into shares at a later date, do not qualify. Capital losses on bonds cannot be used to offset other capital gains.

SIPPs and ISAs pay no tax on bond income or gains. If you hold bonds personally through a Dealing Account, you will account for any tax due via your self-assessment tax return.

There is no stamp duty when you buy bonds.

Permanent interest-bearing shares (PIBS)

Permanent interest-bearing shares (PIBS) are a special class of share issued by building societies. They pay a fixed rate of interest and can be bought and sold on the stock exchange. They have some of the characteristics of a corporate bond, in that they pay a fixed income on a regularly basis, but they normally run for an indeterminate period. Some PIBS, however, have a 'call date', which gives the issuer the right to buy the PIBS back from you if it wants to.

Unlike the fixed-term interest deals that building societies are well known for, PIBS do not benefit from the protection of the Financial Services Compensation Scheme.

PIBS that were issued by building societies that have subsequently demutualised are called perpetual sub-bonds (PSBs).

Payment of returns

Returns are normally fixed, although some building societies will issue floating rate PIBS that pay a certain percentage above a certain price index. That said, the returns are fixed only up to the extent that the building society's financial strength permits them to be paid. Returns are normally paid six-monthly on predetermined dates.

The risks of PIBS

Building societies issue PIBS to raise capital because, being mutuals rather than limited companies, they do not have the power to raise capital by issuing shares. Therefore the ability of the PIBS to continue being able to pay out is dependent on the financial strength of the issuing building society.

PIBS-holders are last in priority to be paid out in the event that a building society becomes insolvent.

Unlike other building society investors, PIBS-holders do not benefit from protection of up to £85,000 from the Financial Services Compensation Scheme in the event that the society goes bust.

The resale price of PIBS can also go down or up depending on other factors in the wider economy. Back in the early 1990s, for example, when bank base rates were in double digits, PIBS paying out 12 or 13 per cent a year were not that extraordinary. These days, with interest rates at historic lows, PIBS paying out at these levels are valuable things, which is why they trade above par.

But be careful about buying PIBS at a premium. Their value is likely to fall in the event that interest rates rise. And if your PIBS have a call date then there is always the risk that the issuing building society will buy them back at face value when that date comes around.

When PIBS go wrong

When many PIBS were launched back in the early 1990s, a number of investors assumed they were as rock-solid as the building societies that issued them. Unfortunately for those who bought PIBS from Northern Rock and Bradford & Bingley, they were.

The interest rates offered were huge. Northern Rock issued PIBS paying 12.6 per cent a year, while Bradford & Bingley issued PIBS paying 13 per cent and 11.6 per cent. To be fair, interest rates were considerably higher back then than they are today, and rates like this were not uncommon. Both of these lenders' PIBS were converted to PSBs when each of the building societies demutualised.

But when the financial crisis hit and both institutions went bust, income payments ceased immediately and it was to be several more years until both sets of PIBS-holders were offered a payout of around 30p in the pound on their original investment.

PIBS-investors were also hit when Lloyds took over HBOS. Some investors were forced to sell their PIBS holdings at lower than market prices.

Then came the case of West Bromwich Building Society PIBS-holders. In 2009 the building society went through a capital restructuring that saw the terms of PIBS rewritten, wiping about 80 per cent off their value. More recently, holders of Co-op PIBS have been given a sharp reminder of the risks inherent in these investments.

The small print in PIBS documents does state that building societies are allowed to alter or stop income payments if making them would breach the society's capital adequacy requirements, which are the financial reserves they are legally required to hold. That is of small consolation to the PIBS-holders who feel they have been made to shoulder a disproportionate share of the burden of restoring the building society to a financially sound footing. On the other hand, PIBS are last in order of priority when it comes to the winding-up of a building society, so they should come lower in the priority order in situations where management are required to trim the society's deficit.

Buying, selling and holding PIBS

You can buy, sell and hold PIBS through your investment platform. The cost of dealing in them will typically be the same as trading any other form of share. PIBS are usually sold in blocks of 1,000, although some can only be bought in larger blocks.

Liquidity of PIBS

Liquidity of PIBS is poor because there is not a lot of trading in them. Spreads between buy and sell price can be as wide as 10 per cent.

Tax on PIBS

Tax on PIBS is the same as for bonds and they can be held in ISAs and SIPPs.

Top websites for research and information

www.digitallook.com

www.dmo.gov.uk

www.fitchratings.com

www.fixedincomeinvestor.co.uk

www.londonstockexchange.com

www.monevator.com

www.moodys.com

www.standardandpoors.com

www.thisismoney.co.uk

14

Cash

The returns you get for investing in cash may be very low indeed, but there is nothing quite like cash when it comes to security and liquidity.

You need cash for your everyday living expenses, but you will also probably have times when you need to hold some of your investment assets in cash, whether for short periods or for several months. This could be while you are taking a pause to rebalance your portfolio, if you think the market does not offer good value, or if you suspect a fall in markets is looming. You might also want to opt for cash if you have a sum of money you want to put to a particular use and don't want to risk losing any of it. Or you could be approaching or at retirement and simply not want to expose yourself to any risk at all.

Cash is about security and access, both of which need to be understood fully when you are putting large sums on deposit.

There are different ways of holding cash, some of which offer better returns than others. There are few, if any, deals available through investment platforms that offer great returns. So, if you have large sums you want to hold on deposit for anything other than a short term, you will almost certainly do better by transferring from your investment platform to a bank or building society direct.

You need to think of a cash account that you hold with your investment platform as akin to a current account that enables you to buy and sell investments as well as to receive investment income such as dividends. These accounts pay low rates of interest and are not intended to be a long-term home for your cash. Each of your SIPP, ISA and Dealing Account will normally have their own unique cash account with your investment platform.

Best-buy savings accounts

You can find best-buy savings account tables at comparison websites such as Moneysupermarket, Moneyfacts and uSwitch, listed at the end of this chapter. If you want to be able to get your money out straight away, look for instant-access accounts.

If you can live with the idea of having to wait before you get your money, go for a notice account, be it 30-day, 60-day, 90-day, 120-day or 180-day. Any longer than that and you are getting into the realm of one-year fixed-rate bonds. Notice accounts carry penalties of a certain number of days' lost interest in the event that you withdraw the cash early. The longer the notice period, the higher the interest they normally pay – but not always. If the market expects interest rates to fall in the next few months, there may be little or no difference between shorter- and longer-term deposits.

Bonus rates

Watch out for bonus rates on comparison site savings account tables. The deals with the highest interest rates usually come with a first-year bonus rate, without which they would be nowhere near table-topping. In fact, some deals with an initial bonus rate fall right down to 0.1 per cent interest as soon as the offer period is over. If you are only investing the money for a year or less, these deals are fine – in fact they are the probably best option.

If you are putting your money away for a long time, however, only use accounts offering early period bonuses if you know you have the discipline to move your money away to another provider the day the bonus deal expires. Always make a diary note for a month or so before the expiry of a bonus deal to start planning your exit strategy and find another market-leading deal.

Alternatively, you can go for a deal without a bonus rate, in the knowledge that you will get a decent-enough rate over the long term. If you know you aren't organised enough to rearrange a new deal straight away, these good but not market-leading rates will work out better for you in the long run.

Cash accounts on investment platforms

Do not expect a decent rate of return from cash you hold in the cash account of your investment platform. These accounts typically pay interest of between zero and base rate, with many paying no interest whatsoever. Some investment platforms pay you more interest the more money you have in the account, but even then it will be below the best high-street rates on offer. With bank base rates at historic lows, that means different shades of not very much for everyone.

There are alternatives to these ultra-low or non-existent interest rates offered by investment platforms, and they are covered briefly in this chapter. All but the most inactive of DIY investors will find there will inevitably be times when some cash is sitting earning little or no interest in a cash account.

The extent to which this interest rate is a relevant factor in your choice of platform will depend on how much you are holding in cash, and how often.

Cash ISA transfer

Cash ISAs are covered in Chapter 3. If you want to move your cash ISA to take advantage of the market-leading cash ISA rates on offer from banks and building societies, you will be able to do so.

To effect the transfer you should be careful not to move your ISA cash into your current account first. If you do, your money will lose its tax-privileged status. Once assets are moved outside the protection of an ISA wrapper they cannot be put in again, other than through using up your current year's ISA allowance. Instead you need to transfer the funds directly from one ISA provider to another.

Security of cash accounts

Cash on deposit with banks and building societies is guaranteed by the Financial Services Compensation Scheme for sums of up to £85,000 in the event that the institution goes bust. The Financial Services Compensation Scheme is a government-backed but industry-funded safety net designed to give savers confidence in the UK savings system.

The level has been increased significantly in recent years. A decade ago it stood at £35,000. In 2008, when banks were collapsing around the world, it was increased to £50,000. Then, at the end of 2010, it was increased again to its current level of £85,000, which is broadly in line with the €100,000 level of protection across the European Union. This level was introduced across the board to stop savers moving their cash to the countries with the highest levels of investor protection.

It is important to understand that savers are only entitled to one lot of £85,000 compensation per failed institution. If you have £85,000 on deposit with a bank and also have a £20,000 fixed-rate bond with that same institution, then you are exposed in the event of it going bust, as you will only get £85,000 total compensation.

Savers in this situation, or who have more than £85,000 in a single bank or building society, may choose to move some of their money to a different bank, so they have no more than £85,000 per institution. If not, you could find most of your life's savings going down the drain if that bank goes bust.

Couples are each allowed £85,000-worth of protection, so joint accounts are covered up to £170,000.

A cash ISA is treated like any other bank account for protection purposes.

Merged banks – one lot of investor protection or two?

Compensation is paid up to £85,000 for each regulated institution. This means investors with assets across bank or building societies that operate under a shared regulatory licence will only get one set of cover.

Check the situation online if you have more than £85,000 with two banks. NatWest is registered as a separate institution to RBS, even though RBS owns it. So each bank is covered up to £85,000. The same applies for Lloyds and HBOS.

HSBC and First Direct, on the other hand, are registered under a single FSA licence. So anyone with £50,000 in each one has £15,000 of unprotected savings.

Banks and building societies that count as one:

- Barclays, Standard Life Cash Savings.

- Co-op Bank, Smile, Britannia.
- Coventry Building Society, Stroud & Swindon.
- Halifax, Bank of Scotland, Intelligent Finance, Birmingham Midshires, AA, Saga.
- HSBC, First Direct.
- Lloyds TSB, Cheltenham & Gloucester.
- Nationwide, Cheshire, Derbyshire, Dunfermline Building Societies.
- Santander, Cahoot.
- Virgin Money, Northern Rock.
- Yorkshire Bank, Clydesdale Bank.
- Yorkshire, Barnsley, Chelsea, Norwich & Peterborough Building Societies, Egg.

Overseas banks

Banks based within the European Union have a similar level of investor protection – €100,000.

But beware of banks that are not based in the EU as they do not have the same level of investor protection, as investors found out the hard way when banks based in Iceland and the Isle of Man collapsed in 2008. At the time, Icelandic banks were guaranteed by their government up to €20,887. The Isle of Man's bank deposit guarantee scheme compensated investors up to 100 per cent of the first £30,000 and then 90 per cent of the next £20,000 of deposits, up to a maximum of £48,000.

Cash funds

Cash funds are pooled investments run by fund managers who invest in 'cash-like' assets with the very loose aim of giving 'attractive' returns with a high level of security. They are also called *money market funds*.

These funds have come under scrutiny from the FSA in recent years because the assets they have invested in have, in some cases, not reflected the risk profile of cash. Some have also suffered from negative yields.

Cash funds are usually far less volatile than equity or bond funds but they still carry risks, and can post negative returns in times of exceptional market volatility.

Don't go into these funds for decent long-term cash returns – cash funds are purely for holding short-term cash on your investment platform while you think about where else you are going to invest it. The rates of return they generate are usually very low indeed. For example, the Fidelity Cash fund, which charges an annual management charge of 0.4 per cent, has an objective of 'pooling the savings of investors to find good rates of interest across banks and financial institutions'. It has an AAA rating from Moody's but the fund's ultra-low-risk approach means that in the three years up to September 2012 it has returned just 0.14 per cent, 0.3 per cent and 0.24 per cent.

National Savings and Investments (NS&I)

These government-backed savings products are as secure an investment as you can find. There is no reading through the small print to find out whether you are covered. They are 100 per cent secure, to the extent that the UK government is secure, regardless of how much you hold in them.

It is no surprise, therefore, that their rates are not great. As well as offering premium bonds for those who fancy a flutter with their interest, NS&I also offer a direct cash ISA account and a direct saver account. Neither are going to top the tables and, at the time of writing, neither even beat inflation.

NS&I used to offer some very attractive products, notably fixed-interest and index-linked savings certificates. These are no longer available as they offered generous rates of return with the security of a government guarantee. For example, index-linked certificates issued in 2007 offered RPI plus 1.35 per cent. These certificates were for a fixed period, but NS&I have offered holders of the certificates the opportunity to roll them over into replacement certificates on less attractive tax-free terms (but nonetheless still reasonable in the current environment).

If you hold some of these they probably offer better rates of interest than you will be able to get elsewhere in the market, so it is worth hanging on to them.

One advantage of National Savings certificates is that they are completely tax free and do not have to be declared on your tax return.

Tax on cash

Interest on cash is taxable as income, meaning you will pay tax on it at your marginal income tax rate.

Tax of 20 per cent is usually deducted at source from cash savings accounts. Basic rate tax payers have no further tax liability. If you are a higher rate or additional rate taxpayer you will have to declare the income on your tax return and will be required to pay the balance.

If you are a 10 per cent taxpayer or do not pay tax at all, you can get your interest paid to you gross by filling out form R85.

While we have covered this before, interest on cash held in a SIPP and in a cash ISA is paid gross with no tax to pay. Interest on cash held in a stocks and shares ISA is paid net of 20 per cent tax deducted at source, with no further tax to pay.

Inflation risk

Aside from the risk of the deposit-holder defaulting, covered earlier in the chapter, the other main risk from holding a lot of cash on deposit is inflation. Since 2008 it has been hard to find non-ISA accounts that will beat inflation without taking advantage of initial bonus rates, and, even then, beating inflation has not always been possible. That has meant money sitting in the bank or building society has actually been shrinking in real terms.

Cash is the most secure way to hold money, but that security comes at a cost.

Useful websites

www.investmentsense.co.uk

www.moneyfacts.co.uk

www.moneysupermarket.com

www.nsandi.com

www.uswitch.com

Investments for the advanced DIY investor

Most DIY investors will want to stick with traditional ways of investing, such as equities, bonds and other securities, whether held directly or in pooled investments through OEICs, unit trusts, investment trusts and ETFs. But there are more complex products and assets out there that can enable you to increase your exposure to a particular asset class while managing the amount of risk to which you are exposed.

Specialised instruments that have historically only been available to professional investment managers are becoming increasingly available to the DIY investor. Structured products, options and contracts for difference allow the DIY investor to access new asset classes in innovative ways, or to increase their exposure to mainstream markets many times over.

Some promise the earth, while others promise to give you your money back when the investment comes to an end. But the one thing all these investments have in common is that they are far more complex than they first appear. That is why they are only to be used by DIY investors who have already developed a genuine expertise in analysing and under-standing financial products.

Structured products

Often described as gravity-defying investments, structured products are plans packaged up by banks that use derivatives to give investors fixed returns in the event that an index, share, basket of shares or other financial measure achieves a particular level during or at the end of the term. They come with two key risks – that the indices being tracked do not do what you had hoped they would, meaning you do not get the return hoped for, and that the counterparty standing behind the derivatives goes bust. Structured products are rarely used by DIY investors.

Enterprise investment schemes (EISs)

An enterprise investment scheme (EIS) is a tax-efficient vehicle for investing in start-up businesses that rewards the investor with tax relief of 30 per cent on their initial investment, plus capital gains and inheritance tax advantages, in return for taking a gamble on a fledgling company. EIS investments are risky – they are unquoted companies, which means they are not subject to the same reporting requirements as listed companies, and they are start-ups, which means their business model is by definition not yet proven. Without the tax relief, most investors would steer clear of them. The majority of DIY investors are unlikely to invest in EISs – they are normally used by very wealthy investors with large tax bills to manage.

Contract for difference (CFD)

A contract for difference (CFD) is a form of derivative that allows you to bet on the price movements of shares or indices without actually owning them. Instead you make a contract with a CFD-provider that determines who pays whom in the event that a particular share price moves either up or down beyond a predetermined point. Because the whole equity is not bought, the investor can get far greater exposure to the market.

Where is the line between investing and betting? You won't get wholesale agreement, but critics will argue that CFDs are to investing what pole dancing is to sport. The risks with these instruments can be huge, so I recommend you steer clear of them unless you are an expert. In the tax man's view, CFDs are investing rather than betting instruments, as gains in excess of the annual allowance are subject to capital gains tax.

Spread betting

Spread betting is another, very similar, way of speculating on movements in share prices and indices. Rather than buy the shares (even though they are held by the provider), you simply take odds from a broker that a share price will move a certain way. Any gains made from spread betting are tax free.

If there is a debate about which side of the investing/betting line CFDs fall, there is no such debate about spread betting. The name gives it away. Racing snails, first throw in at a premiership match, time when the floodlights go out, or movement on shares. Fifty shades of betting – you have been warned.

Useful websites

www.comparestructuredproducts.com

www.londonstockexchange.com/structuredproducts

www.structuredproductreview.com

www.structuredretailproducts.com

four

Putting it all together

16

The tax-efficient DIY investor

There is no point being a brilliant investment-picker if you blow a chunk of your winnings through paying tax you could have avoided. Getting your tax strategy wrong can wipe out years of hard-earned investment gains, so it is essential to put your money in the tax wrapper (or wrappers) to suit your objectives.

It may not feel like it, given some of the statements coming from the government, but while tax evasion is illegal, tax avoidance is not. Avoiding tax does not necessarily mean joining the comedians, pop singers and TV stars in their aggressive offshore tax schemes – for most people it wouldn't be worth it because of the costs involved.

I adopt a simple rule when it comes to tax planning schemes. If I can find reference to it – other than in the context of a tax case – on HMRC's website (www.hmrc.gov.uk) then I will consider it. If I can't, then I don't. You will find plenty of explanatory references to all of the tax wrappers and investments covered in this book on HMRC's website.

I also subscribe to the view that you only have to pay tax when you are doing well. Paying tax is something that should be celebrated. Well, maybe that is pushing it a bit too far.

For the DIY investor, minimising tax is about smart use of the reliefs and allowances that the government has designed to incentivise us to save for our futures. But before we get on to minimising your tax bill, you first need to understand the taxes you are looking to minimise.

The two main taxes the DIY investor needs to bear in mind are income tax and capital gains tax.

Hopefully DIY investing will mean your assets will grow to such an extent that inheritance tax will also become an issue as you approach the end of your life. Here we focus on the two main personal taxes you will pay during your lifetime.

Income tax

You are taxed on your income in three ways, depending on the sort of income it is – general income, savings income or dividend income.

- **General income** – This is earnings from your job, whether received as an employee on a PAYE basis or income from self-employment. It also includes any rent you receive from property, and income from any pension(s) you have.
- **Savings income** – This covers interest from savings accounts and deposit products with banks and building societies, as well as income from gilts and qualifying corporate bonds.
- **Dividend income** – This covers income from dividends paid on your equity and fund holdings.

table 16.1 Income tax rates 2013/14

Tax rate	General	Savings	Dividend
Basic rate	20 per cent	20 per cent	10 per cent
Higher rate	40 per cent	40 per cent	32.5 per cent
Additional rate	45 per cent	45 per cent	37.5 per cent

General income uses the lower bands first.

If taxable general income is less than £2,790, savings income is taxed at 10 per cent until total taxable income exceeds that limit.

Personal allowance

You only pay income tax on income above your personal allowance. These have historically been age related, with over 65s and over 75s getting a progressively larger allowance. But as the government moves towards a £10,000 personal allowance in 2014/15 it is phasing out the age-related allowances.

table 16.2 Your personal income tax allowance 2013/14

Personal allowance (up to age 65)	£9,440
Personal allowance (age 65-74)	£10,500
Personal allowance (age 75 and over)	£10,660

These allowances reduce for higher earners, meaning that if you are under age 65 and earn above £118,880, you get no personal allowance.

Income tax bands

The rate at which you pay income tax is determined by the level of your earnings above your personal allowance in that tax year.

table 16.3 Income rate tax bands 2013/14

Rate	Amount above your personal allowance
Basic rate 20 per cent	£0–£32,010
Higher rate 40 per cent	£32,011–£150,000
Additional rate 45 per cent	Over £150,000

Income tax on savings interest

Savings interest is automatically taxed at 20 per cent. But if you are on low income, you may be able to get the interest tax free or get half of the tax repaid. This effectively means there is a 10-per-cent income tax rate for savings interest. You can apply for tax-free interest on your savings by filling in HMRC form R85.

Income tax on dividends

There is a 10 per cent tax credit on dividends from UK companies, and also some non-UK companies, because the dividends come from profits on which the companies have already paid corporation tax.

Hence, the amount you pay will be 10 percentage points lower than the figures in the right-hand column of Table 16.1.

Capital gains tax

You are taxed on capital gains above the level of your annual allowance, which is £10,900 for 2013/14 for everyone, regardless of age. A capital gains tax rate of 28 per cent is charged where gains, if added to your income, are above the higher rate tax threshold.

This means anyone with a £9,440 personal allowance earning over £41,450 will pay a capital gains tax rate of 28 per cent in the 2013/14 tax year. So, an individual with an income of £36,450 who has a £10,000 capital gains tax liability would see the first £5,000 taxed at 18 per cent and the balance taxed at 28 per cent.

The fact that capital gains tax is charged at a lower rate than income tax means, particularly for income-seeking higher rate taxpayers, it can be more efficient investing for growth and deriving an income by cashing in investments than by investing for income.

table 16.4 Capital gains tax rates

	Tax year 2013/2014
Standard rate	18 per cent
Rate for higher and additional rate taxpayers	28 per cent

Tax reliefs – ISA and pension

The two key ways a DIY investor will get tax relief are through pensions and ISAs.

Pension

Pension contributions paid into your SIPP benefit from tax relief at your highest rate of tax. For people paying tax at 40 per cent, that means it costs £600 of after-tax earnings to pay £1,000 into a pension. Once in the pension, assets grow largely free from income and capital gains tax.

When you come to draw money from your pension, which you are only allowed to do after the age of 55, a quarter of your pot can be taken tax free, with the balance taxed as income when it is drawn. Most people have less income in retirement than when they are working, meaning they pay less tax by tying up their money in a pension. Higher rate tax payers in employment may be basic rate tax payers in retirement.

ISA

ISAs do not give you tax relief when you pay money into them, which means you pay money in out of your taxed salary. But you are relieved from income tax liability for any income they generate. Furthermore, there will be no capital gains tax liability on the growth in the assets held within the ISA wrapper.

Maximising your allowances

When you come to draw money from your portfolio, you want to be able to use the tax allowances available to you to maximum effect. This means making the best possible use of both your income tax and your capital gains tax annual allowances, wherever possible.

Maximising your capital gains tax allowance

One of the most underused tax perks has to be the £10,900-a-year capital gains tax exemption. By investing in assets that grow, rather than pay an income, you can make the most of this generous annual allowance.

By investing in growth assets – sometimes easier said than done – you can withdraw £10,900 of your capital gains each year without paying tax.

Experts warn against letting the tax tail wag the investment dog, and a diversified approach is always recommended, but by having at least some growth assets in your portfolio you will be able to draw down capital gains in years when your income tax rate is high.

table 16.5 SIPP v ISA

	SIPP	ISA
Accessibility	You cannot access any of your money until the age of 55, when you can take a quarter of it as a tax-free lump sum. The rest must be drawn as income, subject to strict Government Actuary's Department limits. But lack of access can be a benefit to long-term saving discipline.	Fully accessible at any time.
Tax efficiency	Tax relief at your marginal rate on contributions and 25 per cent tax-free cash lump sum make SIPP investing more tax-efficient than ISA investing. Most people who contribute into pensions when higher rate taxpayers are basic rate taxpayers in retirement, so gain from tax relief on contributions.	No tax relief on contributions. Same income and capital gains tax benefits as SIPPs while assets held within wrapper. No tax on drawings taken out of ISA.
Divorce	Will be taken into account as part of divorce settlement and divided between the parties.	Will be taken into account as part of divorce settlement and divided between the parties.
Bankruptcy	Cannot be accessed to pay creditors in the event of bankruptcy. Potential for retirement benefits available from the age of 55 to be claimed by the trustee in bankruptcy (TIB).	Will be distributed to creditors in the event of bankruptcy.
Inheritance tax	Falls outside estate. Free of tax if no pension has been drawn at time of death. Otherwise, subject to 55 per cent tax charge.	Falls within estate for inheritance tax purposes at all times.

Unused allowances – gifts between spouses

If you are married or in a civil partnership, you can pass assets to your other half without creating a tax liability, giving your household twice as much tax allowance to play with.

If you are still working, the chances are that your income tax allowance for the current year has been used up. But if you have a non-earning spouse or civil partner, or your spouse or partner is paying tax at a lower rate than you are, simply transfer assets into their name and you will automatically cut your tax bill.

Similarly, even if both you and your spouse or partner are earning and paying a high rate of tax, by giving them parts of your portfolio that are holding capital gains, you can both use a full £10,900 capital gains tax allowance – allowing you to draw £21,800 tax free between you.

Using up spouses' and civil partners' unused allowances

The fact that gifts between spouses are free from any capital gains tax liability means it is relatively easy to move assets around to take advantage of unused ISA or SIPP allowances.

Assets attracting tax at a lower rate

Most DIY investors will stick to simply making full use of ISA and SIPP reliefs, spouse and civil partner allowances and capital gains tax allowances. But if you are paying tax at the higher or additional rate, you may want to consider some of the specialist asset classes that have been designed with tax relief at the forefront of their usefulness.

The main ones are VCTs and EISs, covered in Chapters 11 and 15 respectively. It is worth saying, however, that you should never invest in something just because of the tax relief that is available. If you do, the underlying investment can turn out to be a dud. So treat investments that come with big headline tax advantages with caution.

Onshore and offshore life insurance investment bonds

Life insurance investment bonds are complex tools for tax deferral and are normally only used by individuals who are receiving professional financial advice – hence I have not covered them in any detail in this book.

Onshore bonds are less attractive than they used to be years ago because returns are subject to a minimum tax of between 16 and 20 per cent, irrespective of your tax status. They can be of use to higher rate taxpayers wanting to defer paying tax until a time in the future when they pay tax at a lower rate – for example, in retirement.

Offshore investment bonds can be useful estate planning tools in the event you have large sums of money to give away without attracting an inheritance tax liability, but these too need specialist advice.

17

When it all goes wrong – death, divorce, bankruptcy, complaints and the Financial Services Compensation Scheme

N obody likes to dwell on life's negatives, but it is worth knowing what will happen to your money when significant personal events such as death, divorce or bankruptcy come along, or when an investment or investment provider goes bust.

Death and taxes

Benjamin Franklin's famous quote about death and taxes being the only things certain in life serves to underline just how important inheritance tax planning can be for your loved ones.

This is a book about DIY investing, not about estate planning, so I am going to go no further than explain what happens to the various assets a DIY investor may have built up in the event of their death.

In a nutshell, I would urge you to seek some professional advice and write a will. Intestacy laws do not always lead to the outcomes that you might expect, and society is full of people who have not benefited from their deceased loved one's estate in the way they had hoped they would, often causing years of resentment and hardship for those affected.

Inheritance tax

All your assets held within your ISA or Dealing Account will fall within your estate for inheritance tax purposes in the event of your death. This is not the case for investments held within your SIPP, which can pass to your heirs without raising an inheritance tax liability, though a separate tax charge is levied if you have already started taking benefits.

When inheritance tax is payable

Inheritance tax is payable on all your assets at death above a threshold known as the 'nil rate band'. The nil rate band is £325,000 for the tax year 2013/14 and will stay at that level at least until 2019. Inheritance tax on assets above the nil rate band is charged at 40 per cent.

Included in your estate for calculating inheritance tax are gifts made to other people, including trusts, within the previous seven years, with the tax rate reducing in tiers between 40 per cent and zero the further the date the gift was made from the date of death. These gifts are known as *potentially exempt transfers*.

Exceptions to the inclusion of gifts in your estate are an annual gift allowance of £3,000 a year, gifts to UK-registered charities, regular gifts from income and gifts made more than seven years before you die.

Spouses and civil partners

Spouses and civil partners can inherit unlimited sums from each other without having to pay any inheritance tax.

Spouses and civil partners can also inherit any unused part of the deceased's nil rate band, meaning a married couple or civil partners can always, between them, pass on a total of £650,000 without paying inheritance tax. This flexibility was only brought in from October 2007. Before then, spouses and civil partners could achieve more or less the same result, but they had to pay for estate planning advice and set up a trust to do so. This flexibility does not extend to couples who simply cohabit.

SIPP assets on death

Assets held in your SIPP at the time of death do not fall within your estate for inheritance tax purposes.

Death before taking benefits (uncrystallised benefits)

A lump sum up to your unused lifetime allowance can be paid tax free in the event of death before the age of 75. Any funds over the lifetime allowance can be paid as a cash lump sum, subject to a 55 per cent tax charge.

After the age of 75, all lump sum payments are taxed at 55 per cent. Or, the whole of the fund can be used to provide a pension to a spouse or dependant. The income from that pension will be liable for income tax.

A higher amount may be able to be paid as a lump sum on death if you benefit from one of the various protection measures for those with large pension funds accrued prior to various legislative changes.

Death after benefits have been taken (crystallised benefits)

If you die after you have started taking benefits, a lump sum can be paid to your dependants or nominated beneficiaries, subject to a 55 per cent tax charge. Or the whole fund can be used to provide a spouse's or dependant's pension.

We discussed Sally in Chapter 8. Let's revisit her situation.

example

Sally, aged 60, had £200,000 in her SIPP. She needed £25,000 for a new car, but didn't need the income as she was still working. She elected to crystallise 50 per cent of her SIPP, being £100,000. This provided her with a £25,000 tax-free lump sum, which is what she needed to buy the car, and she elected to take no income from her capped drawdown fund, worth £75,000. Of her remaining SIPP, 57 per cent (£100,000 out of £175,000) remained uncrystallised.

Let's now assume that 12 months have passed and the SIPP fund is still worth £175,000. Sally has received no pension payments in that time and, sadly, Sally has passed away. She leaves a widower, Leon, and two grown-up children, Leighton and Philip.

Sally's SIPP breaks down into two constituent parts:

Uncrystallised – £100,000.

Crystallised – £75,000.

Following Sally's expression of wishes, the uncrystallised £100,000 is paid as two lump sums of £50,000 each to Leighton and Philip. There is no tax to pay on these payments.

Leon, Sally's widower, elects to use the £75,000 crystallised fund to provide a capped drawdown pension. He could have taken the £75,000 as a lump sum, after tax of 55 per cent. But he decided that he would prefer to draw an income, knowing that on his death the residue of the fund can be paid as equal lump sums to his two sons, subject to tax at 55 per cent.

This example highlights the treatment of uncrystallised SIPP funds, where benefits haven't yet commenced, and crystallised SIPP funds where benefits have commenced.

It is worth also looking at what other options could have been open to Sally when completing her beneficiary nomination form:

- Leave the full £175,000 to her two sons. As neither were dependants, they must take the benefits in lump sum rather than pension form – £100,000 tax-free lump sum and £75,000 as a lump sum subject to tax at 55 per cent. Each of these payments could be apportioned however Sally liked between her two sons.
- Leave the full £175,000 to her husband. Leon could have taken the £100,000 as a tax-free lump sum. There would be little merit in taking this as a pension, as this would be tax-inefficient due to the pension payments being subject to income tax. As we have seen, Leon can either use the £75,000 to provide a taxable drawdown pension or annuity, or he could take a lump sum of £75,000 after tax at 55 per cent.
- Any variations of the above.

AIM-listed shares on death

Shares held on AIM become exempt from inheritance tax once they have been held for two years.

Divorce

All your investments, including your SIPP holdings, will be taken into account by the court in the event that you and your spouse or civil partner divorce.

The court can order SIPP and other pension assets to remain in your name, and offset against other assets retained by the other party. Alternatively, the court can also order your SIPP to be split between you and your former spouse, a procedure known as 'pension sharing'.

An ISA or a Dealing Account is treated like any other asset in a divorce.

Bankruptcy

In the event that you are declared bankrupt, the trustee in bankruptcy (TIB) appointed to administer your affairs will be able to take control of all your investment assets, except for those held in your pension where special rules apply. If you are declared bankrupt, or think you are likely to be, seek specialist advice.

Up until recently, the position was that a TIB could not access pension benefits where benefits had not commenced. Where benefits had commenced, then the TIB could use pensions in payment to satisfy creditors. A recent court case in the name of *Raithatha* v *Williamson* disturbed this view when the court ruled that the TIB could force Mr Williamson to commence benefits and then use the proceeds to satisfy his creditors. Unfortunately, the appeal was settled out of court, so what appeared to many of us to be a flawed judgement stands until it is successfully challenged in the courts. This means anyone over the age of 55 who is made bankrupt could see their pension benefits taken by the TIB.

How to complain about your investment platform

Most investment platforms do a pretty good job, but you may find that service falls below the standards to which you are entitled. A strongly worded letter to the platform may sort out your problem, but if you are still not satisfied then you are entitled to take your complaint to the proper authority, as explained below.

ISA and Dealing Account complaints

Complaints about your Dealing Account and your ISA should be made to the Financial Ombudsman Service, or the Financial Services Compensation Scheme (FSCS) in the event that the platform has ceased trading.

SIPP complaints

Sales and marketing complaints about a SIPP provider should be made either to the Financial Ombudsman Service, or the FSCS in the event that the organisation has ceased trading.

If your complaint is about maladministration, you can complain to the Pensions Ombudsman.

However, before going down this route it pays to contact the Pensions Advisory Service – a government organisation that will endeavour to resolve your dispute without having to refer to the Pensions Ombudsman.

Product and provider insolvency and the FSCS

There is always the possibility that one or more of the investment product providers that you use will go bust. Some but not all financial products are protected by the FSCS.

In general terms, the FSCS covers UK-based deposits, investments and insurance policies. Deposits are covered up to £85,000, while investments are covered up to £50,000. Joint accounts benefit from double these figures. Insurance products are covered up to 90 per cent of their value, however great it is.

Cash on deposit in a bank or building society

Bank and building society deposits are guaranteed by the FSCS, a government-backed organisation, for sums of up to £85,000 in the event that an institution goes bust. You are only protected up to the level of £85,000 per failed institution, yet two banks that have merged can be treated as a single bank for the purposes of the FSCS. (Which banks count as a single institution is covered in more detail on pages 202–3.)

Cash on deposit on an investment platform

If the bank your investment platform uses goes bust then you are entitled to compensation up to the FSCS limit of £85,000.

Investment platforms often deposit cash with more than one bank, so it is not possible to monitor this with a view to making sure that you stay within the £85,000 limit with any one bank. Although not tested legally, it is the widely held view that the £85,000-per-person limit would apply to each bank that your investment platform holds its cash with – meaning the more banks it holds cash with, the more protection you have.

Fund manager insolvency

Unit trust and OEIC managers are required by the regulator to put your investments with a trustee or depository rather than actually holding them themselves in their own name. So, if a fund manager does become insolvent then your unit trusts and OEICs would not be affected.

It is just about conceivable that the trustee or depositary used by the fund manager could become insolvent, but we are talking about the very biggest financial organisations in the world, and if they were to go bust the whole global financial system would be in meltdown. Most professionals do not see trustee or depository default as a genuine risk.

In the event of loss caused by a fund manager through negligence or fraud, the FSCS pays compensation up to £50,000 per person per provider.

ETF default

To date, no ETF or other exchange-traded product has ever gone into default, but technically it could happen. Like funds, ETFs place the assets on trust on your behalf with a nominee, meaning they are ring-fenced. If the ETF provider became insolvent, your assets would be protected from its creditors.

Synthetic and leveraged ETFs that use derivatives to pay multiples of the rise or fall in an index could find themselves unable to pay out in the event that the counterparty behind the derivative went bust. (The structure of ETFs is covered in more detail in Chapter 10.) But UCITS rules require ETFs domiciled in the EU to have no more than 10 per cent of the fund's value exposed to a single counterparty risk, so the failure of a counterparty should not be fatal.

Most ETFs are domiciled overseas, in countries such as Luxembourg or Ireland, but even those domiciled in the UK are not protected by the FSCS.

Investment trusts

Investment trusts are simply limited companies whose value goes up and down in line with the market's attitude to the value of the shares they hold. They are not regulated products and therefore do not benefit from FSCS protection.

But there are occasions when compensation can be payable in relation to investment trusts, as happened following the split-cap investment trust scandal of the early part of the last decade. Compensation was available from the FSCS where investors lost money when they were misled into buying a product that was unsuitable, or where the risks of the investment were not fully explained and that loss resulted from the actions of a regulated organisation. In the last decade, compensation was paid where regulated companies had marketed split-cap investment trusts to investors.

Unregulated collective investment schemes (UCISs)

As their name suggests, unregulated collective investment schemes (UCISs) do not, of themselves, benefit from the protection of the FSCS. Compensation can be payable if you are mis-sold one by a regulated firm, such as a financial adviser. But if you invest in a UCIS as a DIY investor you will be doing so on an 'execution-only' or buyer beware basis, which means you will have no recourse in the event that your money disappears for any reason.

Equities

If a company in which you hold shares goes bust you will lose some or all of your money. A liquidator will be appointed and, once all creditors have been paid, the remaining funds (if there are any) will be shared out among shareholders equally. There is no FSCS protection.

Bonds

Bond-holders rank ahead of shareholders but behind secured creditors in the event of a company's insolvency. But, like equities, corporate bonds do not benefit from FSCS protection.

Corporate bonds should be distinguished from 'fixed-rate' bonds issued by banks and building societies, which do benefit from FSCS protection up to £85,000. (The distinction between these two sorts of bond is covered in greater detail in Chapter 13.)

Venture capital trusts and enterprise investment schemes

Neither venture capital trusts (VCTs) nor enterprise investment schemes (EISs) benefit from FSCS protection. If the VCT or EIS loses all its money you will not be able to claim any compensation. But if the fund manager running it goes bust and owes you money, and it is regulated and therefore covered by the FSCS, you will be able to claim compensation of up to £50,000 per person.

Investment platform insolvency

All investments, including cash held by your investment platform on your behalf, are segregated from the platform's own assets. This means that if your investment platform goes bust then your money will not be affected, although you may have to wait a little longer to get access to it.

Useful websites

www.financial-ombudsman.org.uk

www.fscs.org.uk

www.pensionsadvisoryservice.org.uk

www.pensions-ombudsman.org.uk

18

Building a risk-adjusted portfolio

B eing a DIY investor is not just about picking the top shares or funds in a particular sector. You also need to understand which sectors to invest in, and what proportion of your portfolio to put in them. This process is called asset allocation, and it is a crucial factor in building a DIY investment portfolio.

The greater the investment return you want to achieve, the greater the risk you will need to take. But the longer the time frame you set, the greater the chance you will achieve your investment objectives.

Investments can go down as well as up. Well we all know that, but some investments are more volatile than others. Different risks attach themselves to different investments. The biggest risk to investing in cash is not the bank going bust, but inflation. Investing in corporate bonds is typically regarded as being safer than investing in equities, though as we have seen in Chapter 13, these investments are not immune to sharp price movements.

Risks are most concentrated in the individual investments you choose to buy, but there is also the risk that the vehicle you use to hold your investments could turn out to be the wrong one. For example, you could invest the bulk of your savings in a SIPP, only to find you really need access to your money before the age of 55. Maybe investing in an ISA would have been a better option.

Other risks you need to think about include, strange as it may sound, living too long, the possibility that you might become critically ill and any number of other significant and unexpected changes in your personal circumstances.

Investment experts will always tell you that asset allocation is more important to your overall portfolio returns than fund manager or share selection. For example, by investing solely in UK-focused equities or funds you are nailing your colours to the UK economy. If that goes down, your investments go with it. Not only that, but you will miss out on the potentially greater growth elsewhere, such as from emerging markets, bonds, corporate property, commodities, US equities or whichever other sector is having its day in the sun.

Markets are cyclical, with different sectors rising and falling at different points in the economic cycle. Watching everything you have go down in value all at the same time is enough to test the most resolute of long-term investors, and risks tempting you to bail out at the bottom of the market – which is, of course, the worst possible thing to do. By spreading your risk across different asset classes you can smooth out the peaks and troughs in your investment experience, making it psychologically that much easier to stay the course.

Attitude to, or appetite for, risk is very personal and I do find some people are guilty of over-analysing risk, while others just pay it lip service. There is a happy medium.

What is risk?

Risk is a difficult thing to explain or assess objectively. We all know that shares may go down in value as well as up. Corporate bonds are less risky than shares, meaning they are less likely to go down in value but also less likely to go up. Cash on deposit only goes up, but it is likely to go up more slowly than corporate bonds or equities. And that is the point with risk – there is no guarantee that any particular outcome is going to happen, positive or negative.

All you can say about the risk profile of different asset classes is that they are more or less likely to deliver. Equities are meant to out-perform bonds and cash over the long term, yet in the first decade of the new millennium they didn't.

But the fact that risks sometimes don't pay off does not mean we shouldn't bother and put all our money in cash. Because not taking any risk also has its risks – the risk of missing out on bigger returns, and on seeing what you have eroded by inflation. It is a phenomenon known as 'reckless caution', and, usually, the less a person understands about investments and economics, the more likely they are to suffer from it.

Cash is the least risky investment class, followed by bonds, property and then equities.

Figure 18.1 shows the investment return from each asset class over a 20-year period.

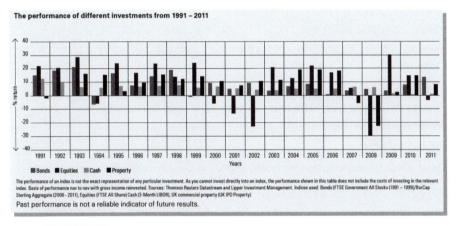

The performance of different investments from 1991 – 2011

The performance of an index is not the exact representation of any particular investment. As you cannot invest directly into an index, the performance shown in this table does not include the costs of investing in the relevant index. Basis of performance nav to nav with gross income reinvested. Sources: Thomson Reuters Datastream and Lipper Investment Management. Indices used: Bonds (FTSE Government All Stocks (1991 – 1999)/BarCap Sterling Aggregate (2000 - 2011), Equities (FTSE All Share) Cash (3-Month LIBOR), UK commercial property (UK IPD Property)

Past performance is not a reliable indicator of future results.

figure 18.1 Investment return by asset class 1991–2011

Source: © The Vanguard Group, Inc. used with permission

Some key risks to consider:

Inflation risk – if your investment return is less than inflation, the real value of your investments will be eroded. This is particularly relevant for cash and bond investments.

Economic and political risk – your investments are likely to be impacted by significant economic or political events. Economic issues that may impact on the return you get from your investments include interest rates, growth of the economy, levels of employment, inflation and political upheaval. When governments increase interest rates, for example to tackle inflation, it will often result in a fall in the value of bonds and possibly also a fall in the value of equities.

Personal circumstances risk – your personal circumstances will most probably change over time and you need to try and anticipate these changes. It is not always easy to do this, and some of these risks may be dealt with by insurance rather than by adapting your investment strategy.

Credit or default risk – this is most relevant when investing in corporate bonds and gilts, but every investment carries some level of risk that the issuer may go bust. Some but not all investments are protected by the Financial Services Compensation Scheme (covered in more detail in Chapter 17).

Shortfall risk – you need to consider the possibility that you don't meet your investment objectives within the time frame you have set yourself.

Currency risk – if you live in the UK and invest in only UK-denominated assets then you won't need to worry about a currency risk. But if you are saving to repay a mortgage on your holiday home in Spain, then this is a very real risk.

Liquidity risk – this is most relevant when investing in obscure investments. You need to ensure you can easily sell your investment when you need to.

Sector risk – one sector may perform very badly, and unless you have a well-diversified portfolio this could really hit your investment return.

Tax risk – tax rules will change over time and you need to ensure that you keep abreast of these changes to ensure you maintain a tax-efficient investment strategy.

Like you did with your investment objectives, try writing down some of the risks you are worried about, using the examples and the risk-profiling tools mentioned here.

Next to each risk, write down your risk appetite. This may be on a scale of 1 to 6, where 1 is when you want minimal risk and 6 is you are happy to be cavalier and accept the consequences. Or you may just rank your appetite for risk as low, low-medium, medium-high or high. I try to avoid using an odd number of rankings as it is just too tempting to opt for the middle one.

Here are some issues to consider when going through this process. You can adapt this list to include any of the other risks mentioned above that are relevant to you:

table 18.1 Risk and risk appetite

Risk	Appetite for risk
Capital value falling by 0–10 per cent	
Capital value falling by 10–20 per cent	
Capital value falling by 20–50 per cent	
Income falling by 0–10 per cent	
Income falling by 10–20 per cent	
Income falling by 20–50 per cent	
Objectives target missing deadline by:	
< 1 year	
1–3 years	
3–5 years	
Objectives target missing amount by:	
0–5 per cent	
5–10 per cent	
10–20 per cent	
I live forever	
I am ill and can no longer work	
Property prices shoot up (I am saving for a house deposit)	
University fees shoot up (I am investing for my kids' tuition fees)	
I lose my job	

Your attitude to risk

Attitude to risk is a deeply personal thing, influenced by our psychological make-up, our experiences of gain or loss and our sense of security in the world.

We all want 'as much as possible' from our investments, but we are not all prepared to take the same level of risk to get a particular return.

This means it is not possible to create a one-size-fits-all asset allocation model for everybody. So it is important to go for an asset allocation strategy that reflects your personality. There are a number of tools to help you work this out.

Risk-profiling tools

There are several good risk-profiling tools available free on the internet. There is a very simple one on the Standard Life website. Put 'Standard Life risk profiler' into a search engine to find it quickly. After answering ten quick questions about your attitude to losing money and seeing investments rise and fall in value, you will be given one of five rankings.

I also like the high-level risk profiler available on the Vanguard website – at https://personal.vanguard.com/us/FundsInvQuestionnaire. This questionnaire is designed for the American market, so talks from a US perspective, but you can easily fill it in on the basis of switching USA for UK. This profiler also goes a step further and gives you a rough asset allocation-split for your objectives.

Your investment objectives

The amount of risk you can afford to take will depend on the length of time you are planning to tie up your money. The risks of the stock market mean you should not really be investing in equities over the short term.

As a general rule, the longer your investment horizon, the more risk you can afford to take. It is also generally the case that the more money you have, the more risk you can afford to take. These two rules should be borne in mind when considering the guidelines set out below.

CNN Money has a useful asset allocation calculator. It is again designed for Americans but it is fully transportable to the UK. For example, with a time horizon of 10 to 20 years and a medium appetite for risk, it suggests a portfolio made up of:

Large-cap stocks – 35 per cent

Bonds – 25 per cent

Small-cap stocks – 20 per cent

Overseas stocks – 20 per cent

In all likelihood, as a DIY investor you need not follow these portfolio construction ideas to the letter, or rather the number. The more complex ones are generally designed for high net-worth individuals with a lot of money. As long as you get a decent level of diversification, across three or four sectors, your portfolio will be in the right ballpark.

These portfolios, constructed from equities, ETFs, OEICs, investment trusts, bonds and gilts, are suitable for your core investment holdings. Once you have your bedrock investments in place in a balanced portfolio, you may start to feel adventurous and experiment with less mainstream asset classes.

Medium-term investing

If you are investing over the medium term, say 5 to 10 years, you should be considering a high proportion of equities, but you should not be investing as aggressively as long-term investors.

Sometimes it pays to invest in a similar asset to the thing you are investing to buy. For example, imagine if you saved for a house deposit for five years, hit your savings target and then found that prices have doubled, meaning you couldn't buy the sort of property you had planned to. By putting some of your portfolio into a residential property fund that provides exposure to the price of UK residential property, at least part of your investment pot would increase in line with your target.

Long-term investing

For periods over 10 years and stretching into decades you can afford to be increasingly risky in your investment strategy, whether in your SIPP or through assets you can access at any stage of your life. You should not go for risky investments just for the sake of it, but you can afford to take higher risks that reward the investor with higher returns.

This means a greater exposure to global equities, whether through funds or ETFs. Actively managed global equity funds can target opportunities in countries where economic growth is greater. The longer your investment horizon, the more you can invest in emerging markets.

Income investing in retirement

While risky assets such as emerging markets are fine for your pension or other retirement savings when there is still a long time before you will be drawing an income, they are generally not a good idea when you are actually in retirement.

As you approach your retirement you will want to transform the make-up of your portfolio from an aggressive growth strategy to an income strategy. This means gradually switching portions of your fund from riskier asset classes, such as emerging markets, smaller companies and technology stocks, towards corporate bonds and dividend-paying blue chip stocks.

If you need absolute certainty of income in retirement then you can buy an annuity from an insurance company. But doing so is a once-in-a-lifetime deal you make with an insurer, and you will be stuck with whatever income they give you for life.

Annuities are very unpopular, not least because increases in longevity have meant the rates they pay out are half what they were 15 years ago. Annuity rates have been depressed further by low interest rates and extremely onerous capital adequacy requirements on insurers, meaning that you are effectively investing in a product that tracks gilts.

Split between asset classes

There are many different rules of thumb when it comes to asset allocation, such as the rule that your equity exposure, as a percentage, should be 100 minus your age. That may work, but it doesn't tell you what the remainder should be in. There are many diverse views on asset allocation splits and there is clearly no right answer.

I have deliberately avoided straying into suggesting what sectors you should and shouldn't invest in, as this changes daily. But the following table provides examples of typical risk-adjusted asset allocations.

table 18.2 Risk-adjusted asset locations

	UK equities	Global equities	Bonds	Property	Commodities	Cash
Higher risk/ aggressive	30 per cent	38 per cent	10 per cent	15 per cent	5 per cent	2 per cent
Medium to higher risk/ moderately aggressive	30 per cent	35 per cent	15 per cent	15 per cent	2 per cent	3 per cent
Medium risk/ balanced	25 per cent	30 per cent	30 per cent	10 per cent	0 per cent	5 per cent
Lower to medium risk/cautious	25 per cent	20 per cent	35 per cent	10 per cent	0 per cent	10 per cent
Lower risk/ defensive	25 per cent	15 per cent	45 per cent	0 per cent	0 per cent	15 per cent

You can find actively managed funds covering the above sectors by searching on any of the websites referred to at the end of Chapter 9. If you want to find a tracker fund then the easiest way to find one that covers the asset class is to visit the website of one of the large ETF providers highlighted in Chapter 10.

If you put ten investment advisers in a room, they will come up with at least ten asset allocations for any given situation. None will be right and none wrong.

For the novice investor who doesn't have much time to research individual investments, it is hard to argue against a portfolio of low-cost tracker funds.

A well-diversified portfolio for someone investing over the medium/ long term for capital growth with a medium-high risk appetite may look something like Table 18.3.

table 18.3 A well-diversified portfolio of investments

Index	Per cent weighting	Notes
UK equity – FTSE All Share Index	35 per cent	Tracks the UK's largest listed companies, representing about 98 per cent of the capitalisation of the whole market.
Global equity – FTSE All World Developed Europe ex UK index	25 per cent	Tracks the performance of all the developed equity markets in the world, excluding UK.
Corporate bonds – Global Aggregate Corporate Bond Index	20 per cent	Provides a broad-based measure of the global investment-grade corporate fixed-rate debt market.
Emerging markets – MSCI Emerging Markets Index	10 per cent	Tracks emerging markets in Europe, Asia, Africa, Latin America and Russia.
UK property – FTSE EPRA/NAREIT UK Index	10 per cent	Tracks UK listed real estate companies and real estate investment trusts (REITS).

There are, of course, very many variations of the above, but you will see that it is a diversified portfolio that can be put together in literally minutes.

Rebalancing your portfolio

There are two reasons why you will need to revisit the asset allocation of your portfolio at regular intervals. First because markets change and experts' views of what a sensible asset allocation strategy actually is can change, and secondly because growth or losses in certain parts of your portfolio can leave it unbalanced. This means you need to monitor the relevance of your asset allocation strategy at least every couple of years, and ideally annually.

Correlation

When looking at different asset classes and sectors, it is helpful to understand how they may be correlated. Some are positively correlated – that is, they tend to move in the same direction. Others are negatively correlated, where a fall in the value of one asset class is normally accompanied by a rise in the other. Correlation is measured on a continuous scale between –1, a perfect negative correlation, 0 where there is no correlation and 1 where there is perfect positive correlation.

Figure 18.2 shows the correlation between some of the major asset classes.

	UK equities	Global equities	UK gilts	Global government bonds	UK corporate bonds	Commodities
UK equities		0.98	-0.44	-0.15	-0.23	0.60
Global equities	0.98		-0.55	-0.27	-0.34	0.62
UK gilts	-0.44	-0.55		0.81	0.91	-0.47
Global government bonds	-0.15	-0.27	0.81		0.89	-0.26
UK corporate bonds	-0.23	-0.34	0.91	0.89		-0.30
Commodities	0.60	0.62	-0.47	-0.26	-0.30	

figure 18.2 Correlation between major asset classes between July 2004 and June 2007

Source: *Shares* Magazine

You will see that UK equities and global equities have the highest positive correlation, whereas UK equities and UK gilts have the largest negative correlation. I have taken poetic licence in my choice of time frame, as since 2008 UK equities and UK gilts have 'behaved' due to exceptional factors such as the credit crunch, quantitative easing and the euro debt crisis.

A final thought on risk and portfolio construction

There is a lot of analysis about model portfolios and portfolio construction, much of which you will choose to ignore. My golden rule, above all others, is to diversify. Spread your assets across several sectors and investment types and you are less likely to come unstuck than someone who goes for a punt on a specific sector of the market with everything they have.

Strategies for investing

n the previous chapter we looked at ways of measuring your personal
appetite for risk and how to use that information to decide how to
spread your investments across different asset classes – a process known
as portfolio construction.

But knowing which asset classes to invest in only gets you halfway there.
It's not just a question of where to invest, but also how you go about it.
And this comes down to knowing what investment style is right for you.

As a DIY investor, you have to choose how to approach investing in the
asset classes you have decided to target – whether through directly held
equities, bonds, gilts and other assets, or through funds. Once you have
decided whether you are going to invest directly or through funds, you
then need to decide the level of ongoing active input you want, whether
from yourself or from a fund manager.

There are many different strategies for investing, many of which are too
complex to do justice to here, though if you are interested there are many
good books that cover this topic in greater detail.

This book is aimed at people who want to invest for their future and then
get on with the rest of their lives, not those who want to become part-time
or full-time investors. So I have only covered the main strategies here. And
I have deliberately not gone into frequent-dealing strategies or day trading
in any great detail. These are highly complex areas and would fill a book
on their own.

There is no definitive answer to the question 'Which is the best strategy?'.
Many people, myself included, use more than one strategy across their
portfolio and, as you will see, some of the strategies overlap.

The fund investor

If you haven't got the time or the inclination to research individual stocks and monitor them on an ongoing basis, then being a fund investor is right for you.

You will be paying fund management charges but you shouldn't expect to pay much more than 0.75 per cent per annum. Once you have read the chapter on building a risk-adjusted portfolio you will have a feel for the sectors you should be targeting. See the chapters on investment trusts, unit trusts and OEICs and ETFs for how to research quality funds.

The financial supplements of all the national newspapers have loads of great articles on funds to buy and funds to sell. You can easily see what financial advisers are recommending by visiting the IMA's website, which shows the best- and worst-selling sectors. Throughout most of 2012, bond funds dominated the best buy list, only to be replaced in the last two months of 2012 by UK equity income and global emerging markets respectively. There is no shortage of information on funds and it is just about finding a source that you like and trust.

The frequent dealer

Everyone likes the idea of easy money. Buying shares, waiting a short period for them to rise in value and selling them at a healthy profit sounds like a great strategy. If only it were that easy.

Making money out of buying and selling shares requires a lot of commitment and effort and should not form the sole focus of your long-term savings. If you know a company well and think its fundamentals mean it should be valued more highly than it actually is, then yes, you may well make money out of it. And if you fancy trying to get rich quick, good luck. But be aware of the risks.

If you think frequent dealing is for you, then do plenty of research before you start investing. There are lots of good books and research out there – the *Financial Times Guide to Investing* by Glen Arnold gives a particularly comprehensive view of most of what you need to know.

Another good way to hone your skills before you start playing the markets with real cash is paper investing. There are a number of websites that will let you trade virtual money rather than lose your own cash learning the ropes. One of the best of these is Bullbearings (www.bullbearings.co.uk).

If you are a frequent dealer, then your selection of investment platform will be crucial. If you are making a lot of trades, then the amount you pay per deal will really start to add up and will eat into your profits. But the real killer is stamp duty, which is 0.5 per cent of the purchase price of each equity investment.

The day trader

Day trading, technically speaking, is buying stocks in the morning and then closing all your positions at the end of the day. It is definitely only for the experts.

Day trading was born off the back of the dot-com bubble at the end of the 1990s, when soaring share prices made it easy to make quick money. People started throwing in their day jobs and did actually make a living trading short movements in share prices, until the bubble burst on the turn of the millennium, after which markets promptly went into a nosedive for a couple of years.

We didn't hear anything about day traders for a while thereafter, but then newspaper articles about them started to re-emerge as memories faded and markets recovered. In fact, whenever markets enter periods of sustained growth, you can be sure the papers will have stories headed 'Return of the Day Trader'. The point is, very few day traders manage to make money at all stages in the investment cycle. If you want to chance your arm as a day trader, good luck to you. There are plenty of websites and books that will claim to show you how.

There is a great book called *The Naked Trader* by Robbie Burns, which tells his story, warts and all, of being a short-term trader.

Market information

Market information is a key factor to bear in mind when buying shares. You are pitting your wits against professional fund managers. If Warren Buffett is selling shares and you are buying, I know whom I would back – no offence intended.

But it is fair to say that DIY investors may have the opportunity to beat the professional fund manager by investing in company shares, either those listed on AIM or those LSE-quoted companies capitalised at sub-£1bn. This is where the chat rooms, tip sheets and specialist financial magazines tend to focus their energies.

Specialist investment magazines, such as *Shares* or *Investors Chronicle*, provide weekly market and company information, as well as a number of share tips.

Websites such as MoneyAM and ADVFN provide lots of research information on individual listed companies, and the bulletin boards such as Motley Fool provide personal observations and reviews.

Some investors like to track whether directors of listed companies are buying or selling shares in their own company – as they will hopefully know more about the company than the market will. There are strict rules surrounding when directors can buy and sell shares, and often there may be a very innocent reason. For example, a director may decide to cash in share options that have just matured. However, a beleaguered chief executive may buy shares to try and help swing market sentiment back in the company's favour. In the main, though, directors buying or selling shares in their own companies is a good indicator, and one that many investors will follow. Two websites that allow you to follow directors' share purchases and sales are www.directorsholdings.com and www.directorsdeals. com.

The long-term buy and hold investor

This self-explanatory way of investing, combined with passive investing, explained below, is arguably the strategy that gives the DIY investor the best chance of good returns over a long period of time.

Buy and hold investing is founded on the idea that markets will give a good rate of return in the long term, in the way that they have done over long periods for most of the last 100 or so years. Buy and hold investors believe it is not possible to beat the market by making short-term bets on swings in valuations because the increased costs of dealing, including broker costs, stamp duty and bid/offer spreads, will more often than not wipe out whatever gains, if any, the investor trying to time the market might make.

Supporters of buy and hold investing argue that markets are so efficient that the price of a share is always accurate, meaning there is no scope for an investor to find undervalued shares. This theory is known as the *efficient market hypothesis*.

Investment legends Warren Buffett, chairman and chief executive of investment giant Berkshire Hathaway, and the UK's own Neil Woodford, of Invesco Perpetual, are both buy and hold investors of sorts in that they hold stocks for a very long time and keep their portfolio turnover to a minimum.

The passive investor

The passive investor has no confidence that fund managers actually add value. If this is an argument that chimes with you, then you are in the company of a growing band of financial advisers and other investment experts.

There have been loads of surveys that have 'proved' this point, though I still believe that certain managers will deliver the goods more often than not.

Central to the theory of passive investing is the efficient market hypothesis, which is essentially the effect of what we all know as 'market forces' – namely that stock prices always settle at their true value, so there is nothing that can be done to find extra value.

The real trick in passive investing is choosing the right index to track. Once you have done this, if you stick with a mainstream tracker fund provider you won't go far wrong. The decision as to which index to track is all about asset allocation, as covered in the previous chapter.

The momentum investor

In its simplest form, a momentum investor buys investments that are on the rise and sells investments that are falling in value. Without stating the obvious, in times of rising markets this strategy works well but when markets are falling, it can be disastrous. There is a bit of momentum investor in all of us. We are often attracted to an investment or market sector because it is doing well and hope we have joined the ride early enough to make some money.

The income investor

Income investing is a strategy for people at a point in their lives when they want to start drawing income from their assets, while preserving capital, rather than growing their fund.

Income investors face a number of big challenges, and changes to interest rates and inflation are but two. Today's low-interest rate environment is forcing income investors to look beyond cash to riskier but higher-yielding asset classes.

They also face the added challenge of generating sufficient income without excessively eroding their capital, which is the income generation engine room. If the capital goes, the income goes with it.

Spreading risk is one of the most basic principles of financial planning, and there is nothing wrong with also apportioning a small part of your portfolio to slightly racier bond-like assets such as preference shares or permanent interest-bearing shares, which can pay higher incomes. But don't bet too much on these higher-risk asset classes unless you can afford to suffer losses if things go wrong.

You can search for the highest-yielding shares in the UK through the *Daily Telegraph* Stock Screener. Be aware, though, a high dividend yield may be masking other problems with a company, so don't buy on the basis of yield alone.

If you do not want the hassle of having to choose which corporate bonds or high-yielding equities to buy, there are plenty of funds out there to serve your needs. I favour spreading your money between both passive and active funds. When going for passive funds, whether corporate bond or equity income, I suggest opting for ETFs because of their generally lower cost.

High-yielding equities may offer a level of protection against inflation that corporate bonds do not, but they also expose you to far more volatility. If we enter another bear market, their value will fall more than your corporate bonds. So it makes sense to spread your risk by spreading your holdings between equity income funds and corporate bond funds.

How much risk you can afford to take for the level of return you want will also dictate the sort of bond holdings you go for. Investment-grade bond funds are more secure than high-yield bond funds, but the returns tend to be lower.

If you simply cannot afford any risk that your income is not paid, then you need to source the best fixed-rate deposits you can find. Generally speaking, the longer you are prepared to tie up your money, the higher the interest rate.

The growth investor

Growth investing is, as you've doubtless guessed, investing to maximise the value of your portfolio, rather than to achieve a steady income.

In its purest form it means going for companies that look to reward investors by increasing their share price by growing their market capitalisation, rather than paying dividends. That means targeting companies that are at a relatively early stage in their development, such as tech companies, rather than mature blue chip companies that pay steady dividends.

Technology stocks have been seen as the classic growth stocks for years, rewarding investors with increases in share price rather than dividends. But you can't avoid being a mature company forever, and Apple's decision in 2012 to pay a dividend for the first time since 1995 has led some commentators to speculate as to whether other big technology companies will follow suit.

Stocks targeted by growth investors often appear expensive in terms of their price-to-earnings or price-to-book ratio. This is because their share price reflects investors' belief in the future earnings potential of the company through its future growth. Good examples of this are emerging markets and commodities-related stocks that are priced on an expectation of continued growth in demand for their services because of the overarching emerging markets growth story.

Smaller companies can be fertile ground for the DIY growth investor. A company with a market cap of £50m has a lot more chance of doubling in value than HSBC or BP. Many frequent traders follow a growth investing strategy, researching the companies they are interested in, banking gains when they come along and then moving on to the next opportunity.

Targets for growth:

■ Technology stocks.
■ Emerging markets.

- Recovery shares.
- Smaller companies.
- Special situations funds.

The capital values of companies paying high dividends have stood up to the difficult financial conditions better than many other sectors. By opting for the accumulation version of an income fund you can get your dividends reinvested into the fund as extra units, thus growing the value of your holding.

The value investor

Value investing involves buying shares in companies that appear to be undervalued in the belief that market forces will eventually force up their value to their natural level.

Value investing is said by many to be the opposite of growth investing. But value flag-bearer, and arguably the most celebrated investor of our times, Warren Buffett, would disagree. Buffett is on record as saying the two are 'joined at the hip'. He can also be described as a buy and hold investor, as he is not a great believer in short-term speculation.

If you are interested in hearing firsthand how this value-investing legend communicates with his investors each year, go to www.berkshirehathaway.com/letters.

Value strategies

Value investors look for shares in companies that have low price/earnings (PE) ratios or low price-to-book ratios. (This terminology is covered in more detail in Chapter 12.) Academic studies have repeatedly shown that value stocks outperform growth stocks over the long term.

But critics of value investing point out this is not always the case, as happened in the late 1990s. These critics also point out that there is no set way to value a stock, and that two analysts might come to a different valuation.

But the basic tenet of value investing – that companies that are cheap in relation to the amount of earnings they return should be a good bet in the long term – is very persuasive. And given it works for the likes of Warren Buffett and a number of successful managers in the UK, it is a strategy DIY investors would do well to follow.

In the UK, you can access funds that operate a value-investing strategy through many of the successful equity income managers.

The *Daily Telegraph* Stock Screener allows you to search for growth and value stocks, as well as high-yielding ones.

The guided investor

Many of the low-cost investment platforms on the market have grown out of independent financial adviser businesses, banks or stockbrokers, so they are used to giving people advice on what investments they should make, and several still have thousands of clients they give full advice to.

When you buy assets through an investment platform you do so on an 'execution-only' basis, rather than on an advised basis. This means you specifically agree that you have not received any financial advice at all, so have no comeback against the investment platform if the product or investment you buy turns out to be the wrong one for your circumstances. In return for having to deal with lower compliance costs, investment platforms have been able to afford to give you the financial services products you want more cheaply.

Because they are aware many customers want to buy investment products but do not know what to buy, several investment platforms have come up with portfolio construction suggestions. These are called 'model portfolios'.

These give suggested asset allocation splits for different types of investors and for different sizes of fund. These asset allocation recommendations are more or less similar to what you would get if you paid to see a financial adviser, so these model portfolios are useful.

The regulator has concerns that some investment platforms' model portfolios are influenced by the payments they receive from the fund managers for selecting and distributing their funds. This suggests there is a risk that by investing in a model portfolio you may end up in higher charging funds that are not necessarily the best for your needs. It is notable that some model portfolios are dominated by dirty share classes of OEICs, with cheaper, clean share classes, investment trusts and ETFs rarely mentioned. By early 2014, any commercial bias should have been eliminated as the regulator bans payments from fund managers to investment platforms.

The ethical investor

Tobacco, gambling, weapons, alcohol, animal testing, pornography, child labour, fossil fuels – the list of activities some investors find unpalatable is long and varied. If you do not like the idea of putting your money into funds that invest in activities that go against your principles, there are plenty of funds available to meet your needs. But you need to make sure you get the right fund for your ethical principles.

Funds are described as light green or dark green, depending on the extent to which they adhere to ethical principles.

Light green funds – avoid companies deriving a high proportion of revenue from animal testing, pornography, tobacco and weapons manufacture.

Dark green funds – adopt a stricter approach, which often excludes companies that have any interest at all in areas ethical investors have issues with. They often seek out companies making a positive contribution to society and the environment.

For full details of the top ethical funds on the market, including their ethical policies and company-filtering techniques, go to www.fairinvestment. co.uk/investing_in_ethical_funds.aspx.

Investment strategies to be avoided

Buying shares that have fallen a long way on the belief that 'surely they will bounce back'

There is no guarantee they will, and in all likelihood the company is on the way out. It happened to a friend, who bought £10,000-worth of Northern Rock in 2008 when their shares were at 75p, having been over 1200p a year earlier. A few months later his money had gone forever.

Short-term plays on the Footsie

Again, just because the FTSE 100 has fallen two days in a row doesn't mean it will bounce back the next. You may say, 'Yes it does, that happened yesterday'. But that is no guarantee it will happen tomorrow.

If someone has told you a sure-fire system for the FTSE, or any other index for that matter, don't believe them. Unless they are driving a Lamborghini and wearing a Rolex, it clearly doesn't work.

Early-stage oil or commodities plays

Getting in early in the one-in-a-thousand company that does become that next fast-growing central Asian energy giant sounds great in theory. But separating truth from fiction on the information that you are getting on these companies is near impossible.

There are many other ways of how not to invest, but a combination of:

■ don't be greedy,

■ don't invest in anything you don't understand, and

■ if it looks like it is too good to be true, then it almost certainly is,

all mixed up with a dollop of common sense, should keep you on the straight and narrow.

20

Choosing a DIY investment platform and getting started

E very report and survey I read suggests that DIY investing is set to become significantly more widespread. The statistics and a few of the quotes contained below are sourced from the 2013 *Direct Platform Guide*, reproduced with the kind permission of investment platform research organisation Platforum.

- The DIY investment platform market was £94.3bn as at September 2012, up nearly 30 per cent from the previous year.
- Revenue models are changing and DIY platform bosses believe they will need to charge explicit fees by 2014.
- There are up to 10m customers whose products are generating a commission payable to a financial adviser. Only 2m are looking for an ongoing advised relationship.
- The average split by product is 17 per cent in Dealing Accounts, 45 per cent in ISAs and 38 per cent in SIPPs.
- The average account size is £26,700.
- There are circa 3.5m DIY investment accounts, for 1.6m customers.
- Only 25 per cent of customers mentioned price as a priority when choosing to invest online.
- As content becomes more important, we will see more publishers work with investment platforms.
- Of the 10.8m holding a risk-based investment, 6.7m tend to mostly self-direct and of these only 2.7m enjoy it. [Note, not all self-directed

investments are carried out through investment platforms, as people who buy investments direct from the provider, e.g. from press advertising, are also included.]

■ Of those who do not invest using an investment platform, one of the major barriers is that the choice is overwhelming and confusing.

I tend to treat industry reports with some scepticism as there is often a hidden agenda, but this report pretty much nails it – except maybe for the bullet about pricing not being important. The final bullet lays down the gauntlet to the investment platform industry. Make investing easy, or risk alienating your potential customer base.

Which investment platform is best for me?

DIY investment platforms can be assessed on a number of measures, but the most important, in my opinion, are functionality, service and price.

Functionality

A DIY investment platform is one that offers broadly the full range of investments covered in this book – namely equities, investment trusts, unit trusts, OEICs, ETFs, gilts and corporate bonds. They will all offer an ISA, a SIPP and a Dealing Account.

Firms known as fund supermarkets or discount brokers are not full DIY investment platforms as they offer only unit trusts and OEICs.

Some of the following features may not be available on all DIY investment platforms, so are worth investigating if they interest you:

Product range – does your preferred platform offer Junior ISAs or Child Trust Funds? Does it offer a competitive cash ISA? Can you access CFDs or even spread-bet via your platform?

Joint accounts – you may want to hold investments jointly with your spouse or partner for tax reasons. Not all platforms can cater for this.

Overseas shares – some may offer a limited range, some a full range and others may only allow investment into UK equities. All platforms will offer funds that can access overseas markets.

Mobile applications – surprisingly few DIY platforms have invested in mobile technology, but a handful have and are reaping the benefits with more customers dealing more often.

Model portfolios – these are normally available in the public area of the platform's website, so you can pick up ideas even if you are not a customer and your chosen platform doesn't offer them.

News and research – all platforms will offer this to a greater or lesser degree, but some provide far more than others. Also, some platforms tend to focus on OEICs and unit trusts whereas others are more equity-focused. You can normally sign up for information or newsletters even if you aren't a customer.

Regular investment/dividend reinvestment – not all platforms have a regular investment facility where you can invest cash held in your ISA, SIPP or Dealing Account into a specific fund or share on a regular basis. You may want to check that your chosen platform can automatically reinvest your dividends received from equities or funds – though all will offer accumulation units of funds where they exist.

Linked accounts – can one person in the family manage all the family's accounts on the platform? I manage my SIPP, ISA and Dealing Account as well as my wife's ISA and my kids' junior ISAs, all via one login on the website and mobile application.

Reporting and data – does your platform offer secure messaging as an alternative to email? Does it offer performance reporting? Sophisticated DIY investors who actively deal in equities will often use Level 2 data to get detailed market information. Is this available? This information can be bought in separately if your DIY investment platform doesn't offer it.

Certificated shares – few platforms nowadays allow you to sell shares where you hold a share certificate, and even fewer allow you to buy shares and hold a certificate.

Shareholder perks – not the benefit they used to be, but if you are interested in these, ask your platform whether or not they will give you access to them.

Service

The assessment of the service standards of an investment platform can be quite subjective. All platforms put their best foot forward in marketing material, but you should treat client testimonials and awards logos littered over a platform's website with a healthy dose of scepticism.

There are several ways in which an investment platform's service proposition will affect your experience:

Website – this is critical and will be your main interface with your investment platform. How easy is it to navigate? How intuitive is it to use? Is the 'search for investments' facility any good? Is the literature easy to understand?

Telephone and email support – try ringing them to ask a few questions that you know the answer to and see how knowledgeable and helpful the staff are. Try emailing and see how long it takes them to respond.

Online or offline – some platforms claim to offer a true online service, but at the first opportunity throw you into an offline, paper-based process. You should be able to apply for and pay money into a SIPP, ISA and a Dealing Account without printing off or signing any paper.

The independent view – try websites such as Motley Fool and Moneysavingexpert to see what other customers think. Go to these websites and put in the name of the platform you are looking at.

Pricing

There are several comparison sites designed to help you compare the pricing of platforms, two of which can be found at www.diyinvestor.co.uk and www.candidmoney,com.

It is easiest to break charges down into product charges and investment charges. For product charges I mean the cost of establishing and running a SIPP, ISA or Dealing Account. For investment charges I mean the cost of buying, selling or holding an equity, fund, bond or any other investment covered in this book.

Product or tax wrapper charges

You may see charges for some or all of the following:

- Set-up or establishment.
- Annual administration.
- Contributions, subscriptions and transfer-in.
- Withdrawals and transfer-out.

These charges may be a monetary amount or *ad valorem*, which means a percentage of the value of the product. They may be a one-off charge or, where a regular charge, could be charged monthly, quarterly or annually, sometimes in advance and sometimes in arrears. Administration charges are normally also subject to VAT, so make sure you check whether the costs quoted are inclusive of VAT or are subject to VAT in addition.

These charges will be deducted directly out of your ISA, SIPP or Dealing Account. If you don't have sufficient cash to pay the charges then you will be given the chance to sell investments or inject some cash into your account. Failing that, the platform will sell your investments, normally on a last-in-first-out basis to pay their charges.

SIPP-only charges

There is far more administration to be carried out on a SIPP than there is on an ISA or Dealing Account. SIPP-only charges are typically a fixed monetary amount and can include costs for:

- Setting up an income drawdown pension, including paying any lump-sum benefits.
- Requesting a review of income levels under income drawdown.
- Income drawdown administration.
- Purchasing an annuity with part, or all, of your SIPP.
- Transferring assets out *in specie*.
- Payment of benefits on death, or if your pension is to be split/shared following a divorce.

Investment charges

Dealing or investment commission – this may be a fixed fee per transaction, with the market level at about £10 per deal, or may be a percentage of the value of the investment being bought or sold.

The rate of dealing commission may vary depending on:

Whether online or via phone – the latter is normally significantly dearer.

Whether in shares or funds – some platforms don't charge dealing commission on funds, due to the attractive ongoing payments they receive from fund managers – which will be banned from 2014, so this may change.

Whether shares are listed in the UK or overseas – the latter may be more expensive, and don't forget there will be a currency exchange cost as well.

How often you deal – many platforms now have a frequent dealer commission rate. Typically, you will need to be dealing more than ten times a month to benefit.

Regular investments – lower dealing commission rates will normally apply for regular investments.

Dividend reinvestments – lower dealing commission rates will normally apply for dividend reinvestments.

Non-standard investments – those involving a paper application form will typically be subject to a higher dealing charge.

Custody charges

Your investment platform incurs a cost when buying and selling investments, but arguably the biggest cost to a platform is for holding the investments on your behalf. Custody charges are exempt from VAT and may be a fixed amount, *ad valorem*, or may not be charged at all.

Custody charges have been quite unusual in the past. Platforms make their money from shares with people who deal regularly, by receiving a regular payment from the fund managers and on cash deposits.

But this cosy world has been turned on its head. Dealing volumes have dropped over recent years and the regulator has announced that platforms will not be able to receive payments from fund managers from 2014. A custody charge is a relatively new form of charge that an investment platform will levy for holding your investment on its platform.

To understand custody charges you need to split funds into two categories – those where the fund manager pays part of their annual management fee to the fund platform and those that don't. We have described these earlier as 'dirty' and 'clean' respectively.

It is highly likely that your investment platform will not make any explicit charge for holding dirty funds. They may even give you some of the money they receive from the fund manager under the label of a loyalty bonus, annual bonus, annual rebate or commission rebate – which is taxable as of 6 April 2013 in a Dealing Account.

You should expect to pay a custody charge if you invest in clean funds, or if your platform rebates all of the payments it receives from fund managers from dirty funds.

To further confuse matters, it is likely that the so-called clean funds will end up paying a rebate to the larger investment platforms. If clean funds carry an annual management charge of 0.75 per cent, then there may be a 0.10 per cent per annum rebate paid to the platform. From 2014, platforms will be unable to keep this payment, which will be used to buy you extra units in the fund.

Other charges

Some platforms charge for corporate actions and some don't. This can be quite expensive if you have lots of equity holdings. Some charge for paper valuations or additional copies of valuations or consolidated tax vouchers, which are used for your tax return. If your platform's charges run to many pages, take this as a warning.

You will typically be charged for a telegraphic transfer of funds – for example if you want your cash transferred from your investment platform to you by same-day electronic transfer.

Cash rates

If you are likely to be holding large amounts of cash on your investment platform for long periods then the cash rate offered will be a factor in deciding which provider to go with.

Interest rates are clearly displayed with the product and investment charges on all platforms' websites.

How do I choose?

Work out what you think your investment behaviour is likely to be over the next few years: what will you be buying/selling, how often, how much cash will you have and which products will you use? Then use a comparison site to help you sift this down to a manageable number of platforms, maybe two or three, and then carry out the wider, other due diligence described above.

A final word

Now you have finished this book there is only one question you need to ask yourself: 'Am I a DIY investor?'. If the answer is no, then you need the help of a professional adviser and you can console yourself with the thought that at least you have avoided what could have been a costly mistake. You will also have a greater understanding of what advisers do for their money.

If the answer is yes, then I wish you good luck as you take control of your financial future.

Appendix

Annuity factors for capped drawdown

Gilt yield	2.0%	2.25%	2.50%	2.75%	3.0%	3.25%	3.50%	3.75%	4.0%	4.25%	4.50%	4.75%	5.0%	5.25%	5.50%	5.75%	6.0%
Age																	
55	4.1%	4.3%	4.4%	4.6%	4.8%	4.9%	5.1%	5.3%	5.5%	5.6%	5.8%	6.0%	6.2%	6.4%	6.5%	6.7%	6.9%
60	4.6%	4.8%	4.9%	5.1%	5.3%	5.4%	5.6%	5.8%	5.9%	6.1%	6.3%	6.5%	6.6%	6.8%	7.0%	7.2%	7.4%
65	5.3%	5.5%	5.6%	5.8%	5.9%	6.1%	6.3%	6.4%	6.6%	6.8%	7.0%	7.1%	7.3%	7.5%	7.7%	7.8%	8.0%
70	6.2%	6.4%	6.6%	6.7%	6.9%	7.0%	7.2%	7.4%	7.5%	7.7%	7.8%	8.1%	8.2%	8.4%	8.6%	8.8%	8.9%
75	7.7%	7.8%	8.0%	8.2%	8.3%	8.5%	8.7%	8.8%	9.0%	9.2%	9.3%	9.5%	9.7%	9.9%	10.0%	10.2%	10.4%
80	10.1%	10.3%	10.5%	10.6%	10.8%	11.0%	11.1%	11.3%	11.5%	11.7%	11.8%	12.0%	12.2%	12.4%	12.6%	12.7%	12.9%

Source: Government Actuary's Department

Index